How to get a Good Degree

Second Edition

How to get a Good Degree

Making the most of your time at University

Second Edition

Phil Race

 Open University Press

Open University Press
McGraw-Hill Education
McGraw-Hill House
Shoppenhangers Road
Maidenhead
Berkshire
England
SL6 2QL

email: enquiries@openup.co.uk
world wide web: www.openup.co.uk

and Two Penn Plaza, New York, NY 10121-2289, USA

First published 1999
This edition published 2007

A catalogue record of this book is available from the British Library

ISBN-13: 978 0 335 22265 0 (pb)   978 0 335 22266 7 (hb)
ISBN-10: 0 335 22265 X (pb)   0 335 22266 8 (hb)

Library of Congress Cataloguing-in-Publication Data
CIP data applied for

Typeset by RefineCatch Limited, Bungay, Suffolk
Printed in Poland by OZ Graf S.A.
www.polskabook.pl

The McGraw-Hill Companies

I dedicate *How to get a Good Degree* to my son Angus – who did.

Contents

List of figures and tables

Figures

Table

Preface: background to this book

This book is for you if you really *want* to get a good degree. It's different from most of the other study skills books around in that the primary focus is on what you can do to ensure that you get a *good* degree, not just any old degree. However, just using your copy of the book won't get you that good degree by magic. Only *you* can work your way to that degree, but this book can help you work out exactly *how* you can get your brain into top gear and increase the odds of your final result being a good one.

You can earn yourself that good degree through what you *do*, not just what you *know*. So in particular, my aim is that this book will help you get your head around how higher education actually works, and in particular how *assessment* in higher education works. The more you know about the assessment culture in which you need to thrive and prosper at university, the better equipped you will be to do yourself justice in the different assessment contexts which add up to the award of your degree. Throughout this book I have listed and discussed the *good habits* of students who get good degrees. You've probably already got (or are fast developing) many of these habits, but I trust that you'll be able to add some more to your repertoire as you use this book.

How did I come to write this book? One way or another, I have been studying what makes learning happen for all of my life. Like everyone, I began at the sharp end as a student, developing my own strategies for successful learning. When I first started as a lecturer, I happened to also hold the position of warden of a hall of residence for several years. Living under the same roof as a hundred students soon showed me the sorts of help they needed – and still need! Whatever you're studying, the main benefit you will derive from your experience in higher education is becoming better at *learning*, and improving your approaches to gaining a genuine understanding of what you study. Such benefits equip you for life, not just for your university experience. It's *your* life. Work well now for *your* future.

I also became very interested in how assessment works in higher education, and have served for many years as an external examiner to programmes in many universities across the UK. For many years now I have been involved in working with university and college lecturers on teaching and learning methodologies. I soon found that the best way to help lecturers to improve their teaching was to focus in on how students actually learn most effectively, in all the different teaching–learning situations that they experience, and how best they could help their students to prepare to be successful in the assessment culture of higher education. My work now takes me throughout the UK and abroad, including New Zealand, Australia, Canada, Sweden, Denmark, and Ireland, working with lecturers on developing their teaching and assessment design, and working with students so that they can do themselves justice in higher education.

In this 2nd edition, I am pleased to build on many suggestions that I have received from students who have used its predecessor, and have extended several parts of the discussion in the book to reflect the significant changes in higher education since 1999 when the 1st edition was published. In particular, this edition contains a great deal more on how you can make the most of all the *feedback* (and in particular *'feed-ahead'*) which is available to you as you work towards your degree. I've also added new thoughts about making use of electronic resources, and virtual learning environments, and the increased gravity surrounding the problem of plagiarism in coursework in higher education.

In this book, my intention is to bring together all of my own learning about studying, teaching, and assessment, and to share it with you, provided you really *want* to do well. There is a lot of good advice elsewhere for those who merely want to survive in higher education (and I have added to this in my own way), but in this book my aim is to help you if you're highly motivated, deliberately setting your sights for a *good* degree. Therefore, probably the most important focus of this book is on the various assessment situations which require you to *show* what you have learned. Knowing much more about how assessment works will allow you to work systematically and purposefully towards putting your best foot forward and being duly rewarded in the qualifications you earn for yourself.

Phil Race

Acknowledgements

I am grateful to the many thousands of full-time and part-time students with whom I have run study skills development programmes, and to thousands of their lecturers and tutors with whom I have worked on their development of teaching methodologies, learning facilitation, and assessment design. In all of this work I continue to learn more about learning itself, and have tried to share all of this in this book.

I am particularly grateful to Sally Brown, not only for making sure that I got down to writing the first edition of this book, and contributing a number of key ideas, but also for her very valuable and insightful comments on draft versions of both editions. I have many people to thank for encouragement and inspiration in my work both with students and with teaching staff, including John Cowan, Mike Thorne, Simon Lee, Viv Lever, Sheelagh Hill, and David Anderson.

I also thank Shona Mullen of Open University Press for continued encouragement and patience, and for valuable suggestions on seeing the completed manuscript of the book. Finally, I am grateful to the anonymous referees whose comments on my original book proposal, and further comments on my plans for this edition, have done much to help me to improve the content and format.

Introduction

Know your enemies: a risk assessment exercise • *Tackling the enemies: don't just work hard, work* smart!

Know your enemies: a risk assessment exercise

Before really starting this book, here's an exercise to help you to identify what could stop you from getting a good degree. Have a go at this straight-away – be honest. There are two dozen statements in the task which follows, and three choices for you to make: often like you, sometimes like you, or not at all like you. Couldn't be simpler – but be honest. Don't tick the column you *think* you would like to tick, tick the columns which actually apply.

How *not* to get a good degree – your risk assessment	This is often like me!	This is some-times like me!	This is not at all like me!
1 I don't take charge of my own learning, and hark back to the comfortable times when other people put pressure on me to keep on track.			
2 I don't keep careful records of when work is due to be handed in, resulting in last minute panics when I learn the news from my peers.			

How *not* to get a good degree – your risk assessment	This is often like me!	This is some-times like me!	This is not at all like me!
3 I believe that what got me by last year will suffice this year – despite me now being at a more advanced stage of my studies.			
4 I don't build in time for the unexpected (bout of 'flu, family crisis, friend in need, and so on) and then get stumped when an emergency or crisis occurs.			
5 I am unable to organize my workloads sufficiently well in order to avoid missing deadlines.			
6 I don't realize that handouts and printed materials are just information – they need to be worked with before they can count as my own learning.			
7 I believe my classmates are studying as little as they claim they are – 'it's not cool to be studying too much'.			
8 I arrive late for, or am absent from, crucial briefing sessions at which detailed information about assignments is given out.			
9 I am easily led away from studying, by classmates with plausible advanced study avoidance tactics.			
10 I don't catch up on what actually happened at teaching sessions I did not attend – even when my absence was unavoidable.			
11 I fail to write down dates of exams, presentations, performances, and other practical tests, then find I have other things going on at the same time, e.g., medical appointments.			

How *not* to get a good degree – your risk assessment	This is often like me!	This is some-times like me!	This is not at all like me!
12 I leave starting assignments to the last minute and then find I can't get hold of the resources I need to complete the task.			
13 I produce assignments in a rush in the last available time, then experience problems with printing, production and/or delivery.			
14 I believe it is a situation beyond my control if I am given multiple assignments with competing deadlines, rather than working out a plan whereby all can be achieved by starting early.			
15 I have artificial expectations of how much I can achieve in any given period of time and then don't allow myself sufficient time to complete tasks properly.			
16 When in the mood, I spend far too long chasing the last couple of marks in a given assignment, instead of stopping at a reasonable stage, and moving on to other work of equal importance.			
17 I am so determined to do a piece of work really well that I spend most of my energy on the research and thinking-through stages, leaving insufficient time to bring it all together for the assignment.			
18 I hand in coursework just hoping for the best, without first having self-assessed it against the given criteria, and improved it accordingly.			
19 I don't make time and space to learn from feedback on previous work.			

How *not* to get a good degree – your risk assessment	This is often like me!	This is some-times like me!	This is not at all like me!
20 I regard critical feedback as failure, and stop trying, when I could have used the feedback as an opportunity to identify how best to develop my techniques.			
21 I find plenty of displacement activities to avoid making a start on the really important task in hand.			
22 I keep putting off starting revision for exams, saying to myself 'it's too early', 'I'll just forget it', and so on.			
23 I feel I have to wait for the right moment or until inspiration strikes, before I put pen to paper or fingers to keyboard.			
24 I have too may other competing responsibilities going on in my life to make it possible to allow enough time for coursework and revision.			
Scoring	Two risk points per entry in this column	One risk point per entry in this column	No risk points
Your scores			0

Discussion: what's your score?

This is simple enough to work out too. Each entry in the 'this is often like me' column counts for two risk points. Each entry in the 'this is sometimes like me' column counts for one risk point. There are no risk points for entries in the 'this is not at all like me' column. Now add up your score.

If your total score is over 48, please enrol for some coaching in addition skills.

36–48: *Excellent* – you've indicated a high level of risk of not getting a good degree – but at least now you already have a good idea of the main enemies. The rest of this book can help you to attack these enemies.

20–35: *Well done* – you're not at such serious risk as others whose scores are over 36. The columns where you scored your risk points should alert you to the main things to address as you work to overcome the main enemies to your mission.

10–19: *Great stuff* – there are at least some hazards which aren't going to be a problem for you – and you now know where the remaining hazards are, and can do something about them. This book should help.

1–9: *Splendid* – you seem to be immune to the majority of the hazards which get in the way of able students getting good degrees. And moreover, you now know one or more hazard to address to work towards complete immunity.

0: *Are you sure?* Do you need any help counting up things in the first two columns of the table? Or have you *really* got none of these enemies to your study ambitions? If so, congratulations – and good luck. You shouldn't actually *need* any luck. In any case, I hope this book will save you from reverting to any risks associated with the hazards in the table.

Tackling the enemies: don't just work hard, work *smart*!

This book is for you if you want to get a *good* degree, and aren't afraid of hard work. If you *are* afraid of hard work, don't use this book! A few students seem to sail forwards to a good degree without having to work hard at all; if you are such a student you probably don't need this book either (or any other study skills advice). Most students, however, who end up with good degrees, work hard for them. If that sounds more like you, this book can help you too.

Some students work very hard and still don't get a good degree, even when they really deserve one. Most such students find out – too late – the differences between working hard and working smart, and fail usually because they don't work *smart* enough. Hindsight is a wonderful way of learning things – but too late! However, this book is full of other people's hindsight, to help you to work smart as well as hard, and to show you *how* to do so.

Towards smartness

Working smart is about making sure that each component part of your studying:

- Achieves high learning pay-off (in other words, is effective).
- Is efficient and economical (in other words, good time management).
- Is balanced (in other words, good task management).
- Is purposeful (so you are continuously focused on where you want to get to).

Smart studying is also about:

- Gaining *control* of your learning, and monitoring it so that you can improve it.
- Gaining skills in *showing* that your learning has been successful (written and oral communication).
- Building up *evidence* of your achievements, matching the intended learning outcomes of your course.
- Keeping your studying in perspective, and making it a natural part of a normal life.

In this book, I aim to help you to adjust your day-to-day studying to increase your achievement of all the factors listed above.

Firsts among many?

There continues to be considerable discussion at present in the UK and elsewhere about whether or not we should actually have degree classification systems, with some students getting first class degrees (and being regarded as winners) and with others being seen as losers. Other countries have adopted alternative approaches, where you either have a degree or you haven't yet got one. Whatever the system, employers want to know how *good* anyone's qualification is, and indeed whether it is awarded by a really reputable institution. So even if degree classification systems such as in the UK change, or become abandoned, society will still require some sort of measure of how good is any degree. Also, high-flying and ambitious students will themselves continue to want and expect recognition and accreditation of their hard work and their excellence. In short, the need to get a *good* degree (however we describe it) will remain with us.

Smartness is a toolkit of habits, not a fashion statement!

It is not enough to work smart (or hard – or both) for the last few weeks before your final exams (though this will be part of what you need to do). Working smart is about developing good *habits*. In this book I will share with you everything I have found out about the habits of people who get good degrees, from students themselves, from their lecturers, and from my own work with both students and staff at many universities around the world. These include their day-to-day ways of going about learning actively in lectures, researching and writing coursework, and many other activities involved in heading for a good degree. I have also based the book on a recognition of all those bad habits which reduce the chance of getting a good degree, including some which *you* may need to diagnose for yourself so you can replace them with better ones.

What kinds of smartness?

Nowadays, learning doesn't just happen (or fail to happen!) in lectures, libraries, learning resource centres, or study bedrooms. It also happens with laptops, computer-rooms, virtual learning environments, and online. Furthermore, students in higher education increasingly learn part-time, through distance learning, or on programmes which require a high level of independent learning, such as with the Open University in the UK. This book is designed to support both traditional full-time on-site learners, and students who may have a higher level of responsibility for planning and managing their own learning. The interactive style of the book is designed to put into practice my belief that learning happens through 'doing' rather than just being the passive recipient of someone else's ideas.

Chapter 1 looks at how you can be smart by gaining ownership and control of *how* you learn. We start by looking at 'what's in it for you?' to get a good degree, and then go on to what *you* think a good degree actually measures. Then we get down to some straight thinking about how learning really works, and what *your* strengths are likely to be.

Chapter 2 is about being smart about how you make the most of a range of teaching–learning situations, and goes into detail about how to work smart in lectures, tutorials, and seminars, with some further discussion of studio work, field work, laboratory work, group work, one-to-one contexts with staff, and work-based learning.

Chapter 3 is new to this edition, and is about making the most of all the feedback you get from lecturers, tutors, fellow students, and anyone else on your way towards your good degree. Feedback is vitally important, and can make all the difference to your prospects if you're smart about how you seek it and (above all) use it.

Chapter 4 is 'Making the most of your learning environment', including not just virtual learning environments, but the people around you, as well as books, journals, and the Internet.

Chapter 5 is called 'Looking after yourself' and is about making smart judgements and decisions regarding a range of issues and factors, including getting involved, being a student rep, lifestyle choices, and managing your stress levels.

Chapter 6 is a really important one: 'Going for gold in assessed coursework', looking in turn at how to excel in essays, reports, peer assessment, self-assessment, group work, research projects, final year dissertations, presentations, assessed seminars, vivas, and work placements. The emphasis is on good habits!

Finally, there's no need to remind you about the importance of Chapter 7, which is about good habits and smartness in revision strategies and exam techniques, and takes you through a critical analysis of which revision processes have the highest learning pay-off, and how to use exams to show that you deserve that good degree.

Don't just read all about it!

Reading is important, but you can't learn to drive a car just by reading books about driving cars well, or even about driving cars badly. You can't learn how to use a computer just by reading the manual – and few computers if any now come with paper-based manuals. Similarly, you can't learn how to work smart just by reading about it in this book, and that is why I have written it not just to be read, but to be *done*. In many parts of the book you will find tasks asking you to rate yourself against various behaviours and practices, or to work out the learning pay-off that is associated with different processes. Then I respond in turn with some discussion about each of the behaviours and practices, so in effect I am trying to work *with* you on your ways of studying. If you just *read* the tasks and my responses, it's not the same as having *done* the tasks and then comparing your habits to my responses. Once you have completed the tasks, it is up to you to turn what you have learned into good habits, and build them into your day-to-day patterns of studying. It is also up to you to monitor each of these habits, and adjust them to make them as effective as possible for *you*.

Your degree is awarded on what you *show* – not just on what you *know*

However well you have learned something, getting a good degree with it depends on getting *credit* for your successful learning, and that depends on you *showing* that your learning has succeeded. You've got to get your learning so that it can be measured to be good in a variety of contexts, and you've also got to make sure that you're *noticed* to be good by the people around you, particularly lecturers, tutors, and so on. In other words, all the bits that add up to the assessment of your degree are vitally important, not least examinations, as are those things that could influence people's opinions about whether or not you really deserve a good degree. Sadly, there are lots of students who deserve a good degree, but don't actually win their prize, because they let themselves down in some of the assessments. In particular, it's really important to learn from each and every opportunity to find out how your learning is actually going, and that's why in this edition I've added quite a lot on making sure that you put feedback to work for you. That is also why, in this book, I have linked all the good habits you need to develop with the gaining of recognition for them in assessed work. Whatever *else* you do at university, to get that good degree you need to aim to show your optimum potential at each and every assessment opportunity.

Learning is for life, not just for university

I wish you success in your bid to get a *good* degree, and I hope that you will find that most of the good habits you systematically develop on your way to this will continue to serve you well in your future employment, and in your life in general. In the final analysis, good learning habits are key skills in life, and are actually more important than just getting a good degree, as you will need to continue to learn throughout your life, for pleasure as well as for work. We human beings are a learning species. To live is to learn. Being in full control of your learning, and making it effective, efficient, and enjoyable is the way of studying that will most enrich your life, as well as helping to guarantee your success.

Onwards and upward

By now you should have an idea about what the main hazards are which could prevent you from getting the good degree you're aiming for, and also you should be realizing that it's not just a matter of working hard, but working *smart*. 'That's all very well,' you may be thinking, 'but *how exactly* do I go about working smart towards my degree?'. That's what comes next. However, first in Chapter 1 we'll think about *why* it's worth aiming for a good degree, and *what* a good degree actually represents. Then, the 'how' question becomes quite straightforward and logical – taking the hard work for granted of course.

1

Why aim for a *good* degree?

Why do you want a good degree? • What is a good degree really a measure of? • How should I go about working towards that good degree? • Taking control of your learning • What factors underpin how you learn? • Five processes for successful learning • What are your relevant strengths? • Taking charge of your time • Taking stock

In this chapter, I'd first like to get you thinking about *why* you're wanting to get a good degree, then we'll explore some of the things which lecturers think are typical behaviours and attributes of students who do indeed get good degrees. We'll also take a look at how exactly *learning* happens. You've learned all of your life, but probably have never stopped to think how exactly this happens best. We'll work out some factors which underpin successful learning, so that you can address your learning all the more consciously from now on. This chapter goes on to give you the chance to self-assess your strengths, so that you can purposefully make the most of these in your quest towards your good degree. All this should help you to sort out where you're starting from, and give you ideas of the particular areas of your studying which could best be improved or changed, so that your ambition becomes a reality.

Why do you want a good degree?

The fact that you're using this book means that you've probably thought about the reasons that you may already have for wanting a good degree. This does not necessarily mean that you've yet decided which are the most *important* reasons for putting all you've got into working towards a successful outcome. Different people have different sorts of reasons for wanting to succeed. The best reasons are the ones that work for you. Let's explore a range of possible reasons, and see which (if any) may already belong to you, which you may be able to add to your own reasons, and which (if any) you may decide aren't good enough reasons for wanting to get a good degree.

Why do *you* want a good degree? Be as honest as you can . . .

Ten reasons for wanting a good degree – some are better than others!	This reason is very like mine	This reason is quite like mine	I don't feel much either way about this reason	This reason is not at all like mine!
1 I want a good degree because I feel I'm worth one.				
2 I want a good degree because I want to prove to myself that I'm up to getting one.				
3 I try to do everything I do well, and working for this degree is no exception.				
4 I want a good degree because I think it will open up more career choices than a not so good one.				
5 I know exactly what I want to do after I get my degree and I need a good one to get into the next stage in my life.				
6 I'm paying a lot to work for this degree and I don't want to waste my money.				

Ten reasons for wanting a good degree – some are better than others!	This reason is very like mine	This reason is quite like mine	I don't feel much either way about this reason	This reason is not at all like mine!
7 I'm spending a lot of valuable time working for this degree and I want to make the time spent as worthwhile as possible.				
8 I want to prove to other people that I can do it.				
9 Other people expect me to get a good degree.				
10 So-and-so got a good degree, and I feel that I'm every bit as good as so-and-so (you may wish to add a name or two to 'so-and-so').				

Now go back through the reasons that you've rated most highly, and ask yourself: 'Will this keep me going on those dark days when it all seems very difficult?' Next, compare my responses to each of the reasons, with your own thinking.

Discussion: reasons for wanting a good degree

1   *I want a good degree because I feel I'm worth one.* This is a good reason, well done if it's very like your reasons. Self-esteem is indeed important; it leads to confidence and confidence leads, more than any other single factor perhaps, to success. However, if you did not rate this reason highly, this does not mean that you can't, or won't, get a good degree. This is just one of many reasons and alone would probably not be enough in any case. Furthermore, the more you take charge of your own studying and focus your efforts towards achieving a good degree, the greater will become your self-esteem and confidence.

2   *I want a good degree, because I want to prove to myself that I'm up to getting one.* This can be a powerful reason for wanting a good degree. It does not automatically mean, however, that you are going to get one. You

need to do more than just *want* to prove to yourself that you're up to getting one – you need to *get* one. The good thing about this particular reason is the fact that the ownership of it rests entirely with you. It doesn't depend on other people, for example, or on circumstances. If you didn't rate this reason highly, it does not mean that there's anything seriously wrong. For example, if you already feel you're worth a good degree, you may not have any need to prove anything to yourself.

3 *I try to do everything I do well and working for this degree is no exception.* This is a good thing to be able to claim. It's a strong starting position towards working for a good degree. It's not the safest of reasons, however. One problem is that getting a good degree depends on more than just a lot of hard work; it depends on doing the *right kinds* of hard work. For example, it's dangerous to work very hard at coursework and not leave yourself a good margin of time to prepare for exams. One of the aims of this book is to help you to decide how to balance your act, so that while trying to do everything well you also make sure that you do everything *that counts* well.

4 *I want a good degree because I think it will open up more career choices than a not so good one.* Of course, this is an absolutely valid reason. If you haven't already decided exactly what you want to do with the whole of the rest of your life, you are probably very sensible. A good degree can be your passport to a much wider range of career opportunities. It can allow you to change fields completely if you wish to. There can be a problem, however: 'When you don't know where you're going, any bus will do'. This means that you may not always be in a position to tune your efforts towards getting a good degree to the next agenda – of getting your first postgraduate appointment (whether it be in employment, or working towards a higher degree). Probably the best position is if this is one of your *additional* reasons for wanting to get a good degree, rather than a major or sole driving force behind your efforts.

5 *I know exactly what I want to do after I get my degree, and I need a good one to get into the next stage in my life.* This is a good solid reason for wanting a good degree. *Needing* to do something is as powerful a motivator in its own way as *wanting* to do it. It can be really useful to keep telling yourself, 'I *need* to do this,' when you come to the tough bits or the boring parts of your studies. Don't, however, let your plans for the next stage of your life blind you to other opportunities which may come along – there may be something on your horizon even better than your present plans. A good degree will still be useful if you change your plans, and in fact could open up even more choices for you in due course.

6 *I'm paying a lot to work for this degree and I don't want to waste my money.* This is a serious reason for wanting a good degree. Now that in most countries students have to fork out (sooner or later) for their higher education, you are right to want to get good value for money. A good

degree will help you to recoup your outlay by securing you more choices of jobs and giving you more chance of getting well-paid employment. However, it's not quite as simple as it first seems. You also need to remember that during the years that you're studying, you're losing out on what you might have earned if you'd got a job straightaway. You're quite likely to be tempted more than once to give it all up and take a job, especially on those dark days when the studying seems hard or the finances seem just too low for comfort. It's therefore useful for this not to be your *only* reason for wanting a good degree, so explore some of the other possibilities carefully and make sure you have some other good reasons too.

7 *I'm spending a lot of valuable time working for this degree and I want to make the time spent as worthwhile as possible.* This is a good reason. The years spent working for a degree are a significant fraction of your life and usually occur during a period when there are many competing significant happenings. It is very healthy to want to get good value for the time you spend studying and this will help you to develop good time management skills, such as checking that each study-related activity you undertake has a significant learning pay-off, and counts in a tangible way towards your goal. However, it is best that this is not your *only* solid reason for wanting a good degree. This is because however good you are at seeking dividends for your investment of time, studying is one of those activities that doesn't lend itself to absolute efficiency all the time. Every good student wastes some time learning the wrong things or not getting to grips efficiently with the right things. If value for time spent is your only barometer, it will be too easy for you to become demoralized and discouraged when you find that a significant episode of time has just not paid off. Therefore, it's best to have some other reasons for your wish to gain a good degree.

8 *I want to prove to other people that I can do it.* This is a very natural reason for wanting to get a good degree, and many successful students have it among their motivators. It can be a very powerful reason for studying well, and sometimes leads to feats of dogged determination. If this is one of your reasons for studying, this is fine, as long as it's not your only motivator. The problem can be that when something goes wrong (such as not getting the grade you expect or deserve in a crucial piece of coursework or maybe underperforming in one of your exams) you feel very vulnerable as though other people's eyes are fixed on you. It's also worth asking *why* you have to prove yourself to other people, and whether getting a good degree is the best way of doing it. What is it that you want from these other people after proving yourself to them? In short, is there too much going on here about other people and not enough about yourself?

9 *Other people expect me to get a good degree.* This is often the case. The other people may include family, friends, colleagues – almost everyone, it

may seem. This is especially true if the other people have already got good degrees and seem to expect that everyone who counts, including you, should do the same. Alternatively, some of these other people may not have good degrees, or any qualifications, and may seem to be living out their own frustrated hopes and ambitions through you. The main problem with this as a motivator is that in some ways it's a no-win situation for you. If you get a good degree, it is *they* who have won, rather than you. If you fail, it is *you* who has let them down! If this was a strong contender in your list of motivators, it's worth thinking about looking for a replacement. You will be well advised in such cases to look for primary motivators that belong to *you*, rather than to other people. It's motivators that you *own* which will keep you going during the more difficult days of your studies. Letting other people down is bad enough, but it's more important to be striving not to let yourself down. It's your life.

10 *So-and-so got a good degree, and I feel that I'm every bit as good as so-and-so.* Many successful students have counted this kind of reason for starting out on a degree programme among their motivators. There's no harm in having role models: plural! However, it's not usually a good idea to have just one or two role models. After all, you may only be modelling one or two particular aspects of the lives of such people. Even worse, what happens if your role model crashes? Are you going to model that too? If the only real effect of so-and-so's success is that it gives *you* the confidence to make a start on getting a good degree, that is fine. Once started, it's really up to you to pave the way towards your success. Things that worked well for other people may not be the things that will work well for you. Therefore it is worth exploring some of the other motivators discussed above, and finding some that belong more to you and are less to do with other people.

What is a *good* degree really a measure of?

Life might be much simpler if there were straightforward answers to this question. In this chapter we will try to triangulate lots of people's views, not least those involved in the assessment processes whereby good degrees are awarded – namely, university lecturers. Let's start, however, by seeing what *you* think. Here are some possible answers – see whether you agree with any of them; for each option, make your choice, then read on.

I think a good degree is really a measure of . . .	Very much so	Only to some extent	Nothing to do with this	I've no idea!
How intelligent I am.				
How hard I work on my studies.				
How well I understand what I'm studying.				
How lucky I am when the exam questions are set.				
How clever I am.				
(Your own thoughts . . .)				

There is something to be said for each of these options, but in general no one of them, nor even all of them, are the prerequisites for getting a good degree for yourself. Let's look in a little more detail at the pros and cons of the main issues lying behind each of the things in the list above.

How intelligent you are

This is a tricky one. If you're really intelligent, you're likely to get yourself a good degree anyway. But it's not as simple as this, because a good degree is not a direct and unambiguous measure of intelligence. Indeed, it is hard to discover ways of accurately measuring intelligence. There are plenty of so-called intelligence tests, and you may well have had fun playing with these. If so, you'll probably have worked out for yourself that there's an art to doing such tests and that practice at doing the tests leads to improved performance in the tests. Does this mean that practising doing intelligence tests increases your intelligence? Or does it mean that practising *anything* improves your ability at it? Probably the latter is the most likely explanation.

However, it all depends what we mean by intelligence. Intelligence can also be interpreted as having the wits to devote part of your studying not just to becoming as expert as you can in the various subjects you're studying, but also to finding out about the rules of the game of getting yourself a good degree – studying *smart*, perhaps. If so, you're already demonstrating a sign of such intelligence by reading this book. However, reading this book isn't enough to get you that good degree; you need to do much more than just read about the rules of the game. Like anything else, you have to *play* the game. This means practising becoming good at the game. It also means taking risks sometimes, and learning from mistakes (at times when it's safe enough to make mistakes, rather than in important exams, for example). So, intelligence may well be involved in getting a good degree, but it takes more than this to be certain that you will do yourself justice.

How hard you work on your studies

If only this were so! Then all you would have to do would be to work really hard from beginning to end of your degree programme, and your efforts would be rewarded. Of course it is partly true that a good degree is a measure of how much you put into your studies, but it's not strictly a measure of how hard you work. It is, however, at least partly a measure of how *well* you work. It's quality more than quantity of studying that gets people good degrees.

There's a limit to how much hard work anyone can or should do. You need to have a life as well as be a successful student. Indeed, if you get the balance wrong and work *too* hard, you're in danger of not achieving your potential.

How well you develop your understanding of the subjects you study

It is an important aim to try to understand things, rather than merely to remember them. If you understand things, they tend to stay with you. This is sometimes called deep learning, as opposed to surface learning, where knowledge is stored up temporarily in your mind and quickly forgotten again when it is no longer needed. In an ideal world, it would be useful if everything you did, you understood and everything that contributed to your good degree, was thoroughly understood along the way. For the most part, it's really, really useful to get things to the state where you feel that you understand them. When you understand something, you don't actually have to *remember* so much about it, as you get into the position of being able to work things out for yourself rather than have to search your memory banks for all the details.

However, there are some health warnings to be linked to understanding. It would be unwise to spend too much time really getting your head around some parts of the curriculum at the expense of other parts. It is really important that you get into the position of being able to *demonstrate* the quality of your understanding of a wide cross-section of the topics and subjects that will contribute towards your degree. Also, there are some things where understanding doesn't come easily, and where it may take quite a few years to really understand them (maybe some time after you've got your good degree). So a sensible balance is to strive to understand as much as possible of your curriculum, but at the same time to make sure that you are competent to *show* that your understanding is well advanced, and to practise on any areas that you don't yet understand until you can show that you are reasonably competent in these too. In fact, your good degree depends much more on what you show for it – even when the understanding isn't there.

How lucky you are when the exam papers are set

There's an element of truth in this. When a significant element of your degree is linked to your performance in a particular set of exams, the questions that confront you are indeed linked significantly to your chance of doing well. If you can get yourself into the position of being able to perform well with *all* the possible questions which could possibly be set, including those that are actually set, you are on your way to not needing luck. But it's still not that simple. Even when you *could* give perfect answers to each and every exam question, there remains the issue of whether or not you *will* produce such answers. Exams definitely measure what people *do* during them, not necessarily what people *could* have done during them. The same is of course true of essays, reports, dissertations, presentations, and anything else that contributes to your overall degree. It's not how well you *could* do them that counts – it's how well you *do* do them that's accredited.

How clever you are

What's the difference, if any, between being 'clever' and being 'intelligent'? Being clever could involve making sensible decisions about how much time to spend on each *way* you adopt to study, and which approaches to use to prepare to give your best performance when it really matters. Yet there aren't any courses about 'cleverness' to help you, and it just seems to be assumed that you're naturally clever enough to learn whatever you need to, to prove that you deserve a good degree. Or could it be that what we're really getting at by cleverness is the business of not just working hard, but working *smart*? That is what this book is really about.

How should I go about working towards that good degree?

The table which follows shows a 30-point set of questions, collected from many lecturers about what they feel are the habits and attitudes of the students who are most likely to get a good degree. Have a go at rating yourself against their views – but don't worry if sometimes you think that a particular habit is not actually necessary – there's a column in the table for you to disagree with these lecturers!

Thirty good study habits and attitudes: how do you rate yourself?	Yes, I do this already	No, I don't yet do this	I don't agree that this is necessary
General approaches and attitudes: do you . . .			
1 Set yourself attainable goals, and keep extending and expanding on them until they are the ultimate goals for getting a *good* degree?			
2 Choose subjects that interest you, rather than the ones that you think are the easiest?			
3 Strike a good balance between work and play?			
4 Find out your weaknesses in your subject, and work at improving them?			
5 Challenge what you read or hear?			
6 Ask many questions?			
7 Try always to make connections between different topics on a course and between different courses?			
8 Learn the subject you do not like first?			
9 Be vociferously curious in all lectures, seminars, and practicals?			
10 Take feedback on assignments seriously and use it as guidance for improvement?			
Working with computers and online: do you . . .			
11 Resist the temptation to surf the net as a distraction?			
12 Keep records of what you find in your web searches?			

Thirty good study habits and attitudes: how do you rate yourself?	Yes, I do this already	No, I don't yet do this	I don't agree that this is necessary
13 Make good use of spell checks and other aids to writing online?			
14 Make good use of being able to edit your own writing on-screen?			
Time management: do you . . .			
15 Organize yourself from day one?			
16 Adopt a normal working day: 9–5?			
17 Make sure you know when assignments are due?			
18 Allow yourself time to do assignments well?			
19 Take a sensible amount of time off to enjoy yourself?			
20 Learn things through the year, rather than cram them all for exams at the end?			
21 Review assignments in detail after feedback has been given?			
Reading and researching: do you . . .			
22 Take a real interest in your subject, carrying out broad and deep research?			
23 Read a lot, not only what you have on your reading list?			
24 Prepare yourself for the kinds of questions that your examiner is likely to ask?			

Thirty good study habits and attitudes: how do you rate yourself?	Yes, I do this already	No, I don't yet do this	I don't agree that this is necessary
Writing: do you . . .			
25 Develop your ability to communicate effectively and concisely?			
26 Avoid wasting time on answering the wrong question in exams?			
27 Make clear notes in a way you can understand them and in a format which you like?			
28 Show boldness and imagination in your writing?			
29 Present work which demonstrates lateral and original thought?			
30 Do all the problems set during the course, and keep/make a set of solutions to these?			

Don't be depressed if some of the questions in that table seem like tall orders! Several of the lecturers also gave the suggestion: 'Work very, very hard!' which may seem rather frightening. However, this book is about helping you to work 'very, very *well*', and to work very efficiently, so that your success may not involve quite as much 'hard work' as some of the suggestions imply. In short, work *smart* as well as hard.

Taking control of your learning

You've been learning all your life. You're already rather good at it, or you wouldn't have got so far as to be thinking about how to get a good degree. Your learning will continue far beyond your degree. The quality of the rest of your life will be influenced strongly by how successful you become at learning. Throughout your career you will need to continue to learn new skills, and to take on board new knowledge. The better you become at taking control of your own learning, the more successful you will be at your job, and at putting your best foot forward every time there is a promotion opportunity. More importantly, most ambitious people *change* their jobs, and even their entire career directions, a few times during their life. Coping successfully with change is an important life skill, and depends very much on being a self-directing, autonomous learner.

Your time at university is the most productive phase of your life for taking control of how you learn. Consciously aiming to develop your toolkit of learning techniques pays long-term dividends, but also helps directly in the short-term by giving you the tools to maximize your chance of being *seen* to be a successful learner through your degree result.

The term 'lifelong learning' has been around for many years. It was often used in the context of continuing education, or professional development, and was formerly seen by many as outside the main business of higher education. More recently, it has been realized by many that the most important outcomes of a period in higher education are not just the subject-specific knowledge or understanding that students develop, but the key learning skills – those necessary for lifelong learning – that accompany such development. Skills such as time management, task management, working collaboratively, communicating effectively, and self-organization are now being systematically built into the curriculum throughout the education system, from school to postgraduate education. This means that all these skills are being developed and *measured* quite deliberately on many degree programmes, alongside students' subject knowledge and skills. Therefore, your degree success is at least as much to do with the way you focus your own development of lifelong learning processes as it is to do with your grasp of your subject or discipline area.

In this book, we will be looking at all the skills that are part of a lifelong learning toolkit, not only because they are important and valuable in their own right, but also because they are directly relevant to putting into practice in your strategy for gaining your good degree.

Much of your learning has already proved successful, and you need to keep it that way. It's quite likely that you haven't given much thought to exactly *how* you learn, but that you have found things which work well for you, and stuck with them. However, if you're really going to be in full control of your own learning, I think it's useful for you to take a little time out to find out more about how learning really works, so that you can make your learning as efficient as you can, as well as effective. Also, knowing how your learning really works can help to make it more enjoyable. Gaining *control* of your own learning is the key factor in helping you to develop the self-confidence and autonomy, which in themselves are characteristics of students who excel rather than survive.

What factors underpin how you learn?

In this section I would like to ask you a number of questions about your own learning, and then share with you the typical answers that are given by students who got good degrees. In fact, I've asked these questions of several thousands of people, face-to-face, in workshop sessions over the last few years, so I have had plenty of opportunity to pick out the most important factors in their answers.

Question 1

(a) Think of something that you know you are good at – something you do well. This can be anything you like; it may be academic or it can be a hobby, a sport, or anything at all. Choose just one thing and jot it down below.

(b) Now think of *how* you became good at whatever it is. Jot down a few key words or phrases to remind you of the processes that were involved in you learning this particular thing successfully.

Typical answers

Successful students' replies about *how* they became good at things almost always contain one or more of the following points:

- Practice.
- Having a go.
- Repetition.
- Just by doing it.
- Trial and error.
- Learning from my own mistakes.
- Learning from other people's mistakes.
- Determination.

The main message to come out of this is that effective learning happens by being active, and *learning by doing* is at the heart of heading towards a good degree. Of course, it's possible to be very active without getting anywhere! Therefore, in many parts of this book we'll be looking at *what* you should be doing and *how* you can make sure that your efforts are focused and productive.

Question 2

(a)   Think of something about yourself that you feel good about – something where you have a sense of pride or self-satisfaction. It can be in any area of your life. Jot down a few words about it below.

(b)   Next, try to write down a few words about why you feel *justified* feeling good about whatever it is. What's the *evidence* which supports your positive feelings about this?

Typical answers

Most people feel good about something! When asked what their supporting evidence is, common answers from successful students include:

- Because other people tell me.
- Praise, compliments.
- Positive feedback.
- Developing my confidence.
- Seeing the results for myself.

This brings the second important factor underpinning successful learning into focus: feedback. Getting a good degree is feedback, but you need to make sure that you don't leave it to chance, and that you get a great deal of feedback on your performance well before the stages which will count towards your good degree.

Question 3

Let's look this time at what can go *wrong* with learning.

(a)   Think of something that you're *not* good at. This may have been the result of an unsuccessful learning experience at some point in your life. Jot down below one thing that is in this category.

(b) Next, jot down a few key words about *what went wrong* – what caused you not to be good at whatever it is.

(c) Finally, try to decide whether it was anyone's fault. If you can decide this, jot down who was to blame.

Typical answers

Learning can go wrong for all sorts of reasons. Let's start with whose fault it can be. If it was *your* fault, you probably already know what you could have done about it. Often other people can be blamed. Sometimes, not surprisingly, teachers of one kind or another are in the firing line. This continues to apply at university. Some of your lecturers will be brilliant teachers, others won't. However, they've all got their degrees, and you are still in the business of working towards yours. To maximize your chance of getting a good degree, you need to take control of your own learning so well that your results don't depend on how good or bad may be the teaching that you experience. Typical responses to (b) are considered further in Question 4.

Question 4

What sorts of things go wrong with learning? Check your own response to Question 3 against the list of nine typical answers, shown below, that students give about the kinds of events that led to them *not* becoming good at something. Decide which column you can tick, indicating whether or not any of the nine causes of unsuccessful learning apply to you.

Cause of unsuccessful learning	This often interferes with my learning	This has sometimes interfered with my learning	This has seldom or never been a problem to me
1 Lack of confidence.			
2 Not getting enough feedback on how my learning is going.			

Cause of unsuccessful learning	This often interferes with my learning	This has sometimes interfered with my learning	This has seldom or never been a problem to me
3 Breakdown in communication: not being able to understand what is expected of me.			
4 Couldn't make sense of the topic – couldn't understand it.			
5 Couldn't see *why* I was learning the topic.			
6 Couldn't see where it was leading to.			
7 Wasn't able to *show* that I had mastered it.			
8 Seemed to learn too many of the wrong things and not enough of the right things.			
9 Didn't like the subject.			

Discussion: some common causes of unsuccessful learning

Probably not many of the answers given in Question 4 apply to your learning, but if there are one or two which have done in the past, it is useful to think about some of the implications. Ignore the responses below to those causes of unsuccessful learning which have never applied to you, but have a look at any which have affected your learning at some time in the past, or which affect it now.

1   *Lack of confidence.* This is a common reason for learning being less than optimal. If this has affected you in the past, or is still with you, many of the suggestions in this book will help you. In particular, when you gain the feeling that you are *in control* of your studies and are developing your own conscious strategy for securing a good degree, you will soon feel more confident about your learning.

2   *Not getting enough feedback on how my learning is going.* It is not surpris-
    ing that this can be a cause of poor learning, as feedback is indeed an
    important part of the learning process. We all need to know how our learn-
    ing is going. Sometimes, the lack of feedback is not the fault of those
    learning. University lecturers are less able to give the amount of feedback
    that they once did, due to larger class sizes and various other pressures on
    their time and energy – particularly the competing agenda of research,
    upon which their funding and promotion prospects depend, much more
    than on teaching and giving feedback to students. However, problems with
    feedback are not all caused by insufficient feedback and are often the
    result of people not being too good at *receiving* feedback. This does not
    just apply to critical feedback, but to positive feedback too. Later in this
    chapter we will look at how to make sure that you make good use of all the
    feedback that comes to you. In various parts of this book, I will also
    encourage you to take charge of the business of getting feedback on your
    own learning. There is a lot you can do to keep a check on how your own
    learning is going.

3   *Breakdown in communication: not being able to understand what is
    expected of me.* This is a very common cause of unsuccessful learning.
    Tackling this problem is therefore a major part of the strategy that you
    need to lead you towards a good degree. One of the most important items
    on your agenda is finding ways of tuning in to the assessment culture of
    each element of your course and of your university as a whole. The more
    you know about how assessment really works, the more you can adjust
    your work to gain marks and credit at every opportunity. In this book we
    will look at all the main assessment processes and instruments you are
    likely to meet and search for ways that you can tune-in to the assessment
    culture, so that you can demonstrate your optimum potential in each of
    the assessment formats you encounter.

4   *Couldn't make sense of the topic – couldn't understand it.* Most people
    remember at least something where this was the main problem. One of
    the problems is simply the word 'understand'. We never really know
    whether or not we understand things. Sometimes, just when we feel we've
    cracked it, we find out that there are hidden depths there that we'd never
    imagined and realize that we had only *started* to understand it. 'Making
    sense' is a better term. This at least implies that there is rarely an end to
    getting our heads round a topic, and that there will always be further
    things that can be learned about it. If this is one of your problems, the
    short message, at this point, is not to worry too much about understand-
    ing everything, and concentrate on showing that you know what to *do* with
    your subject matter, how to *use* it, and particularly how to *show* that you
    can use it. Many parts of this book will help you to find out how best to do
    this and how to get credit for the sense that you have made of everything
    you study.

5   *Couldn't see* why *I was learning the topic*. This is a natural reason for learning not being too successful. We all like to know the purposes behind what we do. We particularly like to have a rationale for anything that involves sustained hard work. Sometimes your lecturers will be good at helping you to develop this rationale, but sometimes it will be up to you. In either case, to take full control of your own learning, it is worthwhile having *your own* reasons for learning each topic on your degree course.

6   *Couldn't see where it was leading to*. This overlaps with point 5 above. If you know where a topic is leading you, it can help you to find the energy to learn it, even if at the time it seems a bit remote from reality. Often, lecturers will explain the links and connections, but sometimes you may need to go looking for them yourself. Syllabus documentation can be useful here and can alert you to when you will need something later in your course.

7   *Wasn't able to* show *that I had mastered it*. This is a very serious, and common, cause of unsuccessful learning. The actual learning is not, of course, unsuccessful, when you have mastered something, but unless you can *prove* that you've mastered something, you can't get credit for it. Many parts of this book address this issue. We will explore how best to ensure that you can *communicate* your mastery, through continuously assessed coursework and in exams. We will also look at the different ways in which you will need to be able to communicate your mastery, ranging from writing in exam rooms against the clock to answering questions verbally when interviewed by lecturers. In assessed situations, you only get marks for what you *show* of what you know.

8   *Seemed to learn too many of the wrong things and not enough of the right things*. This has happened to most people at one time or another. It is particularly the case in the context of exams, when the 'wrong' questions appear on the paper! Getting a good degree depends, at least in part, on minimizing this problem. You need to be sufficiently capable of proving that you have mastered those elements of your learning that are actually assessed. It is certainly unwise to spend a disproportionate amount of your time or energy learning anything that would get in the way of your successful coverage of a good spread of your subject matter.

9   *Didn't like the subject*. We can't be expected to *like* all the topics that we learn. It is perfectly natural to have preferences. However, there may be important parts that you *need* to learn, but still don't *want* to learn. This calls for some self-discipline. What is the difference between wanting to do something and needing to do it? A 'need' can be thought of as a perceived lack. If you know that you lack the necessary knowledge or skills to succeed in your studies of a particular topic, this is still not quite the same as wanting to learn it, but can be quite sufficient as a driving force to lead you towards learning it successfully.

Wanting to learn, needing to learn, and making sense of what you learn: these are the main processes which come to light when we analyse what is missing when learning is unsuccessful. It stands to reason, therefore, that they too are primary factors underpinning successful learning.

Five processes for successful learning

Bringing together the questions and responses that we've explored so far, there are five processes that you can take control of in your strategy for getting a good degree. They are:

1 Wanting to learn: being self-motivated – driving your own learning.
2 Needing to learn: taking ownership of the targets – being clear about your goals.
3 Learning by doing: practice, trial, and error, having a go, experiential learning.
4 Feedback: finding out *how* your learning is going.
5 Making sense of what you're learning: 'getting your head round it', understanding it more and more.

You may be interested to know that this way of describing the central processes underpinning successful learning has become known as the 'Race' model of learning, but it really belongs to the thousands of people who answered my four questions, as you did in the previous section.

It's worth saying a little more about the 'making sense' or 'digesting' side of learning. If you think of the normal physiological meaning of 'digesting', it means extracting what we need from what we eat and drink. We only take from our food that which is useful to us and will energize us for the future. We reject in due course 90-odd percent of our food intake. The rejected parts are the roughage, and we need to make good use of the valuable components. Learning can be thought of as involving mental digesting, where we take forward from each learning experience only the knowledge and skills that we need, and reject or leave aside those parts which were merely a means to this end. As a process to help you get a good degree, digesting is very much connected to making your learning focused and efficient, and spending time working at those parts of your curriculum which are most closely linked to gaining credit and scoring marks in assessments.

How are these factors connected?

The human brain is very sophisticated. We don't just do one thing at a time when it comes to thinking and learning. *All* the five factors discussed above are

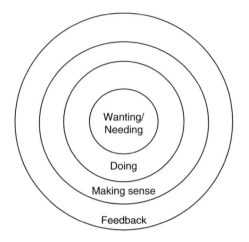

FIGURE 1.1 The 'ripples on a pond' model of learning

going on *all* the time when you study. They all go on, all of the time, as you *live*! There's nothing special about learning here, it's a perfectly natural part of living. *Studying* is slightly different only in that it involves *intentional* learning, rather than incidental learning. I suggest you think of all these processes inter-acting with each other in your mind, like ripples on a pond (see Figure 1.1). They all affect each other. When they are working together, they all enhance each other. If any one of them is missing, the ripple of learning can fade away into nothing.

At the centre of the ripple are the processes of *wanting* to learn and *needing* to learn. Either will do. If you really *want* to learn something, you are very likely to succeed. If you really *need* to learn something, this too is an effective driving force. If you both want to learn *and* need to learn, you should be unstoppable! They are, if you like, where the pebble falls into the pond. They are the source of the energy which radiates outwards and gets reflected back from the outside world. The next part is the learning by doing part, involving practice, trial and error, and so on. Then there's the 'making sense' part – getting your head round what you're learning. The outer part is feedback, coming in from all directions: from your fellow students, from expert witnesses such as lecturers, from resources such as books, learning packages, the Internet, and so on. The feedback needs to be digested, along with the results of the learning by doing stage. At any instant in time, your mind may be busier with one of these processes than with the rest, but they are all still going on under the surface of your mind even then. You can extend the metaphor if you wish, to include learning getting deeper as if the continuation of the ripples causes growing stirring in the deeper layers of the pond. However, one main point that I want you to take away from this metaphor is that these key factors underpinning successful learning continuously interact with each other. The other main point is that you can quite consciously set out to gain ownership and control of all five of them.

How can I harness these learning processes?

All five of these processes lend themselves to harnessing. There is nothing mystical about them. You can decide to do something about them, to bring them to bear on your study strategy. You can develop study habits around them, including those listed below.

Wanting to learn

You can identify those parts of your studies that you really enjoy and then strike your own balance to ensure that you don't *just* study the things that you like, but build in sufficient attention to the other things which are on your syllabus. You can also review your own reasons for studying in general and seek to strengthen your motivation by finding additional reasons why you *want* to succeed.

Needing to learn – taking ownership of your targets

When wanting to learn is not the main driving force, it is useful to identify the benefits that will come to you as a result of your studies. Most subjects have difficult or boring areas where you may find that you have to look ahead to see where your efforts are going to lead you.

Learning by doing: practice, trial and error, having a go, experiential learning

As you progress through your degree you will experience plenty of learning by doing under other people's control. You will be given set exercises, assignments, practical work, and so on, some of which will form the basis of assessed coursework. However, this does not mean that your learning by doing stops there. No one can stop you from building in a great deal more learning by doing under your own initiative too. Throughout this book we will think about the *learning pay-off* of each of many different kinds of practice, and this will help you to build up speed in many of the processes which pay assessment dividends as well as learning ones. The more time and energy you devote to your own agenda of learning by doing, the better able you become to *do* things which prove that your learning has been successful, and the faster you become at proving this.

Feedback: finding out how your learning is going

You will get a lot of feedback from tutors and lecturers, mainly linked to assessed components of coursework. You can, however, seek much more feedback on how your learning is going, particularly by working collaboratively with fellow students, and comparing your learning to theirs. You can also give yourself feedback on how your learning is progressing by building into your normal study habits self-assessment of your own knowledge and skills, to help you to identify in good time those elements that will be the most valuable and important areas to which to devote additional time and effort.

Making sense of what you're learning: 'getting your head round things', increasing your understanding

Of the five processes, this is the one that is most directly *your* responsibility. No one can do your digesting for you! No one is likely to tell you to get on with it. It is more or less *assumed* that motivated students will organize for themselves the actions and processes which lead to making sense of what they are learning. The best ways of checking that you are making sense of what you have been learning is to test yourself out with it. Practice at testing yourself is ideal rehearsal for formal assessments too.

What are your relevant strengths?

What can you bring to bear on the task of earning a good degree? What do you already know about yourself, in the way of strengths, good habits and attitudes that will serve you well in fulfilling your ambition? There are all sorts of possible answers to these questions. Use the following question box to write down short notes about three of your own strengths, which you think will be highly relevant. Then, balance the situation by writing short notes about three 'things to watch out for' that could get in the way of your success.

Three strengths that will help me towards getting a good degree:

1

2

3

Three things that could interfere with my getting a good degree:
1
2
3

Only you will know how well you chose the strengths and weaknesses that you may have jotted down. However, we will continue by looking in a structured way at 20 factors which may work for you or against you, depending how you harness them. In the next task, look at each statement in turn, and make a decision, ticking one of the three columns as appropriate. It's worth your doing this, rather than just thinking about the statements, as we will return again to this list of 20 strengths after you've had time to reflect on your choices.

Select on the following basis:

- This is very like me.
- This is quite like me.
- This is not at all like me.

Please enter ticks in the appropriate columns now, and we will return to these statements later to see if you may wish to change your decisions about where you have placed your ticks after thinking further about the issues involved as you continue working through this chapter.

Task: finding out about your strengths

Strengths?	This is very like me	This is quite like me	This is not at all like me
1 When I start something, I almost always finish it; I stick at things.			

Strengths?	This is very like me	This is quite like me	This is not at all like me
2 I want a good degree for *me*, not just to satisfy other people's expectations of me.			
3 I'm good at organizing my time and finding time to do whatever I know I need to do.			
4 I'm good at deciding what is important and not just getting on with what seems to be urgent.			
5 I'm good at receiving feedback from other people, both when it's positive and when it's critical.			
6 I always try to work out for myself how well I have done something, even when someone else will be telling me later.			
7 I've always succeeded in the past, and I don't expect any problems getting a good degree next.			
8 I don't waste time thinking about doing some work, I just get on with it straightaway.			
9 I believe in planning what I do and spend the first part of my time on anything planning it.			
10 If I can't see what the point is of doing something, I tend to leave it and do something that I can see the point of.			

Strengths?	This is very like me	This is quite like me	This is not at all like me
11 I work best by myself; working with other people just wastes too much time for my liking.			
12 I find it useful to work with other people, as this means I get more ideas than I would if working by myself.			
13 When I do something that is going to be assessed, I find out every bit of information I can about what is going to be looked for by those assessing it.			
14 When I do something that is going to be assessed, I just put everything I've got into it and hope that this will be more than enough to score well.			
15 People tell me that I have a good way with words when I write essays.			
16 I get good feedback when I write reports, especially regarding style, structure, and coherence.			
17 I know myself well enough to recognize my work avoidance strategies and don't let myself get slowed down by them.			
18 I never feel that my learning of something is finished, but that it is sensible to reach a resting level for the present time.			

Strengths?	This is very like me	This is quite like me	This is not at all like me
19 I set myself small-scale targets and break big tasks down into a series of achievable bits.			
20 I feel that there is nothing that I can't do, if I really set my heart on doing it.			

Discussion: auditing your strengths

1   *When I start something, I almost always finish it; I stick at things.* This is something to be proud of, at least under normal circumstances. If this is 'very like you', you have a major strength here. This is one of those strengths that employers love. You are likely to be dependable, thorough, conscientious, and productive. As far as getting your good degree, however, there's just one thing that could be a danger: are you making a habit of starting and finishing the *right* things? There's not much point in being very conscientious about things that don't count much. Many of the suggestions in this book should help you to decide which things are worth sticking at and finishing well, and which things may be better left unstarted.

2   *I want a good degree for me, not just to satisfy other people's expectations of me.* This is important. Well done if you ticked the 'very like me' column for this one. As we've already explored, there are many reasons for wanting a good degree, and the best reasons are those that *belong* to you and are not too dependent on other people. If there *are* other people who expect a lot of you, the best way not to let them down is to expect a lot of yourself and set your own sights high.

3   *I'm good at organizing my time and finding time to do whatever I know I need to do.* This is a very useful skill indeed. If you can manage time, you can manage just about everything else. Good time management is not just a matter of working hard. It's more to do with using your time well and making time for the important things. Studying for a degree could fill all the time you've got twice over and more, so it becomes all the more crucial to make wise decisions about how much time you devote to each particular facet of your studying and to make sure that everything you do is relevant to your ultimate goal: that good degree (and of course all the further goals and opportunities that getting your degree will open up to you). If this is one of your strengths, well done. If not, however, this is not

bad news, as there is a lot you can do to take charge of time, rather than letting time take charge of you.

4 *I'm good at deciding what is important and not just getting on with what seems to be urgent.* This links back to point 3 above. One of the secrets of time management is task management. Task management concerns making decisions about what is urgent, and what is important.

There are four main kinds of task:

- Urgent and important.
- Non-urgent but important.
- Urgent but not important.
- Non-urgent and not important.

See if you can now decide how to strike a sensible balance between urgent and important tasks. Jot down your own further thoughts below, then compare them with my response at the end of this chapter.

5 *I'm good at receiving feedback from other people, both when it's positive and when it's critical.* This is a major strength. If this is already 'very like you', well done, and keep it that way. While it is possible to get a good degree without being good at taking feedback from other people, it's not quite so possible to live a successful life that way. For many people, however, the quality of their degrees depends very significantly on how well they tune in to feedback from other people. After all, other people will be marking your final exam scripts. The more you know about how they will be thinking while they do this, the better you can deliver what they are looking for in those scripts.

6 *I always try to work out for myself how well I have done something, even when someone else will be telling me later.* This is a really useful skill. It's called self-assessment and you may even have to do some of this as an assessed part of your degree. However, self-assessment is too useful just to be something that you do when you are asked to do it. When you try to work out how well (or otherwise) you have done something, you are getting your head round the subject and deepening your learning of it. Also, in the process of working out how well you have performed, you are likely to be looking for feedback and seeing what other people think of what you have tried to do. Looking for feedback is much better than just sitting back waiting for it to come to you.

7 *I've always succeeded in the past and I don't expect any problems getting a good degree next.* If this is 'very like you' it could be good news or bad news! The good news is that since you've always succeeded in the past, you are confident that your success will continue. You may well be justified in your own confidence. I hope that various sections of this book will be useful to you in confirming that your confidence is indeed well-founded. The bad news is that you may be just about to encounter the first situation where you meet your match! In that case (or if you selected the 'not at all like me' option), the agendas in this book should be of great value to you. Knowing more about in what areas you will be required to demonstrate your success will help you structure your activities to make sure you achieve your potential.

8 *I don't waste time thinking about doing some work, I just get on with it straight away.* If this is 'very like you', well done. If not, you can probably already see how useful it is not to waste time thinking about work, but getting on doing it. However, think back to our earlier discussion about what is urgent and what is important. It is worth not just doing any old work straight away, but doing something worthwhile straight away. You may be wise to budget some time for reflection or digesting, if you're intent on working smart and not just hard.

9 *I believe in planning what I do and spend the first part of my time on anything planning it.* Well done if you chose the 'very like me' option for this one. In all sorts of contexts, planning your work is important in setting you up towards getting that good degree. Planning takes time, but it also *makes* time. Planning can help you to save yourself from doing things that would not have been worth doing. Planning can help to make sure that the things you do decide to do are important, worthwhile, focused, and useful. Don't *just* do your planning at the beginning, however. All plans benefit from periodic review and adjustment. You will get further ideas about what is sensible to do well *after* you start working. Plans need to evolve and mature. This too is one of the measures of the skills which lead towards a good degree.

10 *If I can't see what the point is of doing something, I tend to leave it and do something that I can see the point of.* This is a perfectly natural reaction, but it can lead you into danger! Sometimes you will be right in questioning the point of tasks that you are set on your course. At other times, however, the real point of the tasks may not become apparent until much later. It would be better if your lecturers always explained why you were being given particular things to do, but not all of them see it as their job to explain such things. They may feel that you should trust that they would not ask you to do anything without a good reason. You can, sometimes, enquire about the purposes of a task and their responses may be very useful, but they may not always be willing (or have time) to explain

themselves. The best solution is to have a go at such tasks anyway, at least until you have a better idea about whether they are good investments of your time and energy. By all means *also* do things where you *can* see the point.

11 *I work best by myself; working with other people just wastes too much time for my liking.* This is fine as long as you are *really* ahead and not in need of any feedback about how your learning is going compared to that of everyone else around you. It is also fine if you're rather antisocial, and don't much like your fellow students! However, it's a high-risk strategy. *Good* degrees tend to be awarded to people who are able to work well with others, as well as to work effectively on their own. Employers are particularly keen to have evidence that job applicants can work well with people, however good their qualifications may be. More important than any of these factors is the fact that you need feedback on your own learning as part of making your learning focused and efficient. If this statement was 'very like you', I would suggest that you should think seriously about spending at least *some* of your time and energy working with fellow students. This can add to the enjoyment of studying and enable you to make new friends, but can also improve and deepen the quality of your own learning and contribute significantly towards getting your good degree.

12 *I find it useful to work with other people, as this means I get more ideas than I would if working by myself.* If this is 'very like you', well done. This not only paves the way towards your life at university being more sociable and enjoyable, but it also helps you to develop key interpersonal skills which are highly valued by employers, and which can help to get you a good job after your good degree. In several universities there is already a move to build into the curriculum students' development of such 'key skills', and to measure students' development of these along with their subject-related knowledge and skills.

13 *When I do something that is going to be assessed, I find out every bit of information I can about what is going to be looked for by those assessing it.* If this is 'very like you', there's nothing wrong with it. It is perfectly logical and natural to want to know where the goalposts are in the game of playing for a good degree. It is wise to tune yourself in to the assessment culture of your course and of your university. It would be tragic if you worked hard enough to deserve a good degree, but did not achieve your aim simply because you were not *showing* that you deserved it at the times when it mattered and in the ways which were expected or required.

14 *When I do something that is going to be assessed, I just put everything I've got into it and hope that this will be more than enough to score well.* This should work, but doesn't usually! Putting everything you've got into it is not always quite the same as really *thinking* about what is likely to be expected by those assessing you. Most of the marks go with things that

are directly relevant to the task or question as asked, and if you put too much else into your work, the chances are that you will lose marks by irritating your assessors. It is fine to put in that little bit extra, to distinguish yourself from most of the other candidates, but if you go overboard with the extras, the law of diminishing returns tends to apply.

15 *People tell me that I have a good way with words when I write essays.* If this is 'very like you' you're already at an advantage. At least some of the marks for any essay are associated with how well you express your ideas. There are, of course, other marks for how *good* your ideas themselves are, so you need both to score really good marks for essays.

16 *I get good feedback when I write reports, especially regarding style, structure, and coherence.* This is a good indicator of success in coursework. However good may be the content of a report, to score well in assessment you also need to write in a fluent, well organized, and convincing way, and to adopt an appropriate tone and style for the kind of report that you are writing. If your course involves report writing, cultivate this skill and make the most of it to score well with your reports.

17 *I know myself well enough to recognize my work avoidance strategies and don't let myself get slowed down by them.* This is a valuable claim to be able to make. We all have some work-avoidance strategies, but once we recognize them and fight them, we are more than halfway towards conquering them. If this is 'not like you' and you suspect that there are work avoidance strategies that you have not diagnosed for yourself, you should find many of the discussions in this book helpful in enabling you to identify and counter such tendencies.

18 *I never feel that my learning of something is finished, but that it is sensible to reach a resting level for the present time.* There is a lot of wisdom in this position. With many subjects, especially with difficult or complex ideas and concepts, it can take some time to really get your head round them. It is appropriate to do it in manageable stages and to consolidate your learning on one level before moving on to deepen and extend it.

19 *I set myself small-scale targets and break big tasks down into a series of achievable bits.* If this is 'very like you', well done! Even the most daunting tasks are more manageable when broken down into smaller, separate components. In fact, the whole matter of getting yourself a *good* degree is best tackled by breaking the overall task down into a range of separate steps, and devoting time and energy as necessary to each step.

20 *I feel that there is nothing that I can't do, if I really set my heart on doing it.* If this is 'very like you', you're in good company. Setting your heart on learning something well is a manifestation of real motivation, and this works. It can be important not to be too single-minded when trying to master something that is really difficult, however, as there is the risk of spending *too* much time and energy on such a topic, at the expense of several other less demanding topics which need to be mastered too.

Most of this chapter has been about learning, and gaining control of your own learning. Continue to think about how everything else in the succeeding chapters relates to your own learning. When we explore different teaching–learning situations, concentrate on what *you* can do to keep control of your learning in every situation you encounter. When we explore all the different resources available to you (human as well as materials), keep in mind how you can bring each resource to bear directly on your own learning. When we explore all the different ways in which you may be assessed, bear in mind that you need to tune your learning in appropriately to each different assessment format, so that your learning is measured to have been successful.

Taking charge of your time

Earlier in the list we've just finished I asked you to think about the balance between urgent tasks and important ones. Compare your thoughts to mine, as shown in Figure 1.2.

Let's look at how to get your act together regarding task management. Suppose you have inherited quite a lot that's urgent and important, and your main purpose is to clear your backlog and move towards a steady situation where you have time under control as far as possible.

1 *Urgent and important tasks*: these are worth spending time on – say, for sake of argument, 50 percent of the time you can realistically make available to your studies. It would, of course, be better if there were less tasks in this category and we'll head towards this situation soon.
2 *Not urgent but important tasks*: these too are worth spending time on. If 50 percent of your time is spent on urgent and important tasks, maybe 30 percent should be spent on important but not urgent tasks.
3 *Urgent but not important tasks*: these may well have to be done or else they would not have become urgent. However, if they're not important, it's probably best not to spend too much time doing them. About 15 percent of your total available time may be a sensible allocation for these tasks. If they

Urgent and important: 50%	Not urgent but important: 30%
Urgent but not important: 15%	Not urgent and not important: 5%

FIGURE 1.2 Balancing tasks

contribute towards your assessment, it is more important to do all of them, *reasonably* well, than to do some of them brilliantly.

4 *Not urgent and not important tasks*: it's tempting to say 'bin these'! However, that would be rather too prescriptive, and anyway there may be some things here that you really *want* to do. Perhaps the optimum approach would be to use bits of left-over time for the tasks in this particular category that you fancy doing, and let that amount be about 5 percent of your total available study time.

Keeping control of your time

Let's now look at the situation when you're getting your task management under control. Now, you've cleared most of the backlog of urgent and important tasks, and can afford to spend a much greater proportion of your time on tasks that are important but not yet urgent. There will still be *some* urgent and important tasks from time to time – life's like that!

1 *Urgent and important tasks*: now that you've cleared the backlog, maybe you'll only need to spend 30 percent of your available time on this sort of task. Some of this will be last minute bright ideas that come to you, for example second thoughts that are too good to waste shortly before the hand-in dates of coursework, or perhaps a bit of last minute revision before exams when you find out that you're actually about to crack an important concept or idea.

2 *Not urgent but important tasks*: now that there aren't so many urgent tasks crowding your days, you can realistically spend more than half of your available time (say 60 percent) on things that are important without being urgent. The more time you spend on this kind of task, the less likely it will be that they will become urgent. This situation also gives you the feeling of really being in charge of your studies and doing things for yourself, rather than because someone else's deadline is approaching.

3 *Urgent but not important tasks*: there will still be some of these and it remains better to do them than to skip them, especially if they count towards something that is assessed. However, by now your strategy should enable you to polish these off in as little as 5 percent of your available study time.

Urgent and important: 30%	Not urgent but important: 60%
Urgent but not important: 5%	Not urgent and not important: 5%

FIGURE 1.3 Re-balancing tasks

4 *Not urgent and not important tasks*: if your strategy is going really well, you may be able to spend a little more time on these tasks when you want to. However, they are still rather a luxury, so it would be best to aim to keep them down to 5 percent of your available time.

Taking stock

If you've worked conscientiously through the exercises and discussion in this chapter, you should now have a much better idea of your strengths and of the extent to which you already live up to a range of habits linked to the sort of effective studying that can earn you your good degree. I hope too that you've found out some things about learning – things you may never have thought about previously. In this chapter we've been concentrating on learning; in the next chapter, we'll move on to thinking a bit more about *teaching* – exploring some of the main teaching–learning contexts you're working in. Of course, learning remains the important thing. The best teaching in the world is not in itself enough to get you your good degree – learning remains your business.

2

Making the most of your course

Making the most of your lectures • Small group tutorials • Seminars • Studio work • Field work • Laboratory work • Group work • One-to-one meetings with staff • Work-based learning

You will meet a variety of teaching situations during your degree programme, and this chapter aims to help you make the most of all of the main kinds of teaching which you meet. The balance between these varies considerably, depending on your discipline area, what kind of university you are studying with, and the general ethos of your course. To make the most of all the different teaching situations you encounter, the primary requirement is for you to regard each of them as *learning* situations. Never mind the teaching, feel the learning! Not all of your learning happens in such situations as lectures, seminars, studios, and so on, of course; quite a lot of your real learning happens under your own steam, in independent study contexts – for example in your private reading, practising solving problems, talking to fellow students, doing assessed coursework, and revising for exams. All this is over and above the many hours you clock up in teaching situations and there are many suggestions about how you can make the most of your independent studying elsewhere in this book. However, capitalizing on teaching situations means that you can put all of your time to good use.

It is dangerously easy to switch off from learning in teaching situations. However, just because someone else is controlling the situation (for example, a lecturer delivering a rather dull lecture) does not mean that your mind is being controlled for you. You are still in charge of what you think. You are in charge of how you *capture* what you need to take away from the teaching situation. You can plan how to get what you need from it to make your subsequent learning more productive. You can make a good start on your learning while still *in* the teaching situation. If nothing much is happening that is of real value to you (maybe, for example, when you find yourself listening to things that you already know and understand), you don't have to switch off your brain. The choice is yours as to whether you think about and learn other parts of your subjects at such times.

In this chapter, we will explore some of the most common types of teaching–learning situation one at a time, and look at how you can derive the maximum learning pay-off from them, whether or not the tutors who are handling them are brilliant facilitators of learning (relatively few are!). For each type we will ask questions such as these:

- What are the main characteristics of the teaching–learning situation?
- Why is this situation part of your course?
- What are you supposed to be getting out of the situation?
- How do you rate yourself against the habits of students who make such situations deliver high learning pay-off?

In this chapter, we will explore in some depth lectures and small group tutorials. I've also included brief discussions of seminars, studio work, field work, laboratory work, group work, one-to-one contexts, and work-based learning, but return to several of these in much more detail in Chapter 6 on 'Going for gold in assessed coursework', because it's the assessment aspects of these which are by far most important in getting you your good degree. Therefore, some of these contexts are merely introduced in this chapter, so you can see what they mean, and how they may (or may not) fit into the overall shape of your own course or university.

Before continuing with this chapter, I would like you to think about the relative importance of these types of teaching–learning situation in your own degree programme. You may not have all of them in your particular subjects or you may have some extra teaching–learning situations, in which case you should be able to extend and extrapolate the ideas presented in this chapter into these contexts too.

Task: ranking the importance of various learning contexts in your own course

How important do you think each of the following teaching–learning situations is in *your* degree programme? In other words, which contexts do you really need to make the most of, towards making sure that you get a good degree? (And don't worry, you probably won't have at least some of these contexts at all in your own programme.)

Teaching–learning situation	Most important	Quite important	Not very important	Not applicable to me
1 Lectures.				
2 Small group tutorials.				
3 Seminars.				
4 Studio work.				
5 Field work.				
6 Laboratory work.				
7 Group work.				
8 One-to-one contexts.				
9 Work-based learning.				

Discussion: the relative importance of various learning contexts

Most students rate lectures as the most important of the teaching–learning situations they encounter. Thereafter, tutorials and/or seminars are the next most important situations. After these, the other situations tend to be seen as less central to the process of getting a good degree, though any of them can have their part to play if they are components of your own programme. In this chapter, we will explore lectures and tutorials in some detail. For the other teaching–learning situations, which tend to be quite individual and specific in practice, we will explore some broad principles only, and I leave it to you to extend further our discussion of lectures and tutorials into each of the teaching–learning environments that you encounter on your course.

Making the most of your lectures

Whichever teaching contexts you rated as 'important' in the last activity, in just about all degree programmes there are lectures. And they are important. What are the main characteristics of lectures and *how* important are they? Complete the task that follows and then read the discussion.

Task: lecture characteristics

Which of the following characteristics of the lecture situation do you think are very important, quite important, or not really important in the context of *learning* from lectures in ways that will help you get a good degree?

	Very important	Quite important	Not really important
1 A shared experience with lots of other students.			
2 Time, place, content, and pace outside your control.			
3 If you miss a lecture, there is not much chance of catching up.			
4 Lecturers usually regard lectures as a very important part of the course.			
5 Lecturers are often your assessors, setting your exam questions and your coursework assignments.			
6 The content of lectures is normally very firmly based around the intended learning outcomes in your syllabus.			
7 Lectures often focus on subject matter which will be the basis of at least some of your assessment.			
8 In lectures there is not usually much chance for you to ask questions.			
9 In lectures you can often find out a lot more about what exactly may be expected of you in coursework assignments and exams.			
10 Lectures give you a chance to get a feel of how your own learning is progressing compared to fellow students in general.			

Discussion: the relative importance of lecture characteristics

I suggest that numbers 4, 5, 6, 7, 9, and 10 are the ones which are very important. A significant reason for this is that lecturers regard lectures as important. This means that they tend not to have much sympathy towards students who miss lectures. If you miss a lecture, even for a very good reason, the onus will largely be on you to try to catch up. You can of course get the notes or handouts relatively easily – you may be able to download them from the intranet, along with the slides the lecturer used. You also may be able to photocopy the notes made by a willing fellow student who was there. So you may *seem* to be able to catch up. However, any time you miss a lecture, you miss out on the *learning* that you could have done while you were there. While making your own notes during a lecture, it is possible to do a lot of 'making sense' of what you're writing about, so that next time you look at what you have written, much of your thinking during the lecture comes back to you. Looking at someone else's notes is not the same. Similarly, if you are present when handout material is being explained and elaborated upon, the handout will mean a lot more to you when you look at it again afterwards than if you look at a copy of a handout without any stored memories about it. Similarly, if you look again at copies of lecturers' slides, they mean much more to you if you can think back to the lecturer explaining them to the class than if you weren't there.

Why do you have lectures?

There are many reasons why lectures could be part of your course. They are not strictly *necessary* for learning to occur successfully, however. For example, thousands of students succeed on distance learning courses where there are no lectures at all. Think of all the things that *you* know and understand that were not the results of any lecture. Where lectures are part of your course, there are several 'reasons' for them being there, and some of these reasons are better than others. See if you can sort out the best reasons: try the task below.

Task: good and bad reasons for lectures – true-false quiz

This is a three-stage quiz.

First, decide whether you think each of the statements below is true (or nearly true) or false.

Then decide whether each represents a *good* reason for having lectures, or a bad one!

Finally, please read on and compare your views with mine and think about whether you're already making the most of your lectures, or whether you may wish to change how you approach them so that they help you more towards working for your good degree.

Reasons for having lectures?	True?	False?	Good reason?	Bad reason?!
1 Lecturers may feel that the best way for you to learn things that they themselves already know is for you to listen to them talking about them.				
2 Lecturers may feel that not much learning can happen without them doing some teaching.				
3 Lecturers are the best possible people to help you to learn things as they are experts, not only at the subject, but at teaching.				
4 Lectures are tangible events: they are occasions. For the course to 'exist', lectures provide some visible evidence of what the course really is.				
5 Lectures can be used to spotlight the really important parts of each subject, helping you to sort out what you really *need to know* from the material that is simply 'nice to know'.				
6 Lectures are whole group occasions, which can help a large group of students to form attitudes and develop views.				
7 Lectures can be a shared learning experience where you learn things alongside fellow students and can then talk to them about what you are learning.				
8 Lectures are a means of helping students to find out more about the assessment culture and about what constitutes a successful piece of coursework or what makes a good answer to an exam question.				

Reasons for having lectures?	True?	False?	Good reason?	Bad reason?!
9 Lecturers have to be given something to do so that they can be seen to be doing their job and so that their work is accountable in some way.				

Discussion: lecture agendas

As you will have seen, lectures are not all what they may appear to be. Here are my reactions to the agendas above.

1   *Lecturers may feel that the best way for you to learn things that they themselves already know is for you to listen to them talking about them.* They may *feel* this, but there is not a lot of truth in it, except in the cases of those lecturers who happen to be very good at helping students to learn.

2   *Lecturers may feel that not much learning can happen without them doing some teaching.* Many lecturers seem to feel this to be true, but it mainly depends on how good they are at teaching, *and* how good the students are at learning from them.

3   *Lecturers are the best possible people to help you to learn things, as they are experts not only at the subject, but at teaching.* While most lecturers know their subject matter at least quite well, not many lecturers would claim that they are experts at teaching. Lecturers are appointed mainly on the basis of their subject knowledge, as measured through research publications and so on. Some universities also try to find out or to measure how good they are at teaching before they are appointed, but this is by no means easy to do. The first people to find out which lecturers are *not* good at teaching tend to be their students.

4   *Lectures are tangible events: they are occasions. For the course to 'exist', lectures provide some visible evidence of what the course really is.* This may well be true, but has little to do with whether or not lectures are useful as a means of getting *learning* to happen successfully.

5   *Lectures can be used to spotlight the really important parts of each subject, helping you to sort out what you really need to know from the material that is simply 'nice to know'.* This can often be the case in practice, and links firmly to successful learning. Some lecturers are particularly good at helping you to see what the most important ideas, skills, and concepts are. Others are not so good at this and you have to pay much more attention during their lectures so that you can interpret the signals that they give about what is important and what is just background information.

6   *Lectures are whole group occasions, which can help a large group of students to form attitudes and develop views.* This is a valid purpose for having lectures. A whole group occasion can be ideal for letting you see how many people have similar views to your own, and this can help you to get an overall feeling about where you stand in the context of your fellow students in general.

7   *Lectures can be a shared learning experience, where you learn things alongside fellow students and can then talk to them about what you are learning.* This can be true, especially when the lecturers are paying attention to what *you* should be thinking and doing during the lectures, rather than just their own performances. Probably the most important side of these 'shared learning experiences' is what you do with them afterwards – for example, in informal follow-up meetings *you* may participate in after the lectures, where you work out with fellow students what it all really means.

8   *Lectures are a means of helping students to find out more about the assessment culture and about what constitutes a successful piece of coursework, or what makes a good answer to an exam question.* This can be at least part of the rationale for lectures, and can then be a very useful function of large group sessions. When details about the way assessment works are to be shared with students, the fairest way to do this is with the whole group, rather than just with a few students.

9   *Lecturers have to be given something to do so that they can be seen to be doing their job, and so that their work is accountable in some way.* This is a valid reason for having lectures! It is not a *good* one, though, and has little to do with the quality of students' learning. However, as higher education becomes increasingly treated like a business, those in management positions seek to find performance indicators for lecturers, and the number of lectures someone gives is much easier to measure than the quality of them!

Nine more (and better) reasons for having lectures

Even nowadays when you can have your own access to the Internet, source materials, books, handouts, and a range of other learning resources, there are still several things that can best be achieved in large group sessions with classes. Some reasons for continuing the culture of having lectures include the following:

1 To clarify for you the expected learning outcomes, assessment processes, and standards.
2 To provide you with a focus, where everyone (especially if you are part of a large group) gets together regularly.
3 To add the power of tone of voice, emphasis, facial expression, and body

language to printed words or words on-screen, helping you to see what's important and what is not.

4 To provide you with material for later discussion.
5 To challenge your assumptions and beliefs.
6 To change or develop your attitudes and perspectives.
7 To give you a common 'briefing' for major tasks you will be set as you study the subject further.
8 To inspire you and whet your appetite, so that you go away and really get down to studying.
9 To give you the chance to deepen your thinking on things you already know.

What are you supposed to be *doing* in your lectures?

I've asked hundreds of lecturers what they *believe* their students do during lectures and thousands of students what they *really* do. As you may expect, many of the things students do during lectures are far from connected to the content of the lectures. Some of the most common things students do in lectures are listed below:

- Copying down things from the screen or board.
- Copying down things said by the lecturer.
- Reading handouts or copies of the lecturer's slides.
- Summarizing things explained by the lecturer.
- Becoming tired or bored.
- Gazing out of the windows (if there are any).
- Looking at other students.
- Worrying because they can't understand what is being talked about.
- Watching the clock – waiting for lunchtime, for example.
- Doodling, yawning, fidgeting, shuffling, texting, daydreaming – even sleeping.
- Reading things that have nothing to do with the lecture.
- Listening to the match on a personal radio.
- Thinking about coursework soon to be handed in for *other* subjects.
- Actually *doing* coursework due to be handed in for other subjects.
- Worrying about accommodation problems, cashflow problems, relationships.
- Feeling generally unwell – hangover, tiredness, flu, time of the month.

Only one of the things mentioned in the list above is a useful learning experience in its own right: 'summarizing'. This involves processing the content of the lecture, making decisions about the relative importance of different things and generally 'digesting' the material.

Most of the other things in the list above are unproductive in terms of learning pay-off. In particular, *copying* things down (whether from the screen or from what has been said) is not as useful as you may think it is. Most students will admit having been to lectures where they'd copied all sorts of things down (even written down 'dictated' passages) without actually thinking about the material at all at the time. They confirm that if they were to be quizzed about the notes they had just copied out, their answer would have to be along the lines of, 'Sorry, I haven't actually *read* it yet – ask me again later!' It is true that students will often get down to learning what they have copied *later*, but that does not alter the fact that during the lecture itself they were in effect wasting their time and energy on processes with no direct learning pay-off. Even reading handout materials or copies of the lecturer's slides can all too easily have low learning pay-off – we don't actually remember much of what we've read unless we've actually *done* something with it while reading it.

Some more productive lecture processes

What can you do to get the most from your lectures? There are several activities that you can engage in during lectures which can be productive in terms of your learning pay-off from them. In the list below I've linked some things that you can do (or feel) during lectures to the five central processes involved in successful learning: wanting, needing, learning by doing, learning through feedback, and making sense of what you're learning:

- Becoming excited about the subject and enthused (increasing your 'want' to learn).
- Wishing to find out more about things discussed (getting ready to learn by doing things).
- Seeing *why* something is important (finding out why you need to learn things).
- Adding your own notes to handouts or copies of the lecturer's slides.
- Solving problems (learning by practising, trial and error).
- Trying out theoretical principles in practice-based examples (learning by doing).
- Making decisions (learning by doing, also making sense of what you're learning).
- Explaining things to fellow students sitting nearby (learning by doing, making sense of them yourself, getting feedback from your fellow students).
- Asking questions (seeking feedback).
- Working out questions for which you will need to find the answers later (preparing to seek feedback and paving the way for further learning by doing).
- Prioritizing issues and information (making sense of the information, turning information into your own knowledge).
- Summarizing (making sense of the subject, deciding what you really need to learn).
- Making notes in a manner that makes important things stand out from the page (making it easier to regain the sense of it later, learning by doing).
- Answering questions (learning by doing, getting feedback).

What do you actually *do* during lectures?

What you do often depends on how the lecturer conducts the session. Some lecturers seem to want to remain in charge of the proceedings throughout their lectures and tend not to involve students much. Others encourage participation and discussion. Try the task below to see what you can do to derive maximum learning pay-off from lectures.

Task: evaluating what you *do* in lectures

Rate each of the following processes that *you* may be able to do in lectures according to how significant you consider the associated learning pay-off to be. Then compare your ratings to the discussion that follows.

Things you do during lectures	High learning pay-off	Moderate learning pay-off	Low learning pay-off
1 Looking at the lecturer.			
2 Looking at the board or screen.			
3 Listening.			
4 Reading handouts or copies of slides.			
5 Taking notes: copying things down.			
6 Making notes: capturing things for yourself.			
7 Asking questions.			
8 Answering questions.			
9 Writing down questions.			
10 Discussing things with fellow students.			
11 Doing exercises and tasks.			
12 Thinking.			
13 Getting enthused about the subject.			
14 Comparing yourself to other students.			
15 Getting an overview: seeing the big picture.			
16 Spotlighting important details.			
17 Deciding which references to really follow up.			
18 Revising what you've done in previous lectures.			

Discussion: what can you *do* during lectures?

1 *Looking at the lecturer.* There's no guarantee of high learning pay-off from this one! If you *don't* look at the lecturer, you may give the impression that you're not interested, but it is possible to *look* attentive and interested even when your mind is completely on something else.

2 *Looking at the board or screen.* This isn't enough for high learning pay-off. You'll quickly forget most of the things that you see if you just *look* at the board or screen. To achieve high learning pay-off, you need to be *doing* something with what you see.

3 *Listening.* This can have high learning pay-off, but only if you are really listening *actively*. The best way to make your listening active is to give yourself the job of *capturing* what you are listening to. This means making decisions about it, in a form where you force yourself to think and capture your thinking.

4 *Reading handouts or copies of slides.* This is actually of quite limited value – we quickly forget things that we have read unless we've done something more than just reading.

5 *Taking notes: copying things down.* Sadly, the learning pay-off from copying things down is quite low. It's the *copying* that is the problem. This is a low-level task (even if you're very busy doing it!). This includes copying things down onto handout copies of 3-per-page or 6-per-page PowerPoint slides.

6 *Making notes: capturing things for yourself.* This has much higher learning pay-off than 'taking notes'. We will look at some ideas regarding *how* to make notes later in this section of the chapter.

7 *Asking questions.* This is an active process and can have high learning pay-off for the person asking the question. However, you don't always get the chance to ask questions. Even when asking questions is encouraged, it would be impossible for every student to be doing it all the time during lectures! Therefore, even though it is a high learning pay-off process, it is relatively low in frequency, so is limited in its overall effectiveness.

8 *Answering questions.* This can have high learning pay-off for the person answering the question. If the whole class is actively engaged in answering questions (for example, filling in answers on handout materials), the overall learning pay-off can be really significant. Unfortunately, most lectures are not built around getting students to answer questions.

9 *Writing down questions.* This can have very high learning pay-off. Even though you can't always *ask* questions in a lecture, you can always write down the questions you might have liked to ask. This gives you the chance to follow them up later. If you *don't* write down such questions during a lecture, there is every chance that within an hour or two you will

have entirely forgotten what the questions were and then you have no chance at all of following them up.

10 *Discussing things with fellow students*. This can have high learning pay-off. Some lecturers realize this and devise various tasks for students to do *during* lectures that help them to think actively about the topics being covered in the lecture. If, for example, you explain something to other students around you, you necessarily move towards sorting out your own thoughts and ideas about what you are trying to explain, and you will find that you remember such thoughts for a long time after the lecture. However desirable such discussion elements are, not all lecturers like them! You may need to undertake your own discussions with fellow students *after* a lecture rather than during it.

11 *Doing exercises and tasks*. This can have high learning pay-off. In lectures in maths and science disciplines, lecturers often set problems and tasks to be done in the large group situation. These involve learning by doing and also learning from feedback after you have had a try at the tasks. Make the most of such opportunities to do some real learning in lectures. Also, take particular notice of the tasks and exercises themselves: they are often dry runs for things that you will be required to do later in exams!

12 *Thinking*. Thinking *should* have high learning pay-off. Unfortunately, even one's best and deepest thoughts tend to evaporate. It is therefore necessary to *capture* our thoughts before we can claim high learning pay-off. Capturing your thoughts during lectures by making notes of them is the best approach. It is often just as important to capture your own thoughts about a topic as to write down what the lecturer is saying about it. Thinking is also rather difficult to control. How often have you sat in a lecture room and found your mind wandering far beyond the content of the lecture?

13 *Getting enthused about the subject*. This can be the *cause* of high learning pay-off to follow. This is one of the most significant benefits to you of the best lectures you experience. If you are enthused there is much more chance that you will go deeper into the topic after the lecture and research it. This is where the real learning pay-off is delivered.

14 *Comparing yourself to other students*. This can be a very useful thing to be doing in lectures. You can often tell how your own learning matches that of the people sitting around you. Watch their body language for clues to this. Take note of whether other people seem to be able to answer questions that you can't yet answer yourself. It is very useful to have an accurate picture of how your learning is going compared to that of other people. If you're ahead, don't be complacent, but aim to keep ahead: remind yourself that *you* are working towards a good degree. If you find yourself behind other people, the answer is obvious: do something about it!

15 *Getting an overview: seeing the big picture.* This is one of the main purposes of a good lecture. It is one of the hardest things to do on your own. Two factors contribute to the lecture being a good vehicle for seeing the big picture: first, the lecturer should already be in a position to see this picture, and to share it; second, in a large group you are aware of whether everyone *else* is seeing the big picture, and discussions and questions help to clarify the detail of the picture for everyone. Getting an overview delivers high learning pay-off in its own way. When you can see the big picture, you are better able to break it down into its individual components and home in on these in your own learning.

16 *Spotlighting important details.* This can have high learning pay-off. Lecturers often use lectures to spotlight the most difficult or complex parts of the big picture. They often take the view that it is necessary in lectures to take the whole group through such elements, so that they can judge from students' reactions whether or not they are understood properly. It is these elements that are often the basis for subsequent exam questions. Don't forget, however, all those parts of your curriculum that *aren't* spotlighted in lectures. It is usually the case that lecturers believe that you are perfectly capable of learning these parts under your own steam. These too will be tested in exams.

17 *Deciding which references to* really *follow up.* Lectures can be ideal occasions for you to make such decisions. You probably have much of the detail concerning further reading in handouts, course handbooks, and so on. In lectures, however, you've got more than print: you have tone of voice, facial expression, and body language, all of which can give you clues about the most important sources to follow up, and ideas on *how* to approach them.

18 *Revising what you've done in previous lectures.* Some lecturers try to build elements of revision into their lectures. Others, however, assume that when you come into a lecture you're already on top of the content of their previous lectures. It can be well worth your while taking on the responsibility for revising previous lectures, both before coming to another lecture and *during* the next lecture. If you have your previous notes with you, you can spend some of the time during a lecture putting the content into context.

Don't just *take* notes – *make* notes

I've already hinted at the vital difference between note-making and note-taking. The distinction is about not just working hard in lectures, but working *smart*! See if you can decide which is which. Try the task below.

Task: taking notes, or *making* notes?

Decide which of the following 22 things that you may do during, and after, your lectures are closest to note-making and note-taking respectively. Then compare your verdicts with mine in the discussion which follows.

Things you do during (and after) lectures	Note-taking	Note-making
1 Writing down, word for word, things your lecturer says.		
2 Copying down, word for word, what you see on the screen or board.		
3 Putting key ideas that your lecturer says into your own words and writing these down.		
4 Summarizing in your own words the most important information that you are shown on the screen or board.		
5 Writing down your own thoughts about what the lecturer is saying or showing you.		
6 Building up your own mind-map style notes during the course of the lecture, rather than writing your notes in a linear way.		
7 Writing down your own questions with which to test your knowledge and understanding of the content of the lecture.		
8 Writing down questions which other students ask, to remind you of further things you may be expected to get to know.		
9 Copying down worked examples that your lecturer goes through with the class, on the screen or board.		
10 Writing down your own answers to questions posed by the lecturer either orally or as tasks in handout material or shown on the screen or board.		
11 Highlighting the most important words or phrases in handout materials issued before or during the lecture.		
12 Highlighting other materials you have with you, such as textbooks (not library copies), copies of articles, and so on.		
13 Writing your own notes onto handout material or copies of the lecturer's slides, to add detail you want to think about in more depth.		

Things you do during (and after) lectures	Note-taking	Note-making
14 Comparing your lecture notes to those of a few fellow students and adding to yours anything important that they captured but you missed.		
15 Working out what the three most important things were in the lecture and annotating your own notes to indicate these.		
16 Working out what was background information or just 'means to an end' and annotating your own notes to show this.		
17 Getting together with a few other students and making a collective 'digest' of the main points to carry forward from the lecture.		
18 Making a parallel mind-map of the ideas covered in a lecture, after the lecture, from your own notes and those of fellow students.		
19 Downloading from the intranet the slides and handouts for a lecture you missed and reading through them.		
20 Writing out a fellow student's notes of a lecture you missed yourself.		
21 Photocopying the notes of a fellow student for a lecture you missed, then highlighting the photocopy.		
22 Constructing your own notes, in your own words, for a lecture you missed, from the notes of several fellow students who were there.		

Discussion: taking notes, or *making* notes?

1   *Writing down, word for word, things your lecturer says.* This is note-taking, and has low learning pay-off. In general, you won't remember much as a result of this. It is easily possible to become a human photocopier and just to write down what you hear without actually thinking at all about it! Your mind can be on something entirely different. You may still be able to learn from your copied notes later, but you will have to start learning from scratch then rather than from a position where you have already *thought* about what you were writing. There are, however, times when it is worth writing things down verbatim, such as when you need an exact phrase, or definition, and the wording has to be the same as is said by the lecturer.

2   *Copying down, word for word, what you see on the screen or board.* This is similar to copying down what your lecturer says, and is note-taking too. There may be some pressure on you to do this, even though the learning pay-off is very limited. For example, if a lecturer puts up an overhead and everyone around you is busily copying it down, you may feel under pressure to do the same. You may indeed *need* to copy down at least some of it, but much more important is what you *do* with it after you've copied it down. The lecturer may be enlarging on the points and it may be these details that are much more vital than the framework or bullet points on the screen or board.

3   *Putting key ideas that your lecturer says into your own words and writing these down.* This is note-making, and has high learning pay-off. It is a lot harder than note-taking, but infinitely more worthwhile. Putting things into your own words forces your mind to think about things and helps you to start to make sense of the subject. You will find that you remember far more when you look at notes you have *made* during a lecture than when you look at notes you merely *took* during a lecture. There is some risk involved, however. When you're intent on *making* notes, your mind may be so full of what you are doing that you can miss other things that the lecturer says. The best ways round this problem involve following up the lecture with like-minded fellow students (note-makers rather than note-takers), and seeing what they 'caught' in their notes that you missed. It can also be worth comparing your notes with those of some mere note-takers, in case their notes also contain something important that you missed.

4   *Summarizing in your own words the most important information that you are shown on the screen or board.* This too is note-making. It can be more productive to make your own notes about what you are shown than to use up your energies merely trying to capture the words that you see. Sometimes this will mean that you don't manage to capture everything that appears on the screen because you are *thinking* about what you are writing rather than reproducing it. This is not a problem if you are in the habit of following up lectures with fellow students and adding to your notes anything important that you may have missed during your thinking.

5   *Writing down your own thoughts about what the lecturer is saying or showing you.* This is note-making too. Your own thoughts are very important and are part of your learning. If you *don't* capture in writing your thoughts during a lecture, you may never think them again! You can always capture other things, such as what the lecturer said, or what appeared on the screen, from the notes of fellow students, but only *you* had your thoughts. In most lectures, you will find it quite straightforward to choose your times for writing down your own thoughts, such as when there doesn't seem to be anything else that needs to be written down.

6   *Building up your own mind-map style notes during the course of the lecture, rather than writing your notes in a linear way.* This is note-making

at its most advanced level, because you are not only putting things into your own words, but you are making your own structure for the emerging picture. Making mind-map notes is not possible in all lectures of course. Sometimes you need to write things down in a linear sequence, such as when recording solutions to numerical calculations or scientific derivations. Making mind-maps does bring with it some risks too. You could end up missing some of the important information that other students making linear notes have captured (even though you may have done a lot more thinking and learning in the process than they did). The solution is straightforward, however. Work with some students who aren't doing mind-maps until you get confident that you are capturing everything important.

7   *Writing down your own questions with which to test your knowledge and understanding of the content of the lecture.* This is note-making at its most useful. While you're *there* at a lecture is your chance to listen to tone of voice, watch facial expression, detect clues and emphasis, and work out what you are *really* expected to become able to do with the content of the lecture. There's no better way of capturing these thoughts than to turn them into questions and write down the questions, so that you can work towards being in a position to answer them all in due course. The questions are actually more important than the answers. You can always look the answers up, if you've got the questions. If you've just got the answers in your notes, that is no substitute for knowing what questions they are actually the answers to!

8   *Writing down questions which other students ask, to remind you of further things* you *may be expected to get to know.* This too is note-making. When someone else asks a question, the chances are that *you* too will be expected to become able to answer that question. It is more important to capture the question than it is to make notes of any answer given by the lecturer. You can always research the answer to any question on your own after the lecture.

9   *Copying down worked examples that your lecturer goes through with the class, on the screen or board.* This happens a lot in lectures in some subject areas. It is actually just note-taking, but may be quite important. The most useful things to capture are the *questions* or *task briefings* themselves. These are quite often indicators of the sorts of questions that you will be expected to become able to handle on your own, for example in exams. It can be worth storing up all these questions where you can't see the answers to them on the same page! The problem with looking at a worked example as taken down in lecture notes is that you can't help seeing the answer almost as soon as you've looked at the question. This robs you of any real chance to see whether you can actually answer the question without reference to the solution in your notes. When the question is stored somewhere away from the answer, you can have a go at

answering the question and *then* consult the solution to see if your answer was a good one.

10   *Writing down your own answers to questions posed by the lecturer either orally or as tasks in handout material or shown on the screen or board.* This is essentially note-making, and is also learning by doing. It is well worth doing. Be particularly careful to capture the questions themselves, if they are posed orally or on-screen. Then rewrite the questions somewhere else, so that you can practise answering them again later without seeing the solutions or answers.

11   *Highlighting the most important words or phrases in handout materials issued before or during the lecture.* Many students go to lectures with highlighting pens. Some turn their handouts into psychedelic displays, using more than one highlighter colour. This art can be developed even further, with (for example) pink for the most important details, yellow for clues to likely questions, green for things to follow up, and so on. Is it note-making or note-taking? Highlighting a word is not the same as writing it for yourself. It is still someone else's word unless *you* have thought of it and then written it. If you highlight 30 words in a minute you will probably not remember thinking about many of them very much. Highlighting can degenerate into quite a routine activity. You'll know that this has happened if you look at your highlighted handouts and find that you can't really remember *why* you highlighted particular words or phrases. The level of mental activity is probably closer to note-taking than to note-making. However, highlighting can be really useful as a *stage* in note-making, such as when you follow up your highlighted handout with another activity where you really *make* some notes on the basis of your reasons for having highlighted key words and phrases. To make this work well, you will need to process your highlighted materials within a few hours, so that you can still remember the details of your thoughts at the moment of highlighting things. Highlighting with your own code helps you to do this.

12   *Highlighting other materials you have with you, such as your own textbooks (not library copies), copies of articles, and so on.* In its way, this is more like note-making than is highlighting handout materials that are being used in the lecture. This is because *you* are in control of your own reading when looking at materials that you have brought with you, to a greater extent than you are when being led through a given handout along with the rest of the class. Some of the same arguments given above for highlighting handouts continue to apply, particularly those about the need for follow-up processing.

13   *Writing your own notes onto handout material or copies of the lecturer's slides, to add detail you want to think about in more depth.* This is note-making. It is also particularly significant in that when you write onto handout materials you have been given, you are turning them into your

own learning materials. They are no longer identical to everyone else's copies. They are no longer something that was given to you by the lecturer but now contain your ideas, questions, elaborations, and thinking. It is worth developing the habit of always trying to add to handout materials. Pave the way for your future work with them as learning resources.

14 *Comparing your lecture notes to those of a few fellow students and adding to yours anything important that they captured but you missed.* I've already mentioned some of the benefits of doing this in my discussion of several earlier points. This is note-making, and is also likely to be *good* note-making, as you are prioritizing, processing, and further refining the distilled products from the lecture. The learning pay-off from this process is so high that it is well worth structuring your study schedule to make time for it. One reason for it being so productive is that it is in essence combining *revision* with the deepening of your learning.

15 *Working out what the three most important things were in the lecture and annotating your own notes to indicate these.* This is note-making. It is particularly useful in that it is a prioritizing task, and you have to be *thinking* at least a little about *all* the material to get to the position of deciding what the most important parts are. It is much more active than simply re-reading the material you were given as handouts, or re-reading your own notes.

16 *Working out what was background information or just 'means to an end', and annotating your own notes to show this.* This is the other side of the prioritizing task mentioned above. It is just as useful in its own way. In most lectures, there's a fair amount of 'padding' – background detail that is needed to set the scene but which you're not expected to learn in its own right. The best time to decide which is information is just background and which is important is *during* the lecture, when you have tone of voice and other cues to help you make such decisions. However, you can still do this afterwards, but only for a relatively short time while your memory of the lecture is fresh and accurate.

17 *Getting together with a few other students and making a collective 'digest' of the main points to carry forward from the lecture.* By now, you will know that this is note-making! It is a very useful activity to engage in. Chewing over the content of a lecture with a few fellow students has all the advantages of learning by doing *and* getting feedback on your own learning to date. Furthermore, the 'digest' becomes a useful learning tool in its own right. Every time you see it, you will remember some of the thought processes and discussions that went into making it.

18 *Making a parallel mind-map of the ideas covered in a lecture,* after *the lecture, from your own notes and those of fellow students.* This too is note-making in its truest sense, and is by definition a very active process, in that you are translating your existing notes into a different format. This

means that you are really thinking about the content of your notes as you organize and refine them.

19   *Downloading from the intranet the slides and handouts for a lecture you missed, and reading through them.* This isn't much good at all in practice – not even as good as note-taking. You may indeed have captured the *information* linked to the lecture, but just reading it is no substitute for having been there listening, thinking, and (particularly) making sense of the materials by annotating them during the lecture.

20   *Writing out a fellow student's notes of a lecture you missed yourself.* This is no better than note-taking at its worst! Besides, if you do this, all you end up with is a copy of the fellow student's notes, which may only be a pale reflection of the lecture that you missed. There's no tone of voice, body language or any other cues as to what was really important.

21   *Photocopying the notes of a fellow student for a lecture you missed, then highlighting the photocopy.* This is only a little better than note-taking. The highlighting process has potential benefits, but not nearly so strong as those when you're highlighting your own notes and can still remember what your thoughts were as you made the notes.

22   *Constructing your own notes, in your own words, for a lecture you missed, from the notes of several fellow students who were there.* This is probably your best option when you have to miss a lecture. It's the triangulation that is important. Comparing and contrasting notes made by fellow students will tell you quite a lot more about the content of the lecture that you missed than would any one set of notes. When done well, reconstructing notes in this way can be described as note-making.

Developing good habits for lectures

How do you rate yourself against ten habits of students who work smart in lectures, and make them yield high learning pay-off? Rate yourself now, using the table below, and note particularly where you may wish to make some improvements to your lecture technique.

Evaluating your lecture habits

Ten good habits for lectures	Very like me	Quite like me	Not yet like me!
1 Checking back to the previous lecture before coming, so that you remember the context.			
2 Doing any work between lectures that was set by the lecturer and bringing it with you.			

Ten good habits for lectures	Very like me	Quite like me	Not yet like me!
3 Always turning up for lectures, on time.			
4 Making notes rather than taking notes.			
5 Downloading handouts and slides from the intranet (when available) and bringing printouts to the lecture to annotate during the lecture.			
6 Listening actively, rather than just hearing.			
7 Looking for the big picture.			
8 Helicoptering down (i.e., focusing in) to the detail.			
9 Following up each lecture within a few days, revisiting your own notes and handouts (and copies of slides where available).			
10 Continuously seeking to apply what you have learned in lectures.			

Small group tutorials

What are the main characteristics of small group tutorials?

Tutorials are quite different in many ways from lectures, and vary considerably in nature and structure across disciplines. For example in maths and science subjects, tutorials often take the form of problems classes, with students working through practice examples, which may be from past exam papers. In other subjects, tutorials are often the occasions where in-depth discussion follows up ideas and concepts which have already been introduced in lectures. Often, work is set in advance of tutorials and students are expected to turn up having done this work! It's really worth making sure you turn up, since if you are absent from tutorials you may find it difficult (more so than missed lectures) to find out exactly what you missed. The following list gives you some ideas about how tutorials are meant to support your learning.

Ten ways tutorials can increase your learning pay-off

1   There is usually a much smaller number of students compared to lectures or seminars.
2   Tutorials are much less formal than lectures and you should be able to participate actively.

3 You should be able to influence the pace and the content of tutorials.
4 Tutorials are normally regarded by lecturers as being your best opportunity to sort out any problems you are having with the content of the course as a whole.
5 Tutorials are usually linked to subject matter which will be the basis of at least some of your assessment, and often involve dry-runs of likely exam questions.
6 Tutorials may be linked directly to coursework assessment and particularly to your opportunity to get detailed feedback about coursework that has already been assessed.
7 Your performance or participation in tutorials may contribute towards your coursework marks.
8 Tutorials may be an opportunity for you to distinguish yourself from other students and earn the reputation of being someone who is heading for a good degree!
9 Tutorials may be your best chance to ask questions about things that you don't yet understand.
10 Participating actively in tutorials may give you opportunities to explain things you already understand to fellow students who don't yet understand them – which in fact is a very good way of deepening and consolidating your own learning.

Why are small group tutorials part of your course?

There is no agreed definition of a tutorial, and this is probably wise, as tutorials should fulfil one or more quite different roles. These include:

- Providing you with opportunities to learn by doing, practising applying things that have been covered in lectures, handouts, and learning packages.
- Addressing your motivation, helping to increase your confidence in your ability to handle the curriculum successfully.
- Providing you with feedback from other students as well as from the tutor, helping you to find out more about how your learning is progressing.
- Giving teaching staff opportunities to find out what problems students in general may be encountering with the subjects they are learning.
- Helping you to 'digest' or make sense of the concepts you are learning.
- Allowing you to ask questions which you may not be able to ask in large-group sessions.
- Inspiring your confidence when you have problems – a problem shared is a problem halved (at least).
- Providing you with customized support when you need it.
- Providing group learning opportunities, helping you to learn from other students.
- Helping you to develop good relationships with tutors and other students.
- Helping you to develop a questioning, lateral-thinking approach.

- Allowing tutors opportunities to share with you their enthusiasm for subjects.
- To provide feedback to students and gather feedback from students.

It can be seen from the list above that the potential value to you of tutorials is very high and that tutorials can provide a very significant driving force to enable you to build on your learning from lectures, learning resources, and independent study.

What do lecturers want you to do in tutorials?

The key factors lecturers are looking for in what you do during tutorials are:

- Contributing: asking questions, talking to fellow students, participating.
- Being prepared: having done set work, read up about the topic, and so on.
- *Not* pretending to understand things when you don't.

Tutorials are opportunities to show lecturers that you are one of the students who is heading towards deserving a good degree. They notice the differences between motivated, conscientious students and the rest. Asked what 'bad' students did regarding tutorials and why, a group of lecturers came up with the following points.

1 Lack of preparation: for example no idea of the topic of the tutorial (caused by mis-prioritization and/or laziness, lack of ambition, lack of enthusiasm for the subject, immaturity).
2 Signs of exhaustion, hangover, yawning (mis-prioritization).
3 Unwillingness to talk (shy, under-confident, unmotivated, fear of embarrassment, or sometimes lazy).
4 Arrogance (sometimes covering up inadequacies).
5 Absence (this can be lack of motivation, poor prioritization of activities, irresponsibility, lack of knowledge about the objectives of tutorials, or sometimes because students hate the tutor!).
6 Pretending to understand when they didn't (covering up inadequacies or lack of work).
7 Not taking an interest or not taking tutorials seriously (some students don't seem to see the purpose of tutorials and regard them as 'time filling' between other activities).
8 Dominating the discussion or being too argumentative (personality clashes, sometimes insecurity).

Not all problems are caused by students!

The same lecturers who diagnosed the student behaviours shown above also listed some of the things that *tutors* do, which cause tutorials to be less than successful. These include:

- Talking too much.
- Too much digression from the purpose of the tutorial.
- Concentrating on particular students.
- Letting one student talk too much.
- Ignoring particular students.
- Not knowing (or finding out) what the students do and don't know.
- Intimidating students with an over-critical approach.
- Being distracted from tutorials (phone, knock on door, and so on).
- Giving tutorials lower priority than lecturing or research.
- Not following up students' questions.
- Limiting the scope of tutorials to their own specialist field areas.

Telling your tutors that they are letting you down is not the best way to make a favourable impression! There may be ways of giving feedback so that the situation can be improved, such as through student representatives on course committees. However, the best (and safest) way of improving the quality of tutorials, and the learning pay-off that they can deliver, is for *students* to be seen to take them seriously, prepare well for them, and invest in them. You can play your part in this.

Task: developing good habits for tutorials

How do you rate yourself against the habits of students who make small group tutorials deliver high learning pay-off? Rate yourself against the following key habits and check whether there are any habits you should take steps to build into your own way of approaching tutorials.

Eight good tutorial habits: do you?	Always	Sometimes	Not yet!
1 Turn up for tutorials, on time!			
2 Contribute actively and positively.			
3 Avoiding being seen as a show-off or know all!			
4 Learning from fellow students as well as from the tutor.			
5 Looking for clues to the assessment agenda.			
6 Being well prepared for each tutorial.			
7 Showing enthusiasm and interest.			
8 Showing creativity and lateral thinking.			

Seminars

What are the main characteristics of seminars?

Seminars are in some respects not unlike tutorials, and indeed in some universities the two terms are used somewhat indiscriminately to describe similar events. The most usual difference characterizing seminars is for students (individuals or groups) to be given the responsibility for preparing to lead discussions, or giving presentations then answering fellow students' questions, Sometimes, students' seminar work is assessed, perhaps using peer assessment alongside or instead of tutor assessment. Sometimes, students' overall contribution to a programme of seminars is estimated, with attendance and participation being key indicators.

Some of the most common characteristics of seminars include:

- Fewer students than in lectures, but more than in tutorials.
- Seminars usually address a designated topic, known in advance by the group.
- If you miss a seminar there is not much chance to catch up.
- You may be asked to take responsibility (sole or collaborative) for preparing and delivering one or more seminars, and your performance or participation in seminars may be the basis for some assessment.
- There is more chance for you to ask questions than in lectures.

Why may seminars be part of your course?

The reasons for including seminars in courses are wide ranging and include:

- To allow a wide range of topics to be addressed in depth, by smaller groups of students, to deepen your learning of aspects of subject material introduced to the whole class in lectures.
- To pass over responsibility in turn to different students so that overall *all* students are involved in going into one or more particular aspect of the syllabus in depth.
- To allow students to take on the responsibility for researching selected topic areas and preparing to lead a discussion on them or give a presentation on them.
- To help students to develop their skills at independent work or working collaboratively with one or two other students.
- To allow students the opportunity to rehearse and practise presentation skills.
- To help to identify those students whose performance is indicative of what is expected for a good degree.

Sometimes, large classes are subdivided into a number of parallel seminar groups. For example, a class of 200 students may be split into ten seminar groups each containing 20 students. The seminar groups may stay together for the duration of the module or even the whole course, allowing group dynamics to develop, or they may be rearranged for each seminar element to allow students to mix and learn more from each other. Seminars are often facilitated or led by the lecturers who are delivering the module or course, but usually with the support of teaching assistants, postgraduate researchers, and sometimes other lecturers. This often means that although seminars are running in parallel they may be quite different in nature and content.

What are you supposed to be getting out of seminars?

The students who get the most out of any particular seminars are undoubtedly those who prepare them and present them. Other students may essentially be an 'audience' rather than anything else, and may not be expected to learn as much from seminars as from lectures or tutorials, but rather to deepen and extend their learning through the extra detail and depth that they experience by watching their colleagues going into particular elements of the subject in depth.

Different lecturers have their own expectations of what will be delivered through seminars. Some lecturers simply expect seminars to be a way for students to discuss and debate matters arising from what has been covered in lectures. Other lecturers may give detailed briefings for the content of a seminar programme, and prescribe in advance the topics and tasks that will form the basis of a coherent programme of seminars, with the purpose of deepening in a systematic and comprehensive way the syllabus coverage. Some lecturers will clarify that, in examinations, the content of the seminar programme will be assessed alongside the content of lectures and referred reading.

One important thing to remember about seminar programmes, especially if your lecture groups are large, is that seminars (like tutorials) are parts of your course where at least some of your lecturers and tutors have the opportunity to get to know individual students. This means that students who are obviously heading for a good degree tend to be noticed, as do students whose motivation is low or absent. Therefore, it is worth making sure that your own involvement and participation in seminars works for you rather than against you in raising your tutors' expectations of you accordingly. It is clearly advantageous to be an active participant in seminars, even when just in the 'audience' rather than presenting the seminar yourself. At the same time, you need to be the right *kind* of active participant and not just someone who always seems to have an awkward question to ask.

Elsewhere in this book I have given some suggestions about making sure that when it's *your* turn to give a seminar you make the most of your opportunity to gain credit both for your preparation and your performance on the day. For the present, however, let's look briefly at some of the habits which tend to distinguish students who are conscientious and visibly involved when *being at* other students' seminars. If you are already participating in a seminar programme, try the task that follows, which asks you to rate yourself against how well you are *seen* to be demonstrating these habits.

Task: good seminar habits

Rate yourself against the following good habits regarding participating in seminar programmes.

Good habits regarding seminars	I'm good at this	I'm OK at this	I'm not good at this
1 Turning up regularly, and punctually, for other student's seminars.			
2 Listening to what fellow students say, even when I have different views to theirs.			
3 Participating actively in seminars that I'm not actually giving myself.			
4 Having something to ask when questions are invited.			
5 Doing some research of my own in advance on the topic so that I have something to offer.			
6 Contributing *without* putting other students down, especially when disagreeing with them.			
7 Making summary notes during and after the seminar, capturing important detail to add to my lecture notes and other learning materials.			
8 Observing well and learning about communication skills by watching others practise them.			
9 Being seen by all present (not least tutors) as a useful and valuable member of the group.			

Studio work

Studio work is used a lot in disciplines such as art and design, drama, media studies, and architecture. It may be entirely absent and replaced by other teaching–learning situations if your main disciplines are in the maths, science, or engineering areas. On the other hand, if you are studying topics including art, design, media studies, and many related disciplines, studio work could be important. Where it *is* part of your course, it is likely to be a vital part of your experience and well worth investing in.

What are the main characteristics of studio work?

- Supervision by lecturers or tutors may be intermittent and you may be expected to take on a significant level of responsibility for organizing your own work.
- Your main human resource may be technical and support staff, who can be extremely valuable in helping you to develop the skills you need for studio work.
- You may have some choice about when you attend and for how long.
- You will have much more control over the pace at which you learn and the fine detail of the content.
- If you are absent there may be a good chance of catching up.
- Your performance or participation in studio work may be the basis for some assessment, but possibly not in proportion to the time you spend on it.
- There may be much more chance for you to ask questions than in lectures.

Why may studio work be part of your course?

The reasons for including studio work vary widely across disciplines. Some fairly general rationalizations include the following:

- To allow you to learn by doing, at your own pace.
- To allow you to learn from your mistakes.
- To allow you to work independently or with other people, or both.
- To provide you with opportunities to get detailed feedback on your work.
- To allow lecturers, tutors, and support staff to get to know you and your work in more detail.
- To allow lecturers and others to judge your potential.
- To allow you to prepare work which will in due course be assessed.

Good habits when doing studio work include:

- Managing your time there well. This is important in that studio work can easily eat deeply into your total available time. Just being there is not the same as working effectively while there. Don't just work hard in studios, work smart, and let it show!

- Working under minimal supervision. Studio work can give you the chance to show that you can take on the responsibility for organizing and managing your own programme of work, and at the same time decide wisely when you need advice or support.
- Using what's available creatively. Resources and equipment are often limited. While it may be tempting to grumble and protest that you could do much better 'if only . . .', the students who make the most of studio work tend to be those who accept the situation in which they find themselves and put to best use the resources which *are* there rather than wishing for resources which are not available.
- Actively seeking help when you need it. This is much smarter than just waiting for someone to pass by and notice that you are stuck.

Field work

Field work can be very enjoyable. It can be a welcome relief from formal lectures, busy tutorials, demanding seminar programmes, and searching for literature in libraries. Sometimes, field work can be literally 'out in the field', especially in disciplines such as geology, archaeology, botany, zoology, agriculture, and so on. Alternatively, it can be out in 'fields' such as business, industry, commerce, law courts, hospitals, and so on.

What are the main characteristics of field work?

- You may be working more or less on your own, or with some fellow students, with only intermittent support or supervision from tutors.
- Time and place are more or less fixed: field work may take quite a lot of organizing by tutors.
- If you are absent there may be little or no chance of catching up.
- Usually linked to subject matter which will be the basis of at least some of your assessment, but assessment pay-off may not be high considering the time you could spend doing field work.
- Could be a good training ground for research work.
- You will probably be assessed on the basis of a report or presentation *about* the field work, but maybe also on some aspects of your actual performance during the work involved.
- Usually plenty of opportunity for you to ask questions.

Why may field work be part of your course?

The reasons for including field work in degree courses are wide ranging, and very dependent on the particular disciplines and topics you may be studying. Typical reasons include:

- To give you the opportunity to learn by doing, in real-life environments.
- To help you to see the links and chasms between theory and practice.
- To provide you with opportunities to work at your own pace.
- To give you the chance to demonstrate your individuality.
- To provide you with opportunities to take responsibility for your own learning.
- To help you to develop research-related skills and techniques.
- To bring together several different themes, topics, or disciplines.
- To allow you to accumulate *evidence* of putting theories into practice.

Good habits when doing field work include:

- Just getting on with it. Field work can make demands on your time and energy, and sometimes you can't see exactly why you are required to undertake some of the tasks that it involves.
- Following the brief carefully. Whatever *else* you may do in your field work, the tasks and instructions included in the brief will be important.
- Preparing for it and following it up. Field work can be made much more efficient by thinking about it before you start on it, so that when you start, you are working towards identified goals and targets, rather than floundering around trying to get your act together.
- Keeping good records. Field work can be very busy, and when something new and important comes up it is easy to forget what happened earlier.
- Writing it up fast. Field work can take a lot of writing up, and if the task is left too long it becomes much slower, as your memory of what you saw and did will have faded.
- Maintaining and demonstrating curiosity. This is what tends to get you noticed. Curiosity is one of those factors which distinguishes students who are heading for good degrees from their classmates.
- Whatever you are investigating in your field work, keep asking the questions:
  - Why am I doing this?
  - Why am I doing this *this way*?
  - How else could I achieve this?
  - What am I observing?
  - What *else* am I observing?
  - What *else* could I try doing?
  - What does it all mean?
  - What am I trying to capture as I go along?
  - How can I best accumulate evidence for my thinking and actions?

Laboratory work

In some disciplines, particularly science and engineering, you may well spend more time in laboratories and workshops than in lectures, tutorials, and seminars put together. Laboratory work can all too easily take over your whole life if you are not careful. It is therefore important to look carefully at the main characteristics of such work and at why you are expected to undertake it, as well as what you are expected to show for it.

What are the main characteristics of laboratory work?

- Supervision mostly undertaken by postgraduate demonstrators or research students, under the overall control of lecturers.
- You may have some choice about when you attend and for how long.
- Primary focus on learning by doing.
- You will have a lot of control over the pace at which you learn and the fine detail of what you learn.
- If you are absent there may be a good chance of catching up.
- Your performance or participation in laboratory work will be the basis for some assessment, but possibly not in proportion to the time you spend on it. Your assessment may be based primarily on reports that you write *after* attending the laboratory. The content covered through the laboratory work programme may also be reflected in exams.
- Good opportunities to ask questions; demonstrators may be able to explain things to you – when lecturers could not or would not!

Why may laboratory work be part of your course?

The reasons for including laboratory work in degree programmes reflect the characteristics outlined above. They include:

- To allow you to put theories into practice.
- To give you the chance to learn by doing.
- To allow you to try things out, including making mistakes, in a safe environment.
- To help you to develop research-related practical skills.
- To allow you to develop your skills relating to managing your own learning within a given environment.
- To give you the chance to generate your own data, and then interpret it and communicate it to others.

Good habits when doing laboratory work include:

- Getting through the prescribed work quickly to leave time for further attempts. It is just as important to do laboratory work *well* as to complete all of it. You will often find that it is worth making a 'rough' attempt at an experiment, or at certain parts of it, before getting down to your 'final' definitive attempt.

- Making use of all the resources available. Laboratory work briefings will normally give you a good idea about which resources you are intended to be using. However, using any *additional* resources or facilities could be one of the features that distinguishes *your* laboratory work from that of those around you.

- Tolerating zero backlog of reports: write up within the week. It is far *easier* to write up laboratory work straightaway, not least because you don't have to stop and try to work out what you actually did. The longer you leave it, the more time it takes to write up. This can lead to backlogs. Then you could still be working off your backlog of report writing when you really need to be doing other more important things, not least preparing for forthcoming exams. The habit of zero backlog tolerance is one of the surest indicators of students who are heading towards good degrees. Many of the people who mark laboratory reports can tell you that there is usually a strong correlation between good marks and early submission.

Group work

Your degree course may or may not involve you directly in collaborative work with fellow students. Sometimes practical and laboratory work is necessarily done on a group basis, especially if student numbers are too high for the space, facilities, and equipment available. In some subjects, there are things which are *best* learned by working with fellow students rather than on your own.

What are the main characteristics of group work?

- Work where the primary intentions are to get you collaborating with fellow students, gaining team skills, and helping (and being helped by) fellow students.
- There may or may not be a tutor present, with a small number of students compared to lectures or seminars.
- Time and place may be for you to arrange with your fellow students.
- If you are absent you may find it hard or impossible to find out exactly what you missed.
- Usually linked to subject matter which will be the basis of at least some of your assessment, and often involving coursework where the *products* of the group will be assessed and perhaps also your individual contribution measured.

Why may group work be part of your course?

There are many good reasons for getting students to work together for at least some of the time that they are working towards degrees. These include:

- To allow students to learn from each other.
- To help students develop a range of skills which will be needed later in their careers.
- To help students to find out how their own learning is going, by comparison with their peers.

Good habits when doing group work include:

- Not making enemies in group contexts. A group can be quite fragile and conflict can develop which takes away most of the potential benefits. A little tolerance can go a long way in a group situation.
- Collaborating rather than competing. Especially when the overall *product* of the work of the group is to be assessed, it is important to put aside competitive tendencies within the group (though of course there can be healthy competition *between* groups).
- Reading up, on your own initiative, about the features of good group behaviour and practising them.
- Learning from other people. This includes allowing shrinking violets in the group to blossom. Just because someone is reticent does not mean that they have fewer good ideas than everyone else.
- Not being smug or complacent. No one really likes such people, and the groups that work best are those where everyone is open and free with ideas, and not satisfied with doing an adequate job of the group work, but aiming to do a *good* job of it.

One-to-one meetings with staff

One-to-one meetings with staff are sometimes rare and can be intimidating. They vary enormously in nature and in purpose.

What are the main characteristics of one-to-one meetings?

It is not possible to be too specific here, and any combination of the characteristics listed below may arise.

- One-to-one encounters with individual lecturers, often in their own offices, such as one-to-one tutorials or progress-monitoring meetings.

- Short individual consultations with a lecturer immediately after a lecture.
- Meetings by appointment at your request, to sort out a problem.
- Meetings about a specific issue, such as a supervised project.
- One-to-one meetings with staff in field work environments.
- A pre-arranged visit by a member of staff to your work placement location.
- Pre-arranged meetings with a lecturer or tutor as part of a personal tutorial system.
- Meetings with a lecturer or tutor in which assessed work is returned to you, along with feedback on your work.
- Chance encounters with a lecturer or tutor, in a corridor, laboratory, or anywhere else!
- The situation could be controlled by the member of staff, such as when giving you feedback or seeing you about a problem with your work.
- The situation could be mainly controlled by you, such as when bringing specific questions or enquiries to a tutor.

The nature and frequency of one-to-one meetings with university staff varies widely. When class sizes are very large there may be few such meetings. The likelihood of such meetings is greater in the final year of a course than in the first year. In some universities, the culture favours one-to-one meetings with tutors, while in others they are rare occurrences.

Making the most of talking with your tutors

It can feel rather strange to have the undivided attention of lecturers or tutors. You may feel somewhat in awe when in the presence of these great people, with all their qualifications, experience, and fame – not to mention their importance in deciding sooner or later what sort of degree you have earned for yourself! Some of them seem quite intimidating, especially when they look you in the eye and wait to hear what you are about to utter. It is quite easy to become tongue-tied, clumsy, and awkward – or at least to *feel* that you must be coming across like this.

You may, of course, not have any such problems. You may be the sort of student who can talk to famous people as easily as you can order a pizza. See how you rate yourself at talking with tutors by completing the following task.

Task: making the most of talking to your tutors

Rate yourself on each of the following characteristics you may have regarding talking to tutors (you may well, of course, have different reactions to different tutors). In the final column, enter 'more' or 'less' if you'd like to change particular one-to-one characteristics. Then compare your verdicts with the discussion which follows.

Your characteristics?	Very like me	Sometimes like me	Not at all like me	I'd like to be more – or less – like this!
1 I find it easy to talk one-to-one with just about all the staff that I meet one-to-one.				
2 I don't seem to have one-to-one meetings with staff at all on my course.				
3 I'm very aware that I need to make a good impression and this makes me very nervous.				
4 I find that it helps if I write down in advance exactly what I want to ask tutors in one-to-one situations.				
5 I often come away from one-to-one situations quite frustrated that I haven't said what I wanted to say.				
6 I tend to notice only the critical or negative things that staff say to me, and I don't remember much of any positive feedback they give me.				
7 I sometimes get very embarrassed after a one-to-one meeting and replay the conversation in my mind endlessly, wishing I had made a better impression.				
8 When I want to see a lecturer to ask a specific question, I write down the question and send it along with my request for an appointment.				

Your characteristics?	Very like me	Sometimes like me	Not at all like me	I'd like to be more – or less – like this!
9 I try to catch lecturers immediately after lectures to ask any questions I have.				
10 After a one-to-one meeting, I make brief notes to capture the main things I have learned from the meeting.				

Discussion: attitudes regarding one-to-one interactions with tutors

1 *I find it easy to talk one-to-one with just about all the staff that I meet one-to-one.* If this is 'very like you' well done. If you find it easy, so will they, and that way the partnership between you will be better.

2 *I don't seem to have one-to-one meetings with staff at all on my course.* If this is 'very like you', it is probably not at all your fault. It could be because of large class sizes or alternatively because it's just not how your particular course operates. It will be worthwhile making the most of your next-best opportunities to talk with staff, such as in small group tutorials or seminar groups and in any practical or field work contexts that are available to you.

3 *I'm very aware that I need to make a good impression and this makes me very nervous.* If this is 'very like you' you're far from alone. Staff are well used to students trying to make a good impression, and may even be flattered a little at being regarded with such awe! However, don't worry too much about making that good impression. Staff are busy people and don't remember all the impressions that are made on them.

4 *I find that it helps if I write down in advance exactly what I want to ask tutors in one-to-one situations.* This can be particularly helpful, especially when you have more than one question to ask. It is otherwise very easy to get so involved in discussion about the first question or issue that other things slip your mind. Even better, try sending or giving your tutor your list of questions. Even tutors like to be able to be seen to be well prepared and prefer not to be put on the spot.

5 *I often come away from one-to-one situations quite frustrated that I haven't said what I wanted to say.* This is quite natural and is cured only by practice. There are usually two related issues: saying *what* you really want to say and saying it *how* you want to. Even well-chosen, well-rehearsed words don't always come out in one-to-one contexts according

to our plans. Practice helps us to become better at monitoring the effect of our words on other people, and when the effect is not as we wish it to be, choosing additional ways of communicating our ideas to them.

6   *I tend to notice only the critical or negative things that staff say to me, and I don't remember much of any positive feedback they give me.* This problem is shared by many students (and professional people too). It is human nature to notice criticism rather than praise. Both are usually equally valuable. Many tutors try hard to balance the two and are at pains to tell you about things you have done well as well as about any shortcomings in your work. Since it's the praise that tends to get forgotten, it is worth making brief notes about it immediately after a one-to-one feedback episode with a tutor so that you can build on it in your future work. Also, try to regard critical feedback as useful and look for ways in which you can demonstrate that you have taken it on board in your future work.

7   *I sometimes get very embarrassed after a one-to-one meeting and replay the conversation in my mind endlessly, wishing I had made a better impression.* This may be bordering on the neurotic! Yet, many of us do this, not only in the context of one-to-one meetings with tutors, but in all sorts of other meetings with 'important' people. It is, of course, useful to reflect on any meeting and to learn from it, but the 'endless replaying' is not a further learning experience. Think about whether the other person is likely to be doing the same. For busy lecturers, the probability will be approaching zero! Once you've learned what you need to from an unsatisfactory encounter, ditch its memory and move on.

8   *When I want to see a lecturer to ask a specific question, I write down the question and send it along with my request for an appointment.* Lecturers usually appreciate this. In two ways, this *values* lecturers: first, by seeking an appointment rather than invading their time arbitrarily and, second, by sharing the agenda rather than springing it on them. Sometimes, if or when they may not have time to make an appointment for you, they will send back a note with the answer that you need or at least some suggestions to be going on with.

9   *I try to catch lecturers immediately after lectures to ask any questions I have.* Some lecturers tolerate this, but most prefer you to seek them out in other ways. There is every chance that immediately after a lecture the lecturer will have something else to go and do straight away, perhaps another lecture, a meeting, or a phone call, and so on. Collaring lecturers at the end of lectures is not usually the best way of letting them know that you are interested in their subjects, other than for you to give *them* very quick positive feedback (they quite like to be told 'I really enjoyed that, and feel I've learned a lot from it'!). If you have questions, it is better to try to make an appointment with the lecturer, as mentioned above.

10   *After a one-to-one meeting, I make brief notes to capture the main things I have learned from the meeting.* This is an excellent habit. What you learn during such meetings may be even more important than things you learn in lectures and tutorials. Since it is not a note-making situation, the tendency is to think that you can carry forward what you have learned from the meeting in your mind, but memory tends to be short-term unless you set out to *capture* what was important. It may only take a minute or two to jot down your main learning points, but do it!

Good habits when in a one-to-one context include:

• Valuing, seeking, and using one-to-one opportunities.
• Listening well and capturing the scene.
• Radiating interest and enthusiasm.
• Seeing one-to-one contexts as opportunities to develop a partnership.

Work-based learning

Many degree programmes contain elements of work-based learning. Courses of this sort have sometimes had the name 'sandwich' courses, with the 'filling' of work-based learning being placed somewhere in the middle of the course. Some such courses have a whole year of work experience at the centre of the course, others have a shorter period, and some courses have more than one shorter placement. Even some degree programmes which don't call themselves sandwich courses still make use of some elements of work-based learning at some point in the programme.

What are the main characteristics of work-based learning?

These vary from course to course, but include one or more of the following:

• Periods of the course where you work in a normal work environment, which could be in commerce, industry, local government, or at an educational institution, possibly even your own university.
• The arrangements for your placement are normally agreed between your university and the employer for whom you are working; alternatively, you may be encouraged to find your own work placement opportunities and have these duly agreed and accepted by your university department as sufficiently relevant and at the right level to be part of your degree experience.
• There will be times when you act as a normal employee of the organization you are working at, at least during the normal working day.

- Your day-to-day supervision will be entrusted to one or more work placement supervisors, normally employees of the company or organization in which you are working.
- The overall responsibility for your work placement may rest with a tutor or lecturer at your own university who may visit you on-site two or three times during your placement, talking both to you and to your work placement supervisors.
- The job will be relevant to at least part of your degree programme, allowing you to see how theory is put into practice in the outside world.
- You are required to build up evidence from your work placement showing what you have achieved and how you went about it.
- You may need to spend quite a lot of time out of work hours writing up your work experience for your university.
- A major intention is for you to build up employment-related skills and attitudes, and to accumulate evidence for your development of these, to make you more employable after you have achieved your degree.
- You may be paid an amount proportional to the level of work you are undertaking, but may also be responsible for your own accommodation and living expenses during the period of your placement.
- There is a fairly strong possibility that if your work is found valuable by your employer you may be made an employment offer for when you have been awarded your degree.

Why may work-based learning be part of your course?

If work-based learning is included in your course, the main reasons could include:

- To enrich your educational experience by allowing you to see how at least some of the topics you are studying relate to practice in the world outside.
- To give you the opportunity to develop your self-organizational skills, communication skills, and interpersonal skills in real-world contexts.
- To make you more employable after you have got your degree.
- To allow you to undertake work which would be impossible to arrange on a university campus, for example using specialist or unique equipment, working alongside professional people, learning specialist skills, and so on.

Good habits when undertaking work-based learning include:

- Aiming to make it work, even when it doesn't seem to! Work-based learning cannot always be directly relevant to a given degree programme. Tutors go to considerable lengths to try to locate suitable employment opportunities for students, but can't always find ideal placements. If you find yourself in a non-ideal situation, the best approach is to use the time to learn as much as you can without protesting at the irrelevance of any part of the work that you are expected to undertake. The placement will be for a limited time, and even if you are not finding it satisfying, it is still likely to be a useful element on your CV for future usage.

- Keeping evidence of achievements and failures. Work-based learning is a transient experience and at the end of your placement you need to be able to prove that it worked for you, and for the organization in which you were working. This necessitates keeping tangible evidence, not only of your successes, but also concerning things that did not work out.

- Using it as an opportunity to reflect on your experience and to systematically gather evidence of your reflections. In many disciplines, the ability to reflect is highly valued, not least by employers, and it is good to be able to show that you have become skilled in logging your reflections effectively.

- Valuing people around you and not putting them down. Some students make themselves unpopular with their employers and with the staff around them by being too assertive. If something has been done for years in a particular way and you think you know how it could be done better or more efficiently, you may find yourself treading on people's toes if you are too forthright in your exhortations for change.

- Being resourceful and seeing every disaster as an opportunity for learning. This is good practice for a lifetime where mishaps will continue to occur, and for developing the attitude which enables you to continue to learn as much from things which go wrong at first as from things which go right straight away.

3

Building on feedback

Is feedback the weak link in the chain? • Formative and summative feedback • Audit your own channels of feedback • Getting better at receiving feedback: face-to-face praise and criticism • More about critical feedback • What do you do with written feedback on your work? • Working out what written feedback really means! • Using feedback to make action plans • Conclusions

You can only really know how your progress towards getting a good degree is going if you get feedback. Actually, the real crunch is making sure that you not only *get* lots of feedback, but that you systematically *use* it to improve and develop your work continuously.

Task: very short, but important

Don't skip this little task. You'll see why when you read the discussion below – but do the task first.

Here is a quotation – someone else's words . . .

Everything should be made as simple as possible, – but not simpler

That's the quotation – now your task. Who said it? There's no reason why you should know, but your task is to *guess* who it may have been. Write your guess down below . . .

Now that you've written down your guess, please look at the very end of this chapter on page 104 to see whether you guessed correctly or not.

Discussion

Now you will know whether you guessed right. Either tick what you wrote down above, or cross out what you wrote and enter in the right name alongside.

Now for the point of all of this. Feedback only really works after you've done something. If you guessed correctly, you'll remember the name of the originator of the quote for a long time and will probably be rather pleased with yourself. If you guessed wrongly, you're even better off – you now know who said what was quoted *and* you know the name of someone who didn't say it too!

If, however, you simply *thought* about who it may have been and then checked at the end of the chapter to see whether you were right or not, you will very quickly forget both what you thought and what the correct answer was. And hopefully you will probably feel just a little guilty that you didn't do the task as asked.

Is feedback the weak link in the chain?

In the National Student Survey used in the UK from 2005 with final year students, their views on feedback have consistently shown that feedback is often the least satisfactory aspect of their experience of higher education.

In particular, students responded that feedback:

- Reached them too late.
- Did not contain sufficiently detailed comments on their work.
- Did not often enough help them to clarify things that they didn't understand.

Many institutions in the UK are already responding to these three weaknesses and working towards giving students better feedback more quickly. However, there is a lot you can do to make feedback work better for yourself, not least by:

1 Relating your own work carefully so that it matches well evidence of achievement of the intended learning outcomes for each module and course.

2 Self-assessing your work against the assessment criteria which link to these intended learning outcomes and gaining feedback on how good you become at this self-assessment.
3 Being alert and receptive to all the different ways you get feedback – in other words, not just written comments from tutors on your assessed work.

Formative and summative feedback

'Formative feedback' is the name given to the sort of feedback which you gain along the course of your studies, which can help you develop your approach, and fine-tune your efforts towards getting that good degree. Formative feedback can be, for example:

- Comments written by lecturers on your coursework.
- Emails from lecturers about your work.
- Discussion of your work in tutorials and one-to-one meetings with tutors.
- Comments from other students on your work.
- Handouts given to you after completing a piece of work.

'Summative feedback' is what we call the feedback on things which you can no longer change. This includes:

- Exam marks or grades.
- Marks or grades on assessed coursework.

You can, of course, learn from summative feedback too. If you get a low mark or grade for an exam or a piece of coursework, you may well be able to find out more about *why* you didn't do as well as you would have liked to – but you may not necessarily have the benefit of formative feedback to help you to do better next time.

Feedback and feed-ahead

'Feedback' is when you find out what was good about what you did, and what wasn't so good, and as we've seen can be formative or summative. 'Feed-ahead' is when you also find out about what you can do to learn from what you did, particularly from formative feedback, so that you make your next attempt at doing something similar better. 'Feed-ahead' is also often called 'Feed-forward' – you can see why.

Audit your own channels of feedback

As mentioned above, written comments on your coursework represent only one of many avenues of feedback available to you on your learning. By using all available channels purposefully, you can increase the impact of feedback on your work towards getting that good degree. The task below aims to alert you to a wider variety of channels of feedback so that you don't let any of them slip by you unnoticed.

Task: How I use the available channels of feedback on my learning

Feedback channel	I always use these well	I sometimes use these well	I'm not good at using these	These aren't available to me
1 Written comments from tutors on your essays, reports, assignments, and so on.				
2 Front-sheets giving overall feedback from tutors on your work.				
3 Summary reports issued by tutors on the work of the whole group.				
4 Grids where tutors rate my performance against each assessment criterion.				
5 Grids where tutors rate my achievement against each intended learning outcome.				
6 Emailed feedback comments direct to me from tutors.				
7 General feedback comments emailed by tutors to the whole group.				

Feedback channel	I always use these well	I sometimes use these well	I'm not good at using these	These aren't available to me
8 Overall comments posted by tutors on discussion boards in the virtual learning environment.				
9 Face-to-face feedback from tutors to the whole lecture group on matters arising from an assignment.				
10 Face-to-face, one-to-one feedback on my work directly from tutors to me.				
11 Face-to-face feedback on my work from tutors to small groups, e.g., in tutorials and seminars.				
12 Peer feedback comments gained from fellow students in formal peer-assessment contexts.				
13 Peer feedback comments I gain from fellow students on my own initiative.				
14 Feedback I gain from other people (mentor, friend – anyone!) who are not fellow students.				
15 Feedback arising from my own self-assessment of my work against the intended learning outcomes associated with the work.				
16 Feedback I gain from self-assessing my work against the published assessment criteria for the work.				
17 Other sources of feedback you use or could use . . .				

Perhaps as a result of this audit, you are already determined to make better use of some feedback channels you had not thought about before? The more, the better! Next, we'll explore, not just the available channels, but more importantly, what you actually *do* with the feedback you can put to work towards getting your good degree.

Getting better at receiving feedback: face-to-face praise and criticism

As we have already seen, feedback is a vital part of learning. For all sorts of reasons, however, people do not always make the most of the feedback they receive from other people. Some of the feedback that you receive is from expert witnesses, your lecturers. The feedback may not always be 'right', but it is always worth taking notice of any comments, verbal or written, that can help you form a better picture of how your learning is going. Let's think in particular about face-to-face feedback about your work from lecturers, such as you might receive from them in tutorials or one-to-one meetings. Try the following task to explore how you personally respond to face-to-face feedback from lecturers – and indeed from other people.

Task: your reactions to face-to-face feedback

Think about how you receive face-to-face feedback from other people, and particularly from lecturers, tutors, supervisors, and so on. Rate yourself on each of the following possibilities, then consider your decisions in the light of the information provided in the next section.

Reaction to feedback	Very like me	Quite like me	Not like me
1 When I receive a compliment, I tend to laugh and react in an embarrassed way.			
2 When I receive a compliment, I tend to shrug it off and say that 'it's not really special'.			
3 When I receive a compliment, I thank the person who gives it to me and try to take it on board.			

Reaction to feedback	Very like me	Quite like me	Not like me
4 When something I have done is criticized, I go on the defensive.			
5 When something I have done is criticized, I feel hurt and demotivated.			
6 When something I have done is criticized, I thank the person for their feedback and try to take it on board.			
7 When something I have done is criticized, I feel that it is *me* that is being criticized.			
8 When something I have done is criticized, I probe for more details about what is *really* the cause of the negative feedback.			

Discussion: receiving and using feedback

In many cultures, people are not good at receiving feedback, whether positive or critical. Even though most people agree that feedback is important and useful, they rarely really *use* it as well as they could. They tend to shrug off complimentary feedback for example, often laughing in embarrassment. This amounts to rejecting the feedback and not really taking it on board. It also means that, in the nicest possible way, the person giving the feedback has been rejected. People giving compliments are sometimes taking risks, and if their feedback is rejected they are less inclined to take further risks. The channel of communication is being closed down if their feedback is not being received. Simply responding with phrases such as, 'Thank you for that,' or, 'I'm glad you liked that,' can solve the problem. The feedback has then been received and the channel of communication remains open for further positive feedback.

In the case of critical feedback, the situation is even more problematic. Many people get defensive or even hostile when they feel that they are being criticized. They feel that they are being criticized personally, even when it's only something that they have *done* that is being criticized. Even if they say nothing, it is usually very plain to the person giving the critical feedback that a hostile or defensive stance is being taken. The feedback is not really being taken notice of and the channel of communication is being closed down. Furthermore, few people giving critical feedback begin with the most important element; they usually test out the waters with something that is not particularly important. If communication then fails, the *real* feedback may not even be expressed at all. It takes a little practice to *thank* people for their critical feedback, but in doing so, the feedback is being logged for future action. It is possible to go further and to gently probe for yet more detail about the feedback. Questions such as, 'Tell me more about what I could have done instead,' or, 'What was the most important difference I could have made?' are ways of keeping the communication going until all the available feedback has been given and received.

Another problem with oral feedback (positive or negative) is that our human memory does not seem to be particularly accurate. We tend to remember only certain parts of it. If you've received three elements each of positive feedback and critical feedback in an interview with a tutor, the chances are that after a while you will remember two of the negative parts and maybe only one positive part. The simple way round this problem is to log the feedback very soon after receiving it. Make notes under both headings (positive and negative) and try to ensure that you don't lose sight of one category because of preoccupation with the other one. Also, turn *both* kinds of feedback into action-planning notes to yourself. With positive feedback, write short notes along the lines of, 'I'll try to do *more* of this'. With critical or negative feedback, write yourself some recommendations about how you can address the cause of the feedback in future.

Written feedback causes less problems, in that at least it exists on paper, and can be looked at again and again, and digested. Make the most of written feedback, because it is a prime way of learning how to improve your performance. Many students just ignore the words and look at the mark or grade that they have been given; that *isn't* the way to get a good degree! Tutors marking coursework often go to some lengths to make sure that there is positive feedback as well as criticism. Unfortunately, it is sometimes only the critical feedback that students seem to notice. The valuable learning that could have been derived from the positive feedback is often lost. In particular, students often take too much notice of the mark or grade that they have been awarded – but this is only *summative* feedback. If it is a good mark or grade, they are tempted not to bother to read the feedback. This means that they often miss valuable suggestions for further improvements to their work or details of exactly *what* they had done really well. In other words, they miss out on the benefits which could have come from taking on board the *formative* feedback. Similarly, in the case of poor marks or grades, many students are too disappointed with the result to get down to the task of going carefully through all the feedback which may have been provided. The feedback is more important than the score or grade, as far as *future* learning is concerned. Taking really good notice of feedback can help to ensure that strengths are identified and built upon, and that weaknesses are faced up to and addressed in future work.

Getting hurt by critical feedback (spoken or written) is perfectly natural but is not productive in terms of learning. Emotions can be very powerful and, if they take over, serious damage can be done to motivation. It is best to be coldly analytical about critical feedback, at least until you have decided exactly *why* the feedback was warranted and exactly *what* was being criticized – usually only *part* of your work, not the entire piece. Sometimes, after reflecting on critical feedback, you may be justified in concluding that the feedback was after all inappropriate or inaccurate, and that there are no action points for you to take forward into your future work. If, however, the same critical feedback agenda occurs more than once, and from different sources, think hard about the possibility that you indeed have something to learn from it.

As you will have seen from the activity above, feedback (and especially feed-ahead) only works when you *use* it. It is one thing to be given feedback, but only you can make sure that you actually take in on board to purposefully analyse it and improve your future work as a result of it.

More about *critical* feedback

In this chapter, I often use the term 'critical feedback' rather than 'negative feedback' as the latter seems demotivating. However, 'critical' by no means is just 'bad'. If you're asked to do a 'critical review' of something, it would not be wise to simply concentrate on writing or speaking about what is wrong with it; you would be expected to give a balanced view, including what was good about it too. In fact, critical feedback you receive on your work can also be praise, where tutors have looked deeply into your work and found particular things they feel they can tell you about it. That said, most of what you might regard as 'critical' feedback is likely to be about suggestions to improve your work and to remedy deficiencies which your tutors may have noticed.

What do you *do* with written feedback on your work?

Written feedback from lecturers or tutors can be a very useful avenue for alert-ing you to how best you can fine-tune your work towards getting that good degree. Sometimes you'll get comments written directly onto your work or summary comments appended to your work. Sometimes you'll get the oppor-tunity to get face-to-face discussion of these comments, but more often you're likely to be expected to make sense of the written feedback on its own merits.

Now could be an ideal time to revisit how exactly you respond to written feedback on your work. Please do the task below, answering honestly each of the possibilities listed there, then look at the discussion of the pros and cons of the choices you've entered.

Task: what I currently do with written comments from tutors on my work

Decide what you normally do when you get your work back with written feedback from tutors and lecturers. Tick one or more of the columns as appropriate – not least the 'I won't do this in future' and 'I'll do this in future' column where you realize that it would be helpful to adjust your technique regarding using written feedback towards getting a good degree.

What I do with written feedback comments on my work	This is exactly what I do	This is sometimes what I do	This is not what I do!	I won't do this in future	I'll do this in future
1 I look first at the mark or grade I've received.					
2 I'm influenced a lot by the mark or grade I receive when I look at the feedback.					
3 If the mark is better than I expected, I analyse the feedback carefully to work out why my mark was better.					
4 If the mark was worse than I expected, I analyse the feedback carefully to find out why my mark wasn't so good.					
5 If I don't like the tutor very much, I don't take much notice of the feedback.					
6 I take careful note of positive comments and find out what earned them so I can use this feedback to make future work better.					

What I do with written feedback comments on my work	This is exactly what I do	This is sometimes what I do	This is not what I do!	I won't do this in future	I'll do this in future
7 I get upset by critical comments and sometimes feel bad about such feedback.					
8 I take careful note of the causes of critical feedback and work out how exactly I can avoid these sorts of criticism in future work.					
9 I make systematic comparisons between feedback comments I receive from different tutors and work out which are general trends regarding my work.					
10 I share the feedback comments I receive with fellow students and learn more about the comments they received on their work.					
11 I file my marked work carefully, so that I can return to the feedback comments later and reflect on them.					
12 I make an action plan based on the feedback I've received, and keep this handy to continue to use in future work.					

Discussion: what you currently do with written comments from tutors on your work

Looking back at the choices you made in the task above, check out the discussion below to see if you are making optimum use of written comments on your work and making the most of such feedback to help you towards getting the good degree you're aiming for.

What I do with written feedback comments on my work	Discussion comments
1 I look first at the mark or grade I've received.	This is natural. Few people can resist this! However, your emotions can run high when having just received a 'judgement' such as a mark or grade. This is just *summative* feedback – you can't alter it. It's much more important to be able to learn from the reasons *why* you got a particular mark or grade, so that you can make your next mark better. When possible, it is productive to *avoid* seeing the mark or grade, and looking straight at the feedback comments, then trying to work out what your mark or grade is *before* looking at the actual one. However, this is sometimes very hard to do in practice – unless your tutors are aware of the value of this chance to make sense of feedback and withhold marks for a week or so to give you the opportunity to try to work your mark out for yourself.
2 I'm influenced a lot by the mark or grade I receive when I look at the feedback.	Most people are. But this can distract you from making optimum use of the feedback. For example, if the mark was high, you may fail to find out *why* you did so well and therefore miss out on the chance to gain such success routinely in future. Or if the mark is low, you may be too demoralized to make best use of the feedback, using it to work out how you can ensure that you get better marks in future on similar work.

What I do with written feedback comments on my work	Discussion comments
	It can be useful (assuming you can't avoid seeing the mark or grade) to give yourself a little time to get used to the mark you've got and allow your feelings (whether high or low) to settle down, and only then go on to analyse the feedback systematically and dispassionately.
3 If the mark is better than I expected, I analyse the feedback carefully to work out why my mark was better.	This is what you should aim to do. Look carefully at the positive comments and see what earned you the good result. But also remember to look systematically at the critical comments to see how you can continue to improve your work even more.
4 If the mark was worse than I expected, I analyse the feedback carefully to find out why my mark wasn't so good.	This too is what you should aim to do. But you sometimes need to have given yourself time to get used to the fact that you didn't do as well as you had hoped before getting down to the very useful task of *finding out exactly why* this was so. Then, you are better able to look objectively at the critical feedback comments, making notes of how to avoid causing such comments to be given to you in future. Don't, however, be so intent on looking at the critical comments that you don't give yourself the chance to learn from positive comments as well – there will usually be both kinds of feedback on your work.
5 If I don't like the tutor very much, I don't take much notice of the feedback.	This is perfectly natural. You're bound to like some tutors more than others. But some of the tutors you don't like so much may well be markers of your exam answers too. (And, of course, so may some of your favourite tutors.) However, part of your key mission to getting that good degree is to learn from *all* the feedback you get – even from tutors you don't like or respect very much. In particular, analyse the feedback to work out any changes you can make to your future work so that such people would rate your work more

What I do with written feedback comments on my work	Discussion comments
	highly. Making adjustments to counter *their* critical comments may indeed help you to secure higher grades from other tutors too.
6 I take careful note of positive comments and find out what earned them so I can use this feedback to make future work better.	This is indeed what you should do. Don't just luxuriate in the praise – work out exactly what you did to earn such praise, so you can do it again all the more deliberately in future work, including in exam answers.
7 I get upset by critical comments and sometimes feel bad about such feedback.	This is perfectly natural, but feeling bad about critical comments won't actually help you much towards getting that good degree. You may need to give yourself a little time to heal your hurt feelings before doing the next step, which (as you will know yourself) is to work out what you can usefully learn from the critical comments.
8 I take careful note of the causes of critical feedback and work out how exactly I can avoid these sorts of criticism in future work.	This is exactly what to do. Even when you feel overwhelmed by critical comments, it's worth systematically working out what led to the comments (and not just blaming their authors). The more you can learn about how to avoid attracting such comments in future, the better your chance of safely getting that good degree.
9 I make systematic comparisons between feedback comments I receive from different tutors and work out which are general trends regarding my work.	This is a wise thing to do. Some tutors will be 'harder' than others (but so will some examiners). Sometimes what pleases one tutor will annoy another. Your aim should be to please as many tutors as possible for as much of the time as possible, so that when it comes to exams your chances of pleasing your assessors are maximized. Besides, the general trends are likely to be significant, and can be a really useful basis to go about developing your work systematically towards earning that good degree.
10 I share the feedback comments I receive with fellow students and learn	This one takes some courage. You may feel some reluctance to let other students see the feedback comments you received on your

What I do with written feedback comments on my work	Discussion comments
more about the comments they received on their work.	work, particularly if you got better grades than them. But you can learn a lot from praise they received on things you didn't do yourself – and even more from critical comments they received on faults or mistakes you didn't make yourself. All in all, the more you can put your own feedback comments in perspective – the more you can find out about the bigger picture – the better are your chances of aiming to ensure that you come out with the good degree you're aiming for.
11 I file my marked work carefully so that I can return to the feedback comments later and reflect on them.	This is sensible on one level. As you're pulling your act together for exams, for example, it is really useful to remind yourself of the sorts of ways where you earned praise, and even more to ensure that you remember what to do to avoid some of the critical comments you've received on coursework. However, there is a risk: that you won't actually get round to returning to the feedback and re-learning from it. That is why it can be useful to get into the habit of making action plans – please see below.
12 I make an action plan based on the feedback I've received and keep this handy to continue to use in future work.	If you already do this – splendid. For more ideas about how best to do this, please see below. Continuously developing action plans on the basis of feedback can help you to distance the feedback you receive from individual tutors from your feelings about the particular tutors, and from the high or low marks you were awarded for particular pieces of work.

Working out what written feedback really means!

There are several ways you can set about finding out what tutors actually mean regarding particular comments on your work. The most obvious option is simply to ask them – but there are dangers on this route. In particular, if you question something that a tutor has written you risk one or more of the following possible instinctive reactions to your query.

- 'Oh dear, so-and-so is challenging my feedback. Probably thinks it's unfair or wrong.'
- 'Grumbling about the grade I guess. Am I going to be asked why the mark wasn't higher? I really can't have everyone doing this. Best not say much in response to this query.'
- 'Attention-seeking behaviour! I haven't got time for this. I don't like attention-seekers! Students need to become able to work out what I mean.'

For all sorts of reasons, tutors don't always quite manage to say what they mean when they're writing feedback comments on students' work! Not least, they sometimes want to be kind, and to avoid giving feedback which may be demoralizing. Perhaps the problem with written or on-screen feedback is that you don't have other clues to what tutors actually mean, such as you would be able to gain in face-to-face contexts through:

- Tone of voice.
- Body language.
- Facial expression.
- Eye contact.
- Emphasis on particular spoken words.
- Use of pauses to give you time to think.
- The chance for you to ask what tutors really mean.
- Tutors being able to respond to puzzled looks on your face, and explain what they mean.

In short, sometimes you'll need to take steps to find out what exactly your tutors mean by feedback comments on your work, in particular critical comments. Other things you can do to work out what feedback comments really mean include:

1 Look carefully at the comments and the aspects of your work they relate to and try to work out for yourself exactly what is being commented upon and how you may be able to respond to each feedback comment in your future work (especially future work for that particular tutor or exam answers which may be marked by this person).

2 Compare the feedback comments you have received with those received by fellow students on the course or module. Ask them what *they* think tutors mean by particular comments. This will at least give you some more information about the standard of your own work and probably will make you feel better about your own work when you notice critical feedback comments on other students' work which were not written on your work. However, there may still be some guesswork regarding what the tutors may actually mean by their comments.

For example 'perhaps you could have put this better' against a point you have made *could* really mean, 'I haven't a clue what you're trying to say here!' and probably does *not* mean, 'This is fine, there's no need to make the point better than you have done already'!

Some further ways of working out what particular feedback comments really mean are suggested below, in the context of developing action plans into a systematic approach to making optimum use of the feedback you receive on your work, combined with deliberately seeking yet more feedback from other people. *All* feedback is potentially useful.

Using feedback to make action plans

As mentioned in the discussion above, it can be really productive to extract the essence from all of the written feedback you receive on your work and combine this with additional things you may pick up from face-to-face feedback from tutors and from discussions with other students about their feedback.

One way of going about a systematic and productive approach to making the most of feedback is to prepare for yourself a simple pro-forma, and have copies of it available for each episode of feedback on your work so that you can collect together the complete pro-formas as an ongoing record of how your work is developing. In other words, you can take charge of the process of keeping track of how your work is progressing towards earning you the good degree you're aiming towards. All the better if you have copies of such a pro-forma ready to use each time you gain feedback, so that capturing the essence of the feedback becomes a matter of routine rather than a luxury.

This also gives you the opportunity to separate your *reflections* on particular instances of feedback from the actual individual pieces of work, so that you distance yourself from the first thoughts you got when receiving the feedback, and move onwards and upwards with the significant trends, enabling you to continuously adjust your approaches.

A possible pro-forma is suggested below – but all the better if you design one of your own, customized, as you know about how you currently use feedback – and pointing towards how you want to make optimum use of feedback to get you firmly towards the good degree you want. You may indeed want to design a much shorter pro-forma than that given below. My reason for including a fairly wide range of possibilities is to give you more choice in deciding what exactly is going to work well in practice for you – it's *your* feedback and it's *your* good degree we're working towards at the end of the day.

Feedback Action Plan		
Date:	**Piece of work:**	**Mark or grade:**
	Most significant feedback comments:	*What these really mean: (e.g., after asking the tutors, after discussing with other students, or after reflecting further on the work and the feedback)*
1		
2		
3		
Extent to which I *agree* **with the feedback**	**Positive:**	**Critical:**
	Things I did which attracted positive feedback:	*Things I did which attracted critical feedback:*
1		
2		
3		
Notes about any recurring trends regarding the feedback I am receiving		

Date:	Piece of work:	Mark or grade:
	Things I can do to build on the positive feedback in my future work:	*Things I can do to address the critical feedback in my future work*:
1		
2		
3		
Additional feedback	*Further positive feedback I've obtained on this work from other people*:	*Further critical feedback I've obtained on this work from other people*:
Source 1		
Source 2		
Source 3		

The single most important thing for me to keep doing *in my future work on the basis of this feedback*:

The single most important thing for me to improve *in my future work on the basis of this feedback*:

Conclusions

I hope after working through this chapter, you're now convinced that feedback on your work (and on your learning in general) can be really useful in helping you towards your ambition to get a good degree. The more you know about how your work is progressing right from the beginning of your studies the better. Feedback can alert you to what is going well so that you can purposefully build on your strengths. More importantly, feedback can alert you to the hazards which may otherwise stop you from getting that good degree.

I hope also that you're now prepared not just to *wait* for feedback, but to *seek* feedback. In the next chapter, we'll look in more detail at all the sources of feedback and help around you, from the people and resources that make up your overall learning environment.

Response to the short task at the beginning of this chapter

The quotation is commonly attributed to Albert Einstein, 1879–1955 – but I haven't been able to track down exactly where or when he said it or wrote it!

4

Making the most of your learning environment

Making the most of the people around you • Making the most of your learning resources • Conclusions

This chapter is about using all the resources – including people – around you, to help you achieve your ambition to get a good degree. As with most aspects of studying for a good degree, you need some good *habits* to make optimum use of all of your resources. It's not enough just to *know* how to make good use of a resource. It is the regular, systematic way in which you make use of all of your resources which counts. Your university will have its own virtual learning environment – or VLE – the name given to the wide range of linked software, hardware, and electronic databases that are accessible from most computers on campus, perhaps even from your own laptop or desktop machines. Most of your study modules will have elements of them which you are expected to undertake independently using the VLE. Some study modules may be entirely VLE-based, left to you to work through, and assessed in the VLE context. You're bound to meet the term 'blended learning' which is about making sure that the parts of your studying which you do with the VLE link seamlessly with other parts where you attend lectures, tutorials, seminars, laboratories, and so on.

Furthermore, the term 'resource-based learning' is sometimes used for those parts of university courses where the curriculum is delivered using print-based learning materials, or computer-based materials on the VLE rather than being covered in lectures, tutorials, seminars, and so on. In general, an increasing part of the curriculum involves students taking on much more of the responsibility for making sure that their learning gets done under their own steam, and is effective and relevant. Naturally, how well you do such elements of learning under your own steam is important and can be a crucial aspect of your work towards a good degree.

You can indeed regard human beings as part of your learning environment – there are two kinds of learning resources: human and non-human. There is of course a lot of overlap, as human resources can help you make good use of the non-human ones. Indeed, for the purposes of this chapter, we will start by looking at how you can make the most of the *people* around you and then move on to how to get the best value from all the other resources that you will find in your university and far beyond, on the Internet for example.

Making the most of the people around you

A university is a learning organization. It is full of people as well as books, computers, journals, laboratories, and so on. We will start by looking at how you can get the most from the people. There are many categories of people in your university. The most obvious category consists of teaching staff, including lecturers and teaching assistants, along with other staff who get involved in at least some teaching, such as research students, postgraduate demonstrators, part-time or 'sessional' staff, and even professors! The latter tend to be relatively senior (but not necessarily 'old'!) academics who have a distinguished record of research or teaching, who are quite influential in universities, and who may be looking out for signs of students who are heading towards a good degree, not least as possible candidates to consider for research opportunities in due course. Many universities also have 'teaching fellows' who have been recognized for the quality of their teaching.

Not all the academics in universities regard teaching as their main job. For many of them, research is more important, not least because that's where the money lies. Without research funding, many university departments would not exist. The fact that not all your lecturers regard your studies as the most important thing in their lives means that to get the most from the people around you, you need to spread your net wider than just lecturers. The following sections explore the different ways you can make use of the expertise not only of lecturers, but also library staff, learning support staff, fellow students, postgraduate demonstrators, project supervisors, and so on. The order in which we will discuss them is not important. You need to decide how best each category of staff can help you.

Task: making the most of the people around you

How well do you think you make use of the human resources around you? For each different category below, decide how well you think you make the most of them. (Don't worry if some of the categories do not apply to your own course.)

Category	I make really good use of these	I sometimes make good use of these	I don't really make good use of these
1 Lecturers.			
2 Library staff.			
3 Learning support staff.			
4 Technical staff.			
5 Information technology staff.			
6 Fellow students.			
7 Postgraduate demonstrators.			
8 Mentors.			
9 Project supervisors.			
10 Workplace supervisors.			

Next, explore each of the relevant categories in turn, looking at the habits adopted by successful students and comparing these to your own interactions with the human resources around you.

Lecturers

Good habits when interacting with lecturers include:

- Accepting that they are very often experts in the subjects they teach.
- Realizing that some of them are much better at teaching than others!
- Recognizing their role in the design of your assessments.
- Regarding them as people from whom you can learn a great deal.
- Responding to the fact that they are often very busy people.
- Being reasonable about the demands you make on them.

You will see a fair number of lecturers on your way towards your degree. However, for at least some of the time you are in their presence, you are just one of a number (sometimes a large number) of students in their lectures and there will probably be some lecturers who never get to know *you* to any significant extent. Some of your lecturers will be more approachable than others. You will also meet some of your lecturers in less formal teaching–learning situations than lectures: tutorials, practical classes, seminars, and even one-to-one encounters. Some of your lecturers will be really keen to help any students showing interest and enthusiasm. You will soon be able to tell which lecturers fall into this category. A little caution is also useful, however. Some lecturers will feel that it is up to you to work out what they really want.

Your lecturers in general are people who are likely to be able to help you a lot. To have reached their positions in the university, they themselves have been successful students. Most of them will have got one or more good degrees of their own. Some of them will have got their degrees very easily and may not understand why anyone could possibly find their subjects difficult, boring, complex, or anything other than addictively fascinating! Most of them will have higher degrees and could have spent years going deeper into their research specialisms since then, with teaching, for some of them, just being a necessary chore that they are required to do from time to time. In short, as far as getting *your* good degree, *and* in the subject matter involved, your lecturers are two-stroke expert witnesses on both the subject matter and the processes you need to use.

Importantly, at least some of your lecturers will be involved in setting the coursework assignments and exam questions upon which your assessment will depend, so they are key people as far as helping you towards getting a good degree. They know what they are looking for in terms of what a good degree actually entails. Some of them will share this agenda with their students, but others may take the view that it's up to the students to work out what is really being looked for to earn a good degree. In short, your lecturers are likely to be quite a diverse range of people, all of whom have important information which could help you along your way to a good degree, but only some of whom are likely to be willing to share this information with you. They are busy people and your opportunities to find out how their minds work, especially regarding assessment, are somewhat limited.

Library staff

Good habits when taking advantage of the expertise of library staff include:

- Valuing their expertise.
- Asking them important questions and not troubling them with trivial enquiries.
- Remembering that some of them will be specialists and graduates in your discipline.
- Treating them with courtesy.

Library staff are harder to find than they used to be in many academic libraries. It is less common now to find them sitting at help desks around the stacks. The staff of a university library comprises a wide-ranging group of people, both in what they do and in how well qualified they are. Subject librarians, for example, will normally have at least a first degree in the subjects they are responsible for in the library. Many also have higher degrees. They often know as much about the subject matter as your lecturers, sometimes more, and in fact usually have a broader understanding of the discipline, as they tend not to have specialized to the extent that happens to lecturers deep in research.

Subject librarians also know the stock – paper-based and electronic. They have a very good idea about which sources are authoritative and respected. They know not only the books, but also the electronic journals, websites, online databases, search possibilities, and the range of computer-based packages in their collections. They usually also know the lecturers teaching their specialist subjects and are aware (for example) of how helpful or otherwise most lecturers are to students.

Not all library staff are subject librarians. There will be technical staff looking after the equipment and the computing side of things. There will be administrative staff who look after the procedures for issuing books, cataloguing the collection, re-shelving the stock, and so on. It is quite important not to get into the situation of asking the wrong people the wrong kinds of question. For example, a subject librarian is not the best person to ask about how to un-jam the photocopier. They may indeed be quite prepared to help you with this, but such tasks are not really using their expertise appropriately. Similarly, administrative staff are not the people to ask about which text on Socratic thought is the best one for your level 3 course, unless they happen to be graduates in a relevant discipline. They may well help you to find out where the relevant books are, but you need different expertise to help you decide which sources are best. Therefore, before asking library staff about something important to you, it is sensible to find out if it is the right person that you are speaking to. There's no quicker way, when in doubt, than to ask outright, 'Are you the right person to help me find out about . . . please?'

Library staff *like* to be helpful, but often get fed up when students (and staff) seem to want them to just do the work for them. Therefore, ask library staff for advice, but not in a way that implies that you expect them to go and find the best book for you. Ask questions in ways that acknowledge their professionalism and expertise – and value their opinions.

Despite the feeling that with the Internet the whole world is at your finger-tips whenever you sit at a networked computer anywhere on your campus, it remains useful for you to get to know the staff in your library. This means that you need to go there sometimes! Some students are never seen in the library unless they really need to be there, for example to find some source materials urgently for an impending or overdue assignment. Such students tend to be a pain to the library staff. They much prefer to be really helpful to someone whom they've often seen and sometimes talked to. If you know your subject librarian (if there is one), and get on well with the staff who supervise the computing facilities in your library, when you have an urgent need you are in a much better position to know who to ask about what, and when to get on with it yourself, rather than standing looking sheepish hoping someone is going to do it for you.

'Have you a moment or two to advise me on the some interesting sources for a project I'm doing on "Transport in developing countries"?' is the sort of question that could help you save a lot of time, and which may help you find sources other than the ones you would have found on your own. Such extra gloss can be part of the difference that makes for a good degree.

Learning support staff

Good habits when making the most of learning support staff include:

- Recognizing that they are experts in learning.
- Realizing that they may be specialists in particular problems students can face.
- Allowing them to ask you sufficient questions so that they can find out how best to help you to study effectively.
- Thanking them for their efforts to help you.

Learning support staff are primarily there to help students with particular learning problems. They may include specialists in a wide range of areas, including dyslexia, visual impairments, auditory impairments, anxiety, panic attacks, mental health problems, physical disabilities, and so on. That said, most learning support staff are only too willing to give support and advice to any student who is finding studying problematic. Such staff usually have excellent links with other support staff such as counsellors and careers advisory staff, and are in a good position to suggest to students with related difficulties that these colleagues can really help them.

In different institutions, learning support staff are located in different places. These can include:

- A student support office.
- A disabilities or equality unit.
- A learning resources centre or library.
- The Students' Union.

In some institutions, there are learning support staff distributed across the schools and faculties and in such cases most students will have been introduced to their local learning support staff member(s) in departmental induction. In many institutions, learning support staff also work with lecturers and tutors, and are represented on all the key committees and boards, not least helping staff to design the curriculum well, including ensuring that exams and other assessment processes work fairly and equitably for students.

Among the many things learning support staff can do to help you towards getting a good degree is that they can alert you to a wide range of available study skills development materials. This book is just one example of a wide range of such resources, many of which go into considerable depth about particular aspects of studying and could be really useful to you if you have particular study needs related to the discipline you are studying.

It is important to realize that learning support staff are there to help you – and indeed anyone who can benefit from their help. Don't feel embarrassed or ashamed to ask for advice when you feel things are getting you down or if you encounter a particular study problem. Just because you're intent on working towards a *good* degree does not mean that you'll never have any problems. In fact, some of the most distinguished scholars have battled with all sorts of problems – and still do. With the right kinds of help and support, there is no reason why just about any problem should interfere with your ambition to get a good degree. Indeed, universities have staff available to help with every imaginable problem. When one is reminded that around a third of the total population will have, at some time in a lifetime, a mental health problem, it is comforting that support staff such as counsellors are there to help us – staff as well as students. These people, along with learning support staff, are highly professional, very well trained, and, where appropriate, conduct their work with students (and staff) in a totally confidential manner. No one is going to broadcast that you've been to seek help from any of them. There's no shame or embarrassment. Perhaps the most gratifying talent of many of these professionals is that they're excellent listeners. Better listeners than your lecturers, better than your fellow students, better even than your friends or family. Sometimes we all really need someone to listen to us as we talk a problem or issue out of our systems. And that in itself is often all that is necessary. Talking about a problem to someone who is listening (and who cares, and who doesn't call us 'stupid') helps us to express the problem – and as we do so we often realize that in fact it isn't the huge beast that we thought it might be, but something that can be tackled quite systematically and calmly.

There's also another huge advantage of working through problems of any sort with the help of skilled professionals. When the problems are solved, you can walk away from them. That's how it works. You may never see them again. They're always, of course, pleased if you smile at them should you pass them in the street or in the refectory, but they're happy to be strangers who happen to have played a part in your life, then let go. It's not so easy to back away from friends, relatives, or other people we know after they've done something to help us work through difficulties.

Technical staff

Good habits when working with technical staff include:

- Remembering that many of them are graduates too.
- Watching them and listening to them.
- Valuing them and showing them courtesy.
- Learning skills, systems, and procedures from them.

Your degree programme may or may not involve significant contact with technical staff at your university. If it does not, you may wish to skip this section. For many students, particularly in disciplines such as science, engineering, computing, art and design, and so on, quite a lot of time may be spent in laboratories, workshops, or studios, where technical staff are the people who know a great deal about the equipment, apparatus, and procedures involved. As with library staff, technical staff range widely regarding qualifications, experience, and expertise. Some will be highly specialized and may hold first and higher degrees themselves. Sometimes, you will find it easier to talk to technical staff than (for example) to lecturers. Technicians are often only too pleased to spend time with students who are interested and appreciative of their attention. All of them tend to know more about the equipment around you than you do. This in itself is a good reason for watching how they do things and listening to their explanations. They have often helped many students before you and may have developed the art of explaining in ways that students can really understand.

Technical staff can save you from wasting a great deal of time. They know all the blind alleys that students are likely to go down and can advise you about them in advance. They know (often better than academics) how to get the most out of the available equipment and online systems. They know all the main problems that you are likely to encounter in their area of expertise and can help you to be ready for any such problems.

It is important that you show respect and courtesy to technical staff. Some of them wish that they were academic staff and may be acutely aware of any differences in respect that students show them from that shown to lecturers. Technical staff sometimes go on to become academics themselves. Some already *are* academics, in that they spend some of their time working on research and may well have published their findings along with academic colleagues.

Information technology staff

Good habits when using information technology staff include:

- Saving yourself time learning by seeking their help when you need it.
- Ensuring that they *help* you to do things, rather than do things for you.
- Checking back their instructions and making notes of them.
- Doing what you have been shown on your own straightaway, and repeatedly, until you have mastered it.

Just about all degree programmes make use of virtual learning environments and information technology nowadays, and in most courses it is vital to be able to make the most of computer-based learning packages, electronic communication, and the Internet. Many students entering higher education are already very skilled regarding information technology, not least because of having experience with computers at school, but also as a result of the various aspects of computer literacy which they have developed playing with electronic games of various kinds. However, if you're already well into computers, you will know how long it can take to find out by yourself how to make them do something that you want them to do, and how someone else can often show you very quickly how to do it.

Information technology staff are often spread around most departments in universities, as well as working in such areas as information technology centres, learning resources centres, computing centres, and libraries. They can save you a lot of time. However, to get their help, you normally need to ask for it. It is worth making sure that you know exactly what you want to ask first. Sometimes, students take a very long time to get round to what they *really* want to find out, and this wastes everyone's time. Definite questions such as:

- 'How do I run a spell-check with this package, please?'
- 'Please can you tell me why I can't save onto this floppy disk?'
- 'Please can you run me through how I log on to this system or package?'
- 'Is there a self-help tutorial which I can use to learn about this database?'

are more useful to everyone than vague questions such as, 'Can you tell me all about this system?'

It is far better to make sure that you do things yourself, rather than watch other people do them. Information technology staff are usually good at making students do things for themselves, but it is sometimes tempting to show students how to set up things rather than to talk them through setting them up for themselves. 'Make me do it, please!' is the tactic to employ when you need to get your head (or your fingers) round something new.

When information technology staff explain something to you, write it down straight away, preferably as a series of step-by-step instructions to yourself for the next time you need to do it. This saves you having to annoy them by asking the same question yet again, and saves you time too. It can pay to read back the sequence of instructions to them as a quick way of checking whether you've missed out anything important.

Whenever you've learned something new to do with computers or information technology, there is no substitute for doing the main steps once *again*, on your own, as soon as you possibly can. It can help you even more if you teach it to someone else as soon as you have the opportunity. This may seem like a few extra minutes of unnecessary work at the time, but can save you a significant amount of time when you come to do something similar again. As you repeat your steps, make sure that your written notes are clear enough for you to be able to use them in future, then file them where you will be able to find them again.

Fellow students

Good habits for making the most of your fellow students include:

- Realizing how much you deepen *your* learning every time you explain something to a fellow student.
- Valuing what they know and not making them feel small with what you know and they don't.
- Recognizing their abilities and expertise.
- Being open and sharing information with them.

Probably the most significant resource you have around you consists of your fellow students. Even people studying by distance learning find it valuable to network with fellow students using email, for example. If you spend much of your college life surrounded by fellow students, they can be a very significant factor contributing towards *your* success (and you to theirs).

Try the task below, to find out how well you presently use your fellow students, and to diagnose any areas where it could be worth changing your tactics.

Task: making the most of your fellow students

How do you use your fellow students? Tick whichever column is most like you.

Approaches to working with fellow students	Very like me	Quite like me	Not like me
1 I find it really useful to work with fellow students and do so in many aspects of my course.			

Approaches to working with fellow students	Very like me	Quite like me	Not like me
2 I set up my own ways of working with fellow students, such as study syndicates.			
3 I like working with fellow students, but I'm easily distracted and my productivity falls too much.			
4 I don' t really like working with fellow students as they slow me down too much.			
5 Why should I work with fellow students? I'm competing against them!			
6 I find it really valuable to explain things to fellow students; this helps me to learn them better myself.			
7 I find it very useful to have things explained to me by fellow students; I can often understand them better than my lecturers.			
8 I find that there are a few fellow students that I can really open up to and with whom I can openly share my feelings and views.			
9 I don't work much with fellow students as when I try to they only make me more anxious about my own studying.			
10 I just don't seem able to find the right sorts of fellow students with whom to get down to some useful studying!			

Discussion: making the most of your fellow students

1 *I find it really useful to work with fellow students and do so in many aspects of my course.* If this is 'very like you', you're already making good use of one of your most valuable resources. Some courses provide lots of opportunity for collaborative or team work. However, if you're not on such a course and seem to be getting conditioned to do most of your studying on your own, you may need to think about making your own opportunities to benefit from working with other students.

2 *I set up my own ways of working with fellow students, such as study syndicates.* Many students find that there are major benefits from taking charge of the collaborative-working agenda, and forming their own study

syndicates. Some such groups take their role quite seriously and have regular meetings, agreed agendas, and even keep records of the outcomes of each meeting. Other groups are less formal, but still can achieve significant pay-off in terms of the learning that is achieved by the participants.

3 *I like working with fellow students, but I'm easily distracted and my productivity falls too much.* If this is 'very like you', at least you're confronting an important issue! Working with friends can't be all work and it is perfectly natural to stray from study-related agendas for at least some of the time. It could be that you need to decide whether it's your fault that you're easily distracted or whether the other students with whom you are trying to work are particularly distracting.

4 *I don't really like working with fellow students as they slow me down too much.* If this is 'very like you', it is probably a sign that you're a high-flier anyway. Many students have been 'lone stars' before you and gone on to get good degrees. However, being 'slowed down' is not always a bad thing. Sometimes, when you're working on your own and feel that you're making rapid progress, it can turn out to be *surface* processing that is occurring. Moreover, you may be in danger of not getting sufficient feedback on how your own learning is going. Working through the same thing more slowly can help to make your learning deeper and more permanent. Furthermore, when you're working with 'slower' students, you will get a good deal of feedback about where you stand with your own learning, and you will sometimes be alerted to questions that you would not have thought of by yourself. You may find yourself helping them out with problems which you may yourself have been confronted with later. A compromise is called for; work as fast as you like on your own for *some* of the time, but make some time available to check out how your own learning is going with fellow students as your barometer.

5 *Why should I work with fellow students? I'm competing against them!* This view is not uncommon and there is some logic to it. If this is 'not like you', well done for being sociable! There aren't any marks for sociability in most degree courses, however, though collaboration is increasingly rewarded in many situations. Collaborative working pays dividends in other ways. For a start, not many people really *like* loners who only seem interested in their own destiny. It should not matter at all whether or not the people who make assessment decisions about your work really *like* you; their decisions should be impartial, fair, and valid. Human beings, however, can only *try* to be impartial and fair. More importantly, as part of your strategy for getting a good degree *and* a record which employers will like, you need to accumulate appropriate evidence that you can indeed work well with other people. When your lecturers can say positive things about your interpersonal skills in references which they write for you, it is likely to bring your job applications nearer to the short-listing pile.

6 *I find it really valuable to explain things to fellow students; this helps me to learn them better myself.* If this is 'very like you', well done, you have already discovered the most important benefit of working with fellow students. When you explain something that you have only recently learned to someone who does not yet understand it, the act of choosing your words to get the ideas across is a way of firming it up in your own mind. Furthermore, it helps it to stay in your own memory, as you tend to remember the way in which you explained it, and this is good practice for communicating it again when you need to, including in exams. From your fellow students' point of view, it is often easier to understand things when they are being explained by someone who has only recently learned them, and who has not forgotten what it was like to make sense of them for the first time.

7 *I find it very useful to have things explained to me by fellow students; I can often understand them better than my lecturers.* It is not surprising that lecturers are not always the best people to explain things in an understandable way. It's not that they aren't trying to be clear. It is more likely that they have known things for too long to remember what it felt like to make sense of them for that vital first time. Fellow students, who can still remember how they put their thoughts together when learning about an idea or concept can help *you* to put your thoughts together in the same way. From your point of view, hearing several different explanations from fellow students helps you to triangulate your own thoughts on the idea or concept, and brings you a deeper level of understanding.

8 *I find that there are a few fellow students that I can really open up to and with whom I can openly share my feelings and views.* It is good to have at least a few such people around you during your studies, especially when you reach the more demanding and potentially stressful times before important exams. It is then useful to have some people you can talk to, where you know how each other feels and where any worries or frustrations can be shared openly.

9 *I don't work much with fellow students as when I try to they only make me more anxious about my own studying.* This is one of the dangers of working with fellow students. It is seldom the case that fellow students *intend* to make you anxious about your own studying (or lack of it!), though this has been known to happen. Mostly, it is *your* attitude that may need adjusting, if you have such feelings. One way of addressing the issue is to remind yourself that when you hear fellow students talking about something that you don't yet know, you tend to notice it much more than when they talk about things you already know. You can turn this to your advantage, by making your own notes regularly, jotting down all the things which you think it may be worth you spending some extra time studying.

10 *I just don't seem able to find the right sorts of fellow students with whom*

to get down to some useful studying! This can indeed be the case, and if you find yourself in this position you may need to find ways of compensating for the benefits on which you may be missing out. You may be able to make some use of the limited opportunities available to you regarding working with such fellow students as are available to you, or even to go beyond your own course or university and track down one or two like-minded individuals studying similar topics elsewhere. Email communication can be a valuable way of making up for the lack of feedback from fellow students in such cases, and you may indeed make new friends in the process.

Elsewhere in this book, for example when planning your revision activities as discussed in Chapter 7, I have suggested that working for at least some of the time with fellow students can be a useful component of your own preparations for exams and other assessments.

Postgraduate demonstrators

Good habits when using postgraduate demonstrators include:

- Using them as expert witnesses.
- Finding out about what counts in assessed work.
- Showing them that you are interested.

Whether you meet postgraduate demonstrators or not during your time at university depends mainly on the discipline areas you are studying. In science and engineering subjects, for example, many of the practical sessions you are involved in are likely to be supervised by demonstrators. These are usually research students, working for Masters or PhD degrees, but required to undertake some teaching duties as well. The same or similar people may be responsible for tutorial or seminar elements of your course too.

Postgraduate demonstrators will already have a first degree, usually a good one. Therefore, from your point of view, they can be expert witnesses. They are also likely to know many of your lecturers and may be able to give you useful information about how the assessment systems work in the department in which you are studying. They may even be involved in some of your coursework or exams, and almost certainly will be involved in the assessment of your practical work.

They are usually specializing in their research fields and may or may not be good at explaining things outside their particular area of interest. However, regard them as part of the staff of the department and not just as research students! They are often the people who will get to know some aspects of your work better than anyone else, and their views may well be sought at examinations boards when the 'overall performance' of candidates is being compared to their coursework records. In other words, it is useful to impress them favourably. They soon get to know which students seem really interested, and they also usually know who attends laboratory sessions or tutorials regularly and punctually, and who contributes effectively. In short, it is best to have them on your side.

Mentors

You may or may not have a mentor. If you haven't, it might be a good idea to find yourself one after you've read about the sorts of things mentors can do to support your studies. Good habits when using mentors include:

- Valuing them.
- Not making them feel small when you know more than they do.
- Making agreements with them, then doing what you promised to do.
- Seeking feedback from them.
- Making them feel that they are helping you.

What is a mentor? The usual definitions include phrases such as 'critical friend' and 'trusted colleague'. Other kinds of student supporters include proctors (for example third year students helping first year students with particular areas of the curriculum), who may be students involved in 'supplemental instruction'. A mentor is someone who may be in a role which is intended to support your learning, but someone not usually involved in assessing your work. Not all universities have mentoring schemes for students, but interest is growing in the benefits which mentoring can bring. Some universities have developed systems where, for example, third year students mentor first year students, usually for particular elements of the first year study programme. The roles of such mentors vary a lot across disciplines, but often include running small group sessions with students, or one-to-one meetings with each student under their care, with the general aim of helping to resolve any study problems. You can, of course, find your own mentor(s) too. Anyone with an interest in your studies can help, but it is best if a mentor is not just a friend, as part of a mentor's role is to help you to get down to some serious work when you need to do so – friends may not be firm enough! A mentor is normally someone who has already done at least some of the studying that you yourself are doing, and is therefore in a position to help. A good mentor won't do things for you, but will help you to do things for yourself.

Another reason why some universities get more experienced students to mentor their less experienced counterparts is that the mentors themselves derive valuable learning from explaining things to their mentees. Add to this the fact that mentors can often explain difficult concepts rather more clearly than can lecturers (who may have known them for too long to remember what it was like to feel the light dawning), and the rationale for using mentors becomes even stronger.

Essentially, a mentor is in a helping and supporting relationship with students rather than a teaching one. This is why it is important to make a mentor feel valued. You will get far more out of having a mentor if the person concerned feels that the mentoring support is something that you feel is important to you.

The mentoring relationship is often an informal one and meetings may be quite haphazard. It may be largely up to you to decide how much use you are going to make of a mentor. This is why it is useful to cement the relationship by making a learning agreement between your mentor and yourself. Most mentors have been involved in learning agreements before and will be able to help you devise a workable plan. This may involve regular meetings, and ways of setting the agenda for each meeting in advance, to help the mentor be prepared for what might be discussed. Such agreements can work out very well indeed, making the best possible use of mentors' and mentees' time alike. However, it is vital to carry out *your* part of any such agreement, otherwise your mentor could decide that you are not serious about being mentored.

Mentors are usually in a position where they can give you valuable feedback about how your learning is going. You can show them drafts of assignments that you are working on, and they may well be able to put you on the right lines and save you from wasting energy on blind alleys. They are not usually *required* to give you feedback, so how much feedback you get is largely up to you. Nothing makes a mentor feel better about the relationship than being found by mentees to be providing really useful help and support. That is the main feedback that mentors themselves have, and is the barometer of their mentoring work. Even when a mentor only partially solves a problem, it is important that mentees show their appreciation. Even a little appreciation can open the doors to a great deal of further support and advice.

Project supervisors

These, of course, are only important to you if and when a project is an important part of your degree programme. In such contexts, however, they can be really important people in your life for the duration of your project. Good habits when making use of project supervisors include:

- Going to see them regularly, maintaining your contact proactively.
- Preparing for supervision sessions.
- Going to them with your ideas.
- Being receptive to all their feedback.
- Visibly responding to at least some of their suggestions.

Many degree programmes have an extended project, usually in the final year. Such a project may count significantly towards your overall degree and may well be critically important in reaching the decision about how good a degree you have earned. Your project supervisor is a central person in this situation.

Project supervisors may be lecturers, teaching assistants, or research students. You may have some choice in selecting whom you wish to be your project supervisor or you may simply be allocated one. Whichever is the case, project supervisors tend to be very busy people and are not likely to regard supervising *your* particular project as the central element in their lives, even though it may be of critical importance to you at the time. It may be very much your responsibility to *use* your project supervisor well. There are countless tales of students whose project work failed for one reason or another, where the supervisor's remarks about it were along the lines of, 'Well, I hardly ever saw him/her'. You've got to make sure this doesn't happen to you. It's all too easy to put off arranging a meeting with your project supervisor when you feel you haven't done enough to warrant a meeting – but look at this the other way round: when you *do* arrange a meeting, the pressure's then on you to do something to discuss at the meeting – that can't be bad!

Project supervisors don't like to be taken for granted. It is important not to go to see them and wait for them to tell you what to do. Think and plan before each meeting and take along with you some ideas of your own about how you believe that your project work might proceed. They are much more likely to give helpful suggestions if they feel that you are not just waiting for them to think about *your* project. They will often criticize your plans, and it is then important not to become defensive about your own ideas but to listen to everything that they may suggest. You can usually try out your own ideas in any case, but the more ideas you have to play with, the better will be the outcomes of your project.

One of the reasons for having project supervisors is that problems are *expected* with project work, which is similar to research in this respect. You may well be planning to move on from your good degree into research opportunities; project work is not just excellent practice for this but is your chance to show that you're an ideal candidate for consideration for a research studentship. If there were not any problems to expect in projects, the work would have been done already! It tends therefore to be the case that most times you seek out your project supervisor you normally want, and need, some help. However, what would you feel like towards someone that you never saw unless they needed your help? To avoid giving this impression, it's worth thinking of some answers before you go to your project supervisor with your questions. Work out at least two or three things that you could try to address the problems. Maybe try out one or more of these, so that you can explain what you tried to do and perhaps why it didn't solve the problem. This will help you get into the position where your project supervisor knows you as someone who is resourceful and autonomous, but who will still listen to advice and feedback.

Workplace supervisors

This all depends on whether or not your degree programme includes a work placement. If not, skip this section. If, however, you do have a work placement on your programme, the following discussion may help you to make the most of one or more key people, in this particular context: your supervisors. Good habits when making use of workplace supervisors include:

- Using them to help you to contextualize classroom learning.
- Listening to their experience.
- Avoiding moaning to them about things they can't change!
- Recognizing their value as experts in their own fields.
- Taking problems to them with your own suggestions regarding solutions.

If your course involves a work placement, your workplace supervisor will be a very important person in your life during this time. Workplace supervisors are sometimes lecturers or researchers from your own university, but may alternatively be someone on-site, whom you are able to contact on a day-to-day basis throughout your placement. Supervision of your work placement is quite likely to be done by both sorts of supervisor, one from your university and at least one more local one.

When on a work placement, you are likely to find life very different from university. For a start, you will be expected to be on-site for at least a normal working day, every day! The shock of early morning starts may throw you for a while. However, as a student heading towards a *good* degree, you need to be seen to be able to rise (including literally!) and meet all challenges during your work placement. Whether or not the outcomes of your work placement contribute to how good a degree you are awarded, the experience itself is one of the most relevant parts of your CV when you come to apply for permanent jobs, and you may well wish to use people who have supervised your placement as referees in your applications. This makes it very important to create the right impression. The last thing you want to do is to be regarded as 'all theory and no practice' or 'full of grand ideas that are far from reality'.

Workplace supervisors are rather like project supervisors when it comes to taking your problems along to them. They are busy people and need to be assured that you have tried everything you could think of before seeking their help, and that you have some further ideas about which to ask their advice rather than coming along to them empty-handed and empty-headed!

Making the most of your learning resources

We've looked at how you can make the most of the *people* in your learning environment, so now we'll go on to the 'things'. The terms 'learning environment', 'virtual learning environment', and 'resource-based learning' are heard more and more in higher education nowadays. They are often coupled with such terms as 'independent study', 'flexible learning', 'self-study pathways', and so on, indicating learning that *you* do, often at your own pace, in times of your own choosing, at places you choose, and essentially under your own steam. What all this really boils down to is learning which *you* do, using anything that is not 'directly taught'. You could regard resource-based learning as *all* the learning that you do outside lectures, laboratories, and class sessions. In fact, *most* of your learning is resource-based, where just about all of the responsibility for your learning rests with you. No one is going to stand over you and exhort you to get on with it – it's up to you.

'Virtual learning environments' are about electronic systems such as the Internet, your own university's intranet(s), and a wide range of hardware and software, allowing you to learn at computers and terminals, and to contact tutors and fellow students by email, and to contribute to discussion boards and chatrooms located on university servers and on the web.

There's not really anything new about the concept of resource-based learning. *Most* learning has always happened in a resource-based way, if we include such resources as lecture notes, handout materials, textbooks, journal articles, and so on, in our definition of learning resources. The differences now is that you are quite likely to meet some elements of your degree studies where you are intended to do *all* your learning from learning resource materials, without any direct teaching, and the range of resources has grown dramatically to include computer-based and electronic learning resources.

In the discussion which follows, we'll explore good habits which apply to typical resources in your learning environment, ranging from textbooks and handouts to the Internet and discussion boards. There are so many resources around you that your progress towards a good degree depends a great deal on using all of these wisely and productively, and not allowing yourself to be distracted into spending too much time or energy on particular resources at the expense of others.

Textbooks

Good habits when making use of textbooks include:

- Keeping a good database of your source materials (on computer or on cards).
- Using the index and contents pages well.
- Annotating the books with Post-its, or directly in the text when the book belongs to you.

- Researching your choices of books.
- Asking other people about books.

You've learned a great deal from books already and will continue to do so throughout your education and beyond. It's one of the primary ways of finding information, and then learning what you need of it. You may well feel, depending upon the nature of the subjects that you are now studying, that you spend quite a lot of your life with books. You may also be aware that it is dangerously easy not to spend this time efficiently. Have a go at the next task, which aims to help you to diagnose some of the possible bad habits that can interfere with learning from textbooks, and to alert you to good habits you can build upon. Then read the discussion that follows.

Task: using textbooks and learning from them

Rate yourself on each of the following statements about finding, using, and learning from textbooks.

Statement	Very like me	Quite like me	Not at all like me
1 I don't often seek out books in the library, as I have my own copies of sufficient of the important literature for my studies.			
2 I seem to be forever looking for books in the library, and spend more time looking for them than really *using* them.			
3 I seem to spend a lot of time reading the wrong books!			
4 I find myself spending too much time reading the wrong parts of the right books!			
5 I'm now efficient at information retrieval, and use the online catalogue to search for *relevant* sources by author and topic.			
6 I know my way around the library stock that is relevant to my studies and spend some time just reminding myself of what is there.			

Statement	Very like me	Quite like me	Not at all like me
7 I ask other people about which books are most useful and relevant, and then check these out for myself, along with others I have chosen.			
8 Before I go searching for sources, I make a list of questions that I want to find out some answers to from the sources.			
9 I make good use of the contents pages and the index to find in a book those parts that are directly relevant to my immediate purpose.			
10 I regard it as really important to *capture* the vital information from my source materials, and not just to photocopy large tracts for later perusal.			
11 I keep careful records of the source materials that I have consulted to save me wasting time looking for them again.			
12 I build up an accurate database of facts, figures, and quotations from books where I think I may want to quote from them in my work.			
13 I revisit my sources and give myself the benefit of second thoughts.			

Discussion: good and bad ways to search for books and learn from them

1 *I don't often seek out books in the library, as I have my own copies of sufficient of the important literature for my studies.* It is very useful to have one's own stock of source materials, and this can save a lot of time looking for them (and waiting for them to become available) in libraries. It also shows some measure of dedication to buy a significant amount of the literature that you will be using most. However, there is a significant risk of owning your own copies of most of the literature that you need, in that you may become too dependent on a relatively narrow cross-section of the whole field, and may not distinguish yourself as a student heading

for a good degree, as indicated by relatively narrow reading. Furthermore, you may be missing out on developing your speed and skills at finding source materials in libraries and on databases.

2   *I seem to be forever looking for books in the library, and spend more time looking for them than really using them.* It is really worthwhile to polish up your information tracking and retrieval skills. These are important life skills. You will need them even more if you go on to do research after your first degree. If this was 'very like you', think hard about *how* you go about looking for materials in libraries. Talk to other people (students, staff, librarians) about how they tackle information tracking and retrieval. Find out whether your university has self-teach packages on information retrieval. Try out using online catalogues, narrowing down your search by getting better at choosing the most relevant keywords, and triangulating your search on the works of the most authoritative writers and editors. Don't just walk up to the stacks and browse! This is fine for a *luxury* episode, *after* you've located the sources that are most directly relevant to your searches.

3   *I seem to spend a lot of time reading the wrong books!* Is there such a thing as a 'wrong' book? Well, there is, if we define 'wrong' as inappropriate to your purpose or need. There just isn't the time to read everything that looks as though it may be interesting or relevant. You need to find the 'best' books – in other words, those that are important in the context of your studies, and which are authoritative and respected. Citation indexes can be very useful as a way of finding out which sources are most often quoted. You can then compare the 'right' books with the 'wrong' books if you have time, and if you want to add some extra polish to your own writing about what you have learned.

4   *I find myself spending too much time reading the wrong parts of the right books!* This is a common bad habit. Well done if it's 'not at all like you'! One problem is that the 'wrong' parts are often the most interesting! However, if you plan to make your studying really efficient, you have to regard reading the 'wrong' parts of your source materials as a luxury activity, to be engaged in only *after* getting what you need from the most relevant parts of your books.

5   *I'm now efficient at information retrieval, and use the online catalogue to search for relevant sources by author and topic.* If this is 'very like you', well done. This is a good habit which will repay dividends not only by helping you to track down all the most relevant material, but also by saving you time that you can usefully deploy towards making sure that you get credit for your learning from source materials – in other words, making summaries and making sense of what you are learning.

6   *I know my way around the library stock that is relevant to my studies and spend some time just reminding myself of what is there.* It is good not just to depend upon information retrieval aids, such as online catalogues

and databases. Regard it, however, as a luxury, and don't spend too long browsing the stacks. Turn the activity into detective work. Look for the books that seem to be well used – this may be because they're useful, authoritative, or popular for other reasons. Look for the books where there are multiple copies on the shelves. This can be because they are important or at least because someone *thought* they should be important. But triangulate your detective work with information from catalogues or online databases, which also will tell you about multiple copies; there may be 20 copies of the *best* book and they all may be out on loan!

7   *I ask other people about which books are most useful and relevant, and then check these out for myself, along with others I have chosen.* This is one of the most useful strategies for finding good source materials quickly and efficiently. Many students decide to undertake literature searches collaboratively and then pool their results. This can save everyone time and effort. It is always useful to ask someone who has already studied the subject you are researching (and done so successfully) about which sources turned out to be the most useful, and why.

8   *Before I go searching for sources, I make a list of questions that I want to find out some answers to from the sources.* This is normally an excellent habit. It gets your mind searching for answers rather than just trying to absorb information. Sometimes your questions will only be a starting point and you will find more important questions that you should be addressing as you go deeper into the material. Remember, however, that one way or another your ability to *answer questions* is one of the things that your good degree really depends upon, so all practice at devising and answering questions is useful. Your list of questions can be the ideal starting point with which to interrogate the contents pages and indexes of your selected sources.

9   *I make good use of the contents pages and the index to find in a book those parts that are directly relevant to my immediate purpose.* The contents pages and the index are in many ways the most important and useful parts of most non-fiction works. It is useful to have a supply of slips of scrap paper (or Post-its if you can afford them!) to insert in the pages which seem most relevant to your agenda, and to scan right through the contents pages first, marking your book ready for the next stages. If you're looking for something particular rather than general, the index may be an even better starting point than the contents pages. It is worth finding out about *everything* in a source that may be relevant before looking in detail at any of your selections. This can help you to avoid reading too much material that is merely tangential to your purposes before discovering the part of the book that is really central.

10   *I regard it as really important to capture the vital information from my source materials, and not just to photocopy large tracts for later perusal.* The actual learning pay-off derived from reading is relatively low.

Reading is only a start. The real work, and the real learning, goes with *processing* the information that you find. Just photocopying it is not in itself processing it. A shelf full of photocopied material still has to be started on as far as learning from it is concerned. You can only be really sure that your reading is paying off if you are making decisions as you read. Sort out the really important from the quite important. Sort out too the 'not at all important' and don't waste much time reading it! Make your own summary notes to capture the really important material. Organize your notes systematically, for example on record cards or in a form which you can transcribe to a computerized database of your own if you prefer to keep track of your source materials in this way.

11 *I keep careful records of the source materials that I have consulted to save me wasting time looking for them again.* If this is 'very like you' well done! It's a thankless task searching again for something that you have already seen once. Make sure that your notes contain accurate details of each important source, so that if you refer to it in your own work you have the exact details of author names, title of the source, date of publication, publisher, and place of publication to hand. With journals and maga-zines, make sure you have the volume number (and part number if appropriate) as well. With journals, check up the normal way that the journal is referred to by authors referring to other articles in the same journal, and from other journals.

12 *I build up an accurate database of facts, figures, and quotations from books where I think I may want to quote from them in my work.* This can save you a great deal of time in the long run. It may seem as if it is slowing down your reading, but processing the information from books is where learning really starts. Keep notes of the page numbers (as well as all the information referred to in point 11 above) relating to the most relevant and important parts of the material, especially if you might need to quote from the source. Where you may want to quote word for word, take par-ticular care with your own notes, so that you can tell what is 'quotable' rather than your own digest.

13 *I revisit my sources and give myself the benefit of second thoughts.* It is human nature to take first impressions seriously. This applies to using textbooks too. The book that seems ideal at first sight may appear much less ideal when you have got to know the field a lot better by consulting a number of further sources. Similarly, sources which don't look at all attractive or suitable can turn out to be the really useful ones. Further-more, returning to something a week or two later that you've already used can surprise you. You may find all sorts of useful things that you did not notice the first time, making it worth annotating and adding to your previous notes.

What about 'speed reading'?

Speed reading is much overrated. It's something that you can develop when reading for pleasure, but less likely to be relevant to reading for learning. Don't believe what some people claim about dramatic increases in your ability to read quickly. Things *read* at speed will mostly be *forgotten* at speed! It's the slower *processing* of the important parts of what you read that are where the real learning begins. Speed reading is fine for things that you don't want to remember or that are not important. Your good degree will be more a measure of the *quality* of your reading than of your reading speed. It will also be more a measure of the quality of your reading than the quantity. Besides, in many subjects (including most parts of mathematics and many parts of science and engineering) speed reading is just not an option. You can't *learn* an extended proof or derivation just by reading it quickly! Some such things you can't learn *at all* by just reading them, you have to *do* them to learn them. Similarly, most open learning materials are designed for learning-by-doing, and are not intended merely to be read.

There are, however, two useful speed reading techniques that you *can* adopt:

1 *Speed finding:* it is well worth developing your speed at *finding* the parts of each source material that are going to be worth reading properly. This includes making good use of the contents pages and index. It also includes developing the skill to skim through large tracts of a given source, just getting the feel of what is in it, by looking quickly at headings and subheadings and the first sentence of some of the paragraphs. Don't regard this as a key *learning* strategy, however, even if you find that you're learning quite a lot in the process. The real learning strategies come into play once you have tracked down what is *worth* learning.
2 *'Not talking' reading:* most people first learned to read, at school, by following things in books and reading them aloud. This is actually far, far slower than your eyes can now read, and also far slower than your brain can think. Check that you haven't still got the habit of following printed words at the slow rate at which you can hear them being spoken. It is useful to use this faster kind of reading when you are just getting the feel of what is in a source, but it is crucial to slow down considerably each time you find something that is worth learning. 'Talking reading' is really useful when proofreading your own work. Reading aloud what you have written slows you down and allows you to concentrate on your own words, enabling you to hear repetitions, and find instances of poor phrasing and grammatical errors.

Handout materials, including copies of PowerPoint slides used in your lectures

It used to be the case that handout materials were given out in lectures, and this still happens sometimes. More often nowadays, handout materials are made available to you, electronically, for you to download and print out as necessary. They're often made available *before* lectures, so you can take them to the lecture and edit and annotate them there and then. As well as text-based handouts, many lecturers make available their PowerPoint slides, often as 3-per-page or 6-per-page handouts (or electronic files in this form), allowing you to write notes alongside the slides on the basis of the discussion in the lecture.

Good habits when making use of handout materials include:

- Not missing any!
- Paying particular attention to course or module handbooks, which contain details of the intended learning outcomes, and the assessment criteria relating to these.
- Not assuming that if you've got the handout, you've got all you need.
- Downloading them promptly, and if necessary printing them out and taking them to lectures.
- Actually using them, during lectures and after lectures as appropriate.
- Modifying them, editing them, and adding to them.
- Filing them systematically whether physically or electronically.
- Turning what's in them into questions to practise on as you revise.

You probably have quite a stock of handout materials, whether on paper or as files on your computer. Many lecturers use handout materials for the content that they cover in class sessions, and some issue further materials for you to peruse between sessions. They also tend to assume that if something was in a handout, it is reasonable to expect that *all* students not only *have* it, but also will in due course *know* it. Handout materials (including copies of PowerPoint slides used in lectures) are probably your richest single source of really relevant and central material, in at least some of your subjects. The habits that you develop regarding what you do with handout materials can be central to your strategy for working towards a good degree. Try the next task to work out whether you've already acquired really productive habits with handouts and copies of slides, and then read the discussion that follows.

Task: using handouts and learning from them

Rate yourself on each of the following habits regarding handout materials.

Habit	Very like me	Quite like me	Not at all like me
1 I file handout materials regularly and systematically.			

Habit	Very like me	Quite like me	Not at all like me
2 I make quite extensive notes directly onto handout materials during lectures when I can.			
3 I work out what exactly is being handed out on each occasion.			
4 I add to, and annotate, my handout materials as I follow up lectures, and do so within a week of each lecture.			
5 I make sure that I get copies of any handout materials I missed when they were issued.			
6 I make my own concise summaries of the important information and data from handout materials.			
7 I build up a question bank, writing short, sharp questions with which I can quiz myself on the most important information in handout materials.			
8 I work together with two or three fellow students, regularly debriefing the content of handouts and adding to my question bank.			

Discussion: using handouts and learning from them

Just about all the items in the previous task are linked to useful habits to develop regarding what you do with handout materials you are given. The following discussion elaborates on these.

1 *I file handout materials regularly and systematically.* This, of course is not sufficient, but it's an important step in its own right. There's no point carrying around with you the ever-increasing bulk of notes and handouts that you build up. The pile soon gets too heavy! Besides, when you've assembled a significant amount of handout materials, there's no way that in any one day you're going to get the chance to look at *all* of them. It can be useful to have separate files or ring-binders for each main subject area, into which you file your handout materials along with your own

lecture notes. Alternatively, where the materials are issued electronic-ally, you can make computer folders instead. It can sometimes be useful to take the whole file along to a class session, especially if you know that the session is going to look back over quite a lot of the work that has already been covered. Usually, however, it is enough to carry around with you only the materials from the last couple of sessions, and to file safely all the rest. It also cuts the risk of losing everything if one file goes missing. A single ring-binder with card dividers can be big enough to file the last couple of sets of notes and handouts for several topics, and may be all you need to carry around during an entire week. Another reason for not carrying the whole lot around with you is that students' handouts and notes sometimes get lost (or worse, stolen) when it's too late to do much about it! However you organize your handouts, don't mistake *having* them for *having processed* them. More about this in the responses below.

2   *I make quite extensive notes directly onto handout materials during lectures when I can.* You can't always do this – for example, when handout materials are issued *after* the lecture. When you have the chance, it is an excellent habit to develop, and it helps to prevent you from switching off mentally believing that the subject matter is already captured in the handout material. Making notes as the lecture proceeds allows you to capture your own thoughts and reactions to the material that is already in the handout. It is particularly useful to mark onto your handouts your own questions. If you jot a question down there and then, you will be able to look up or work out the answer to it in due course. If you *don't* jot down the question, you may have quite forgotten what the question was after an hour or two!

3   *I work out what exactly is being handed out on each occasion.* This may have seemed quite an odd statement, and you may not have quite decided whether it is 'very like you' or not. It was intended to get you thinking. We call them all 'handouts', but there are several different kinds of handout. Some are potted digests of all of the most important things that lecturers actually say and discuss in their lectures. Others consist of headlines and bullet points, and are meant to be enough to remind you of the main points discussed, acting as a basis to build upon when writing up your own fuller notes of the lecture. Other handouts include copies of some or all of the overheads or slides used to *illustrate* a lecture, but this does not mean that they 'contain' the lecture itself. Yet other handouts are further information papers, tasks, and exercises involving material *not* covered in the actual sessions. You are quite likely to get several different kinds of 'handout' from different lecturers in the same week. What you *do* with them, both during and after the session, needs to reflect what exactly was being handed out, and what the respective lecturers *intended* you to do with them – they will usually give you advice on this during lectures – keep listening.

4   *I add to, and annotate, my handout materials as I follow up lectures, and do so within a week of each lecture.* If you said 'very like me' to this one, very well done! It is an excellent study habit. It is important to add to and annotate handouts in any case, but it is even more sensible to do this as soon as you reasonably can manage it, and within a week if at all possible. This may seem a tall order, but think about it: if you follow up your lectures relatively quickly, you can still remember lots of the detail when you come to annotate your handout materials. You can also use the exercise to help you get your head round the topic of the lecture *before* the next one is due, and this helps you to make more sense of the next one, and so on. Although it does take some time to build such follow-up work into your study schedule, regard it as *quality* study time.

5   *I make sure that I get copies of any handout materials I missed when they were issued.* Of course, it is wise to catch up on handouts that you've missed, but this is only the start. As you know from the sessions that you attend, the handout is only part of the business. Just as important are all the things you *do* with the handout during and after the lecture. Getting a copy of a pristine handout is not the same as being there. Even getting someone else's annotated copy only bridges the gap partially. Your best option is to try to see the notes that several fellow students made during any session you miss, and to triangulate their notes and comments to gather as much additional information about the session as you can. If there are one or two fellow students whose note-making you really trust (in other words not just note-taking), it can be useful to come to mutual arrangements with them about missed sessions. When you know that you are trying to make notes that will capture everything important, *and* that you may be passing these on to someone else who cannot be present, your notes tend to be much fuller and better (and more legible!). Mutual arrangements mean that you and your collaborators put yourselves out to make a good job of covering for each other's absence.

6   *I make my own concise summaries of the important information and data from handout materials.* Well done if this is 'very like you'. There are two main advantages of making your own summaries from materials that you have been given. First, the act of boiling information down into its most important parts and putting these into your own words helps you to make sense of it much better than just reading someone else's words. Second, when you have a separate summary, you can practise looking at that, and trying to recall all the other important information that is in the original handout. This means that as you get to know the material better, you only need to look at the original handout occasionally. This can make your revision much more efficient by enabling you to work with smaller amounts of well-digested material.

7   *I build up a question bank, writing short, sharp questions with which I can quiz myself on the most important information in handout materials.*

If you're already building up a question bank, excellent! If not, I suggest you start making one today. It's useful to write down questions that occur to you during lectures, so that you can follow these up rather than forgetting them. It is even *more* useful to start devising short, sharp questions about your lecture notes and handout materials fairly soon after each lecture. You can usually think of at least ten such questions, and perhaps up to a hundred or so, for a single lecture. These short questions are the building blocks that make up bigger questions such as those you will meet in exams. If you get to the state where you have no problems at all answering all the little questions, you are automatically in a position to answer any of the bigger ones which may come up. Exams measure, more than anything else, your ability to answer exam questions, so making a question bank is directly paving your way to being able to do yourself justice in your exams. Furthermore, if you build up a comprehensive question bank all through your studies, you are *always* in the safe and reassuring position of *knowing* how your learning is going. You can test yourself at any time, and find out those questions to which you don't yet know the answers, and then *do* something about them. You can also spare yourself from reading material that you don't need to read again, as you can identify such material by the fact that you can already answer all your questions on it.

8   *I work together with two or three fellow students, regularly debriefing the content of handouts and adding to my question bank.* In many ways this is the ideal way to follow up lectures, and to debrief the contents of handout materials as well. In point 7, I suggested you begin a question bank if you have not already done so. This works even better if you do it collaboratively with other like-minded students. Two or three minds will think up a much more comprehensive question bank than one mind alone. A further advantage of building a question bank collaboratively is that you can quiz each other with the questions. You can of course quiz yourself, but it's even more realistic to be put on the spot by someone else firing questions at you in random order. This trains your brain to think of the answers to the questions 'on demand' and is excellent practice for exams.

As you will have seen from the discussion above, there is much more to handouts than may at first seem apparent. There is little value in just getting them and filing them. It is what you *do* with them that matters most. Too many students leave processing their handout materials until the revision stage before exams, and then find that there's far too much material to process properly. Such students don't usually end up with really good degrees! Even a two-page printed handout can have much more in it than you would have been able to write in an hour. Put your handout

materials to work for you as soon as you have them and start learning from them straight away.

Independent learning materials

Your studies can include working through print-based packages or working in your university's virtual learning environment, essentially under your own steam, to learn things alongside what's taught in lectures, tutorials, and other 'taught' parts of your studies. Alternatively, there may be some elements of your studies which aren't taught at all, and the learning is entirely up to you – but, of course, it is still *assessed* sooner or later in exams, assignments, and other assessment formats, including online assessment.

Good habits when making use independent study elements include:

- Paying close attention to the intended learning outcomes and working systematically towards achieving these under your own steam.
- Not skipping the tasks, practice questions, and other activities – learning happens by *doing* things, not just by reading the learning materials (whether online or print-based).
- Making the most of the feedback following on from activities, which often appears on-screen in online materials, or is printed in print-based materials.
- Revisiting problem areas until you're sure you've achieved the intended learning outcomes.

Independent learning, especially using virtual learning environments, is being used more and more as part of normal university courses. Students studying *entirely* by independent learning (not least students of the Open University in the UK – by far the largest university in terms of student numbers) soon get into the swing of how to go about independent learning. If, however, you only meet independent learning for isolated elements of your curriculum, you may not have time to work out for yourself what the rules of the game really are.

The main characteristics of independent learning can include:

- You work through learning resource materials of one kind or another.
- You have freedom to work at your own pace.
- You have freedom to work at your own choices of times.
- You may have freedom to work where you prefer to work.
- You're doing it under your own steam, and therefore have freedom to fail to do it! (Not how to get a good degree!).

One of the most significant dangers with independent learning elements within a traditional course is that you're expected to get on with the independent components, but no one will be pressing you to do so. The materials will be issued to you, or made available to the whole group, and then it's up to you when you start doing the learning, where, and how fast. All you know is that one way or another your achievements gained through independent learning *will* be measured.

What's in it for me, becoming good at independent learning?

Some students feel that independent elements in their programmes are 'not quite fair', and that the university is letting them down by not getting on and teaching them these parts of the curriculum. Other students really enjoy the freedom to learn in their own ways (and, with care, these students usually get good degrees!). There are several direct benefits to you associated with having at least some of your studies in independent learning mode. These include:

- You can make the most of the various freedoms mentioned above.
- You are in control of the pace of your own learning.
- You gain skills in managing your own learning.
- You gain skills in working with virtual learning environments, and increase your confidence regarding the various technologies in use there.
- You become more autonomous as a learner, which is a useful skill to carry forward into other areas of your studies, and into your career in general.
- If you use your learning materials well, you can monitor your own progress continuously as you work through them.
- You can accumulate *evidence* of your self-organizational skills.

What features can I expect to see in independent learning materials?

The best materials are quite different from textbooks in their structure and style. While they still contain the theory, information, and data that you will be using in your learning, they have other additional features which make them more self-sufficient as learning resources. These features may include:

- Statements of intended learning outcomes or learning objectives.
- Tasks and activities, such as self-assessment questions, for you to try for yourself as you work through the materials.
- Feedback responses to tasks and activities, so you can see how you fared in your own attempts at the questions.
- Exercises and tasks to help you gain practice at using what you are learning.
- Tutor-marked assignments, so that your work with the materials can be assessed – these usually count towards your overall coursework marks.

Although some independent learning packages are entirely print-based, it is increasingly common for them to refer to other kinds of learning resource materials, including computer-based programmes, video-recordings, audio-recordings, and sometimes even practical kits. Independent learning on virtual learning environments usually has audio and video elements, along with email opportunities to contact tutors and fellow students, and online assessment elements. Also, some independent learning packages are not designed to be self-sufficient, but make use of one or more traditional textbooks as 'readers', and refer you out to these with specific directions about what you should be aiming to get out of particular sections of the books.

Task: making the most of independent learning

How good do you think you will be at making the most of the principal features of independent learning? Rate yourself against the features listed below.

Feature of independent learning	I know I'm very good at handling this	I think I will be OK at handling this	I don't know whether I'll be good at handling this
1 Working at my own pace.			
2 Working on my own.			
3 Choosing where I study.			
4 Choosing when I study.			
5 Getting used to the technology and equipment.			
6 Making the most of the stated intended learning outcomes or objectives.			
7 Making good use of the learning-by-doing elements.			
8 Learning from the feedback in responses to the tasks and activities.			
9 Doing well at the tutor-marked assignments.			
10 Carrying forward what I learn independently into traditional assessments such as exams.			

Discussion: making the most of independent learning resources

1 *Working at your own pace.* It is important to be effective at working at your own pace, not just in the context of independent learning, but as an overall strategy for managing your own learning, leading you towards getting a good degree. Independent learning elements in your course can help you to develop skills at managing the pace of your own learning. These include not getting bogged down with unimportant material, and devoting your time and energy to those parts of the material that really need your full attention.

2 *Working on your own.* Most independent learning materials are designed for working on your own. It is indeed useful to have some parts of your curriculum where you have to make all the decisions for yourself and take on full responsibility for planning and doing your work. This does not mean, however, that you *must* work on your own. It is still possible for you to find students who are working through the same material at the same time as yourself, and to compare notes with them. As always, it can be very useful to gain feedback from other students, such as by comparing problems and explaining things to each other.

3 *Choosing where you study.* With some independent learning materials it will be entirely up to you where you choose to work with them. However, sometimes the places will be limited – for example if you have to log on to university servers to access the virtual learning environment or the Internet. It is therefore important to make sure that you plan sufficient time to be in the same place as your learning opportunities! Don't, however, let waiting for access to equipment stop you in your tracks. There are always some things you can do while you are waiting for access to equipment.

4 *Choosing when you study.* This is one of your key responsibilities with independent learning elements in your studies. There are usually all sorts of things for you to do that may seem more urgent, or more important, than working through some study materials. Many of these other tasks in your life have *people* as driving forces, such as tutors wanting you to hand things in for assessment, or seminars and tutorials where you want to be *seen* to be working productively and in a well-prepared way. Even the peer pressure of trying to keep up with what other students seem to be doing is a driving force helping you to keep up with your studies. With independent learning it is all rather different as no one but *you* really knows to what extent you are taking on your responsibility of working through your materials. This means that you may have to take deliberate steps to make some time for these studies, alongside all the other things you may be doing on your course.

5 *Getting used to the technology and equipment.* For most students this is not a problem. Practice makes perfect. The best way to learn new systems is to do things with them. It's sometimes hard to work through a list

of instructions, but once you've used a system a couple of times, you'll waste little time re-tuning to it. In any case, there are usually lots of people around to ask who already know the technology.

6   *Making the most of the stated intended learning outcomes or objectives.* These can be really useful. They are normally expressed along the lines of, 'When you've worked through Section 3, you should be able to . . .' followed by a list of the things that you are expected to become able to *demonstrate* to prove to yourself (and to anyone else) that your learning has been successful. The intended learning outcomes are very likely to be closely related to any assessment that you will meet in due course on the content of the independent-learning materials. These outcomes are your principal frame of reference to keep tabs on how your learning from the materials is going. It is best to keep your eyes on the intended outcomes throughout your work with independent-learning materials. Look at them before you start to find out what the agenda is. Keep looking back at them as you study and tick them off every time you are sure that you have achieved one. Look at them again when you come to any tutor-marked work, as this will have the primary purpose of getting you to show a tutor that you have achieved the desired learning outcomes, as they are strongly linked to what tutors will be looking for in your work.

7   *Making good use of the learning-by-doing elements.* These are where you give yourself the chance to learn by experimenting, to practise, and to make mistakes! At least, when you're working alone through independent learning materials you have the comfort of being able to make as many mistakes as you like, in private. It is in *doing* the tasks, exercises, and activities that you really make headway with *learning* from the materials. Just reading them is not enough. They are designed to be *done*, not just to be read. Of course, you need to be sensible about *what* you do. There's no point, for example, doing a self-assessment question when you are absolutely sure that you already know how to do it and what the answer is. Even then, however, it is worth checking the response or discussion about the question included in your materials to make sure that you would have done it well.

8   *Learning from the feedback in responses to the tasks and activities.* Learning from feedback is *always* useful and important, but never more so than when you're working on your own. Well-designed learning materials provide a great deal of feedback. You can only get feedback, however, if you have *done* something to get feedback about. That's why the feedback in learning materials is associated with self-assessment questions and exercises. When you have had a go at any of these, see what you can learn about *how* you did, by comparing what you did with the feedback responses already built into the materials or those coming up on-screen. You will soon find out that one of the main benefits of independent learning is that it gives you the chance to do things *in-correctly* and then to find out *why* you did so. This is one of the most

productive ways of learning how to do things well, and the more mistakes you make when doing tasks and activities, the greater the number of mistakes you're never likely to make again, including when they would count!

9 *Doing well at the tutor-marked assignments.* In some ways, this is just an extension of doing well at normal coursework. The difference is that in independent learning, most of your preparatory work leading up to tutor-marked assignments is likely to have been done on your own, so you may lack the frame of reference to know in advance whether your tutor-marked work is going to be up to scratch. Also, the printed questions of tutor-marked assignments don't carry the tone of voice, body language, and facial expression that can give useful clues to how to go about coursework where briefings are given face-to-face by lecturers. With tutor-marked independent-learning assignments it is even more important to read the wording really carefully and to follow all clues or suggestions about what is being looked for. Return to the intended learning outcomes of the package for guidance about the overall agenda. Look again at the self-assessment questions, which in most independent-learning materials amount cumulatively to practice runs for tutor-marked work. In due course, you are likely to get useful feedback about your actual performance in tutor-marked assignments, and this can be invaluable at helping you fine-tune your future efforts in such assignments.

10 *Carrying forward what you have learned into traditional assessments such as exams.* This can be a problem area. It's a matter of working out an appropriate balance. Check carefully what *proportion* the independent learning component of your studies contributes to the overall programme. Check which other parts of your learning will be assessed alongside this learning and whether there will be compulsory questions on the independent learning material. The main danger is that students sometimes don't take things they learned by themselves as seriously as things they were taught in traditional ways, even when they are of equal importance in an assessment situation.

Libraries, learning resource centres, learning centres, and so on

These parts of universities are now called by several alternative names, reflecting the changes in function and usage and what is expected of students using them.
  Good habits when making use of such places include:

- Going into them!
- Getting to know what's in them for you.
- Making the most of the expert help and support available from library staff.

- Using all the *other* things in libraries besides books!
- Learning information retrieval skills early.
- Getting up to speed at using libraries.

We've already looked at some of the implications for making good use of libraries in the earlier section about textbooks in this chapter. However, it is important to realize that libraries aren't just places where books and journals are stored. They are significant resources in several different ways. For a start, libraries are staffed by people who know a lot about studying successfully. There are experts in your subjects among the staff. There are experts at information tracking and retrieval. Usually these people will not be visible among the stacks, but will work from rooms behind the scenes. This should not stop you from making an appointment to see exactly the right person to help you when the need arises.

Another important consideration about your library is that it is a place in which you can do at least some of your studying. If you prefer to work in quiet or silent surroundings, a library may be a good place for you. If you need a clear surface upon which to spread out your books, journals, and notes, there are such surfaces in most libraries. If you need a place where you can spread out your resources for several days and work hard in solitude, many university libraries have study carrels which can be booked in advance for such purposes. If the heating and lighting are not too good where you live, they are probably much better in a library. If you need to get your head down to some work away from the distractions of your fellow students, libraries usually have corners that your fellow students may not know about! If you need to find somewhere to work *with* some of your fellow students, many libraries have rooms which can be booked for meetings and collaborative work, and non-quiet areas where discussion between students is encouraged. If you need to escape from television or CD players, you can do so in a library. If you want to gain access to email, the Internet, computers, printers, multimedia learning resources, online databases, and so on, you can normally do so in a large library (though your university may have some such resources concentrated in a separate information technology centre or computing centre). Despite all the things that a good library can offer, there are always some students who hardly ever go there. They don't, however, tend to get *good* degrees, and probably are not reading this book anyway! Make the most of *your* library facilities – all of them.

Journals – paper-based and online

Good habits when making use of journals include:

- Establishing which journals are relevant to your studies.
- Skimming for interest.
- Keeping good records of what you find that's important for your studies.
- Using journals quite selectively.

- Photocopying very selectively – only copy what you're really going to use.
- Capturing the most important information efficiently.
- Knowing in which journals to look for papers.
- Being among the first to see new issues of key journals.

Now complete the next task, rating yourself against most of the good habits listed above, and a few more. Then read the discussion that follows.

Task: good habits when using journals

Rate yourself against the habits listed below.

Habit	I'm good at this	I'm OK at this	I'm not yet good at this
1 Establishing which journals are relevant to your studies.			
2 Skimming for interest.			
3 Keeping good records of what you find that's important for your studies.			
4 Using journals quite selectively.			
5 Using journals iteratively – going back to important things again.			
6 Photocopying selectively.			
7 Capturing the most important information efficiently.			
8 Being among the first to see new issues of key journals.			
9 Quoting sources correctly.			
10 Evaluating journal articles well.			

Discussion: good habits when using journals

1 *Establishing which journals are relevant to your studies.* This is something you should do as early as you can, especially in connection with project work where you may be expected to show your ability to survey the field in areas close to your own work. Whittling down the frightening mass of literature into three categories helps: (1) two or three journals which are the key areas for authoritative publication in the field; (2) a selection of other journals which occasionally have key articles, and which more often have interesting but not very important articles; and (3) all the rest, which you will not need to return to often, or at all. Having said that you should establish which journals are relevant, you should also, of course, follow up any suggestions made by your lecturers about sources you should consult, even if some of them seem obscure. Lecturers like to see that their suggestions have been acted upon, and they usually see this when acting as assessors!

2 *Skimming for interest.* It is important to spend some time doing this, particularly with the key journals, and also the next most important group. It is during this stage that you are likely to discover further articles that you can refer to in your own work, and it may be these references that help your work to stand out from other people's work and thereby help you towards your good degree. However, don't skim for interest at the expense of locating the key sources that you need to refer to. Regard skimming as a luxury, to be done after you have done the real work of tracking down the most authoritative and respected sources.

3 *Keeping good records of what you find that's important for your studies.* This can save you a great deal of time. It only takes a few seconds to jot down exactly which journal, which volume, which date, and which pages are the source of a given article. These seconds are insignificant compared to the time searching for the article, finding or ordering the journal, and looking at the article to see if you want to refer to it. Yet many students are careless with the details, and either waste a lot of time finding out all the information once again, or give inaccurate references (which loses marks!). A card index is a good way (and a well-used one by lecturers too) of capturing the essential details of each piece of work that you may decide to refer to.

4 *Using journals quite selectively.* When you refer to other people's work, especially when writing up project work or dissertations, the quality of your coverage of the field is one of the indicators that is used to decide how good your work really is. It is best to show that you have looked at a good range of the available literature, including the work of well-known and respected authors, but not just listing everything that *they* have written. Look out for other work in other journals which may take a different viewpoint, and include references to this too. Also, make sure that your

coverage includes a few unusual but interesting sources. One of the best ways of 'rounding' your coverage is to pay particular attention to articles which review the field well, and chapters in very recent textbooks or edited conference proceedings which do the same.

5   *Using journals iteratively – going back to important things again.* You may not have known what I meant by this one! Let me explain it like this. Suppose you start to research a topic through journal articles and one of the first really relevant-looking pieces that you come across is by Henderson (2007). You may well go on to capture the essential information from it and mentally file the article as 'very important'. After reading another 20 or 30 articles, you may confirm your first thoughts, but alternatively by then you may have found that Henderson is just a minor player in the picture and that Mathias (2004) seems to be your key reference, leading to a range of other sources. You might already have looked at Mathias (2004) just after you discovered Henderson (2007), and dismissed Mathias (2004) as irrelevant. Now, it may be well worth *revisiting* both Henderson (2007) (probably to downgrade your importance rating of the article now that you know a lot more about the topic) and also Mathias (2004) (perhaps to upgrade your importance rating). First impressions are dangerous, and there is always the possibility that 'wrong' first impressions aren't rectified. In short, use journal articles *iteratively*: go back and look at things *again* as your knowledge and understanding develops, and give yourself the opportunity to have second (better) thoughts.

6   *Photocopying selectively.* Being selective saves you money as well as time and energy! It is tempting to want to take away from a library copies of everything that could be remotely relevant to your own work and to postpone the decision about what is really important and what is merely tangential. This is actually a work-avoidance strategy – or at least a work-postponing strategy. Try to force yourself to make your importance rating decisions *before* visiting the photocopier. Some students (and many lecturers and researchers) end up with masses of undigested photocopies, which don't help in the process of sorting out what to quote and what to reject and throw away. Imagine that how good a degree you will be awarded depends solely on the following task: 'Spend three hours in the library, and photocopy only the most important *ten* pages you see in journals relating to the topic you are going to write about'. This is bending the truth only a little!

7   *Capturing the most important information efficiently.* This does not just boil down to photocopying! You haven't captured the information you need from journal articles until you've turned it into something that isn't just a copy. You need to *digest* the most important articles and to work out what you are going to say about them, what you have discovered from them, and what other researchers in the field seem to think of them. This

is where your card index file (or computerized database) comes into its own. Force yourself to make immediate notes about each source. Don't make the notes too long or you may narrow the range of literature that you cover. If you keep such records on computer disk, be particularly careful about backing up your work. Disks can corrupt or get lost. It is dangerously easy to replace a file with something else and to lose a lot of information. Save your database by date every time so that you can easily get to the most recent version before you add to it.

8   *Being among the first to see new issues of key journals.* This is one of the ways in which you can distinguish your work from that of other students and is an indicator that you deserve a good degree. Lecturers who are active researchers often know to the day when to expect a new issue of a journal which frequently has important, relevant work in it. You can do the same. If the most recent references in your bibliography are right up to date, you will impress people assessing your work. If you have discovered important articles that your assessors have not yet seen themselves, you will impress them even more.

9   *Quoting sources correctly.* This earns marks too. Having gone to the trouble of collecting your source information carefully, don't let yourself down by using an inappropriate or incomplete way of listing your sources. The Harvard system is the most commonly used, where in the body of your text your references are along the lines of 'the work of Stephenson (1998b) suggests that . . .', with the full reference in an alphabetical list at the end of your work, and the 'b' letting your reader know that there is a previous reference to the work of the same author from the same year.

10   *Evaluating journal articles well.* This can earn you a great deal of credit and is where your 'capturing the information' pays real dividends. You will be grateful that you didn't just carry home endless photocopies but forced yourself to think about the most important sources, and to make decisions about what they were saying.

Using journals well is extremely relevant to research. Many, perhaps most, students who get really good first degrees go on to study for higher degrees, and for most of these their principal activity becomes research. Think about putting the case the other way round: those undergraduate students who *show* that they have well developed research skills are proving that they deserve good degrees. It can be a steep learning curve, developing your mastery of the literature, but it's a journey well worth making.

Online and computer-based resources

Good habits when using online and computer-based resources include:

- Getting smart quickly.
- Capturing the detail you need in a form in which you can take it away.
- Checking the relevance of each resource to your learning.
- Getting to know when to stop playing and get serious.
- Not getting sidetracked.
- Rationing your time.

Many of the principles that apply to making the best use of textbooks and journals continue to apply to other kinds of learning materials, including electronic ones. In this section, I will just remind you of some of the differences between these and those we have already explored in this chapter, and I will elaborate a little on each of the good habits mentioned above.

Getting smart quickly

This is about learning *how* to get into online and computer-based resources quickly, and also about finding out how to monitor your own usage of them, so that you know when you're learning and when nothing is happening. It is also advisable not to get into electronic materials the slow way – in other words, by trial and error. Try to find someone who has already used them or someone who knows them well, and ask for suggestions about how to make the most of them and where the real gems are hidden.

Capturing the detail you need in a form in which you can take it away

This is particularly important with electronic resources, even more so than with textbooks and journals. With print-based resources, you can photocopy important parts. With electronic resources, you can't usually take the learning experience away from the computer, unless you are able to obtain (legitimately!) copies of the materials and load them onto your own equipment. The actual effect of working through computer-based materials tends to be quite transient, unless you are able to print off the outcomes and follow them up in the same ways that you would process lecture notes and handouts. At the time, when working online you may feel that you've really got the hang of what you're learning, and you may get all the questions and exercises right. A few days later, you may find that you've actually forgotten much of the detail that you learned. The solution is to capture the most important learning points in your own way, such as by making brief summary notes of the things you particularly want to remember, and writing down enough short questions to enable you to quiz yourself on what you have actually retained from your experience of working through the materials.

Checking the relevance of each resource to your learning

This may seem obvious! However, most online or computer-based learning packages are *not* designed specifically for your particular course, at your particular level, or with built-in assumptions about the existing level of your learning and expertise. This means that in most such materials there are going to be many parts which you already know, don't need to know, or don't want to know! Unfortunately, the materials may be so interesting that it is easy to spend a lot of time working with stuff that you don't need. To get a good degree, there are more than enough things you need to focus on and devote your best efforts towards achieving, without using up time doing things that are not relevant. If you find working with an online or computer-based package enjoyable but not relevant, this is fine so long as you classify the time you spend with it as relaxation and pleasure, rather than serious study.

In practice, the best way to establish the relevance of any kind of learning resource material to your own learning is to look carefully at the stated learning outcomes and cross-reference these to those of your syllabus. If the match is good, it may be worth putting the resource material to full-scale use.

Getting to know when to stop playing and get serious

Playing is fine as long as you *know* you are playing. Many online or computer-based packages are intended to be fun; that is how they are designed and marketed in a highly competitive industry. If you really enjoy playing with something and if you know it is *not* central to your learning, you can think about turning it into a reward system for you. For example, allow yourself to play for 5 minutes every time you have clocked up 15 minutes of serious work. This can help to keep you on-task, especially with fairly long and mundane work, such as writing out full essays or long reports. It can also be a welcome relief to play for a while after doing short, sharp bursts of demanding work, such as 15 minutes' worth of adding questions to your question bank, brainstorming an essay plan, or making a summary of one of your last lectures.

Not getting sidetracked

This follows on from the arguments made in the discussion above. It can be helpful if you make a list of the things that you want to find out from a given resource, and check off each item as you encounter it when running through the resource. This helps you to remain in charge of your work, rather than letting the resource seduce you away from your real agenda.

Rationing your time

You will probably need to do this in any case. Online and computer-based resources are usually in demand, if they are useful and enjoyable. You may need to book your time on public terminals or machines in computing rooms. More importantly, you should also ration your time using online and computer-based materials quite logically, according to the proportion that they contribute to your intended learning outcomes on your course.

Email

Good habits when using email include:

- Using it to communicate efficiently and well.
- Checking your inbox regularly where email is used for course communications.
- Using it to gather feedback on your ideas and work.
- Saving important emails so you can see them again when off-line.

Email can be a very useful way of communicating with fellow students on your own course, fellow students everywhere, friends and family, and tutors and lecturers. Some institutions or courses have a strong culture of electronic communication. It saves trees and is regarded as environment-friendly. It is very cheap. You can send messages, around the world, free (or if you have to pay for the connections yourself, for the price of a short local phone call). You can actually send large documents as attachments to the other side of the world in seconds, just as easily as to the next building in your university. You can send people drafts of your reports or essays, and get feedback from them. You can keep in touch with friends in other universities or companies. It's so easy to log on, send, and save messages. It is also a wonderful work-avoidance strategy! I've been known to play with email all day when trying to put off the evil moment of starting to write something that I don't really want to write!

If email is part of your course culture, it is obviously wise to check your messages regularly or you may miss something important, such as details of assignment deadlines or some clues on how to go about a particular piece of coursework. Most lecturers also use intranets or virtual learning environments (networks of computers usually in a single institution and not open to the outside world, unlike the Internet) to put up discussion boards on which to put up lecture notes and other resources. You can usually download these, if you choose to, onto your own memory sticks, CDs, or floppy disks, edit them, personalize them, and turn them into learning resources for your own studies.

With electronic communication, there's even more spam and junk mail than in postal communication. One thing you may need to learn quite quickly is to recognize, ignore, and then *delete* such stuff from your email space, otherwise you will soon use up your allocation of memory, and you will not be able to receive much more important messages when they are sent.

Email can be a good method of communication between busy tutors and busy students. It's sometimes called asynchronous communication, because messages can be sent when the sender has time to do so, and read when the readers have the opportunity to do so. In other words, it is time-unconstrained. Because of this, many tutors welcome email questions from students rather more than they welcome face-to-face verbal questions. The art of getting people to reply to email questions is to keep the questions very short and sharp, and never send more than a single screen of questions. If you send long email messages, most people read the first few lines, then file them to read later (which rarely happens), or just delete them (the most common reaction). So if you have ten questions to ask a tutor, it may be best to ask one or two at a time in separate messages on different days, unless you know that the answers you need are likely to be quite brief.

Many tutors prefer to give feedback on coursework assignments by email rather than in handwriting or in print. In such cases you may receive quite a long electronic message or, more usually, a short email with an attachment such as a Word document. Don't dump *this* kind of long message, and make sure you download and save the attachment! Print it out if you can, so that you can look at it more than once, reflect on it, and act on any suggestions that it contains.

The Internet

Good habits when using the Internet include:

- Having an agenda each time you log onto it.
- Distinguishing between playing and searching.
- Critically evaluating work that you find.
- Tracking and recording your movements.
- Working collaboratively.

The Internet is the most powerful, and the most dangerous, of all the different kinds of learning resources we have discussed. Dangerous? It can turn into a really serious study-avoidance tool! The Internet is, after all, the ultimate learning resource, with the whole world out there, and information and interaction possible on every imaginable subject. When used well, it is a powerful learning tool. The secret of using it well is that you need to be in control of what you are doing with it. This means that you can *choose* to play with it, and browse, explore, follow up interesting leads, and have fun. But it also means that you can *choose* to interrogate the information to find out things that you want to use or refer to in your own work. Getting the balance right between playing and searching in a focused way is the most important thing to keep in mind when using the Internet. Most important, however, is don't put things you've extracted from the Internet directly into your own work – plagiarism detection software will find this out, and plagiarism is a very serious offence in universities. There are essays on most things available on the Internet, some free, and others for sale by credit card. Students can download these and edit them, or use them as they are, passing them off as their own work. Students who do this may be caught, and will then face the rigours of charges of plagiarism. Students who are really good at editing the work beyond recognition may just get away with it, but it's not worth the risk. You can of course *quote* things you've found on the Internet, citing them properly, and including the exact web reference so that anyone reading your work online can go directly to the source to check it.

The Internet is like a vast maze. It is very easy to find something interesting, then to have to retrace your steps for hours to find it again. There are, of course, ways of laying out a trail so that you can find things quickly again. You can store addresses of websites as 'bookmarks' and organize your bookmarks systematically so that you can look up things to which you want to return. It is no use just turning everything into bookmarks, otherwise you will soon have hundreds or thousands of them, and it will be just as hard to find what you want as it would be without them. If you accumulate a large number of bookmarks to relevant Internet sites, you need to classify and organize them in ways which allow you to find them quickly.

One of the most important reservations about information on the Internet is that it is not necessarily authentic, substantiated, or valid! Most of the information that you see in print (textbooks, journals, and so on) has been refereed, which means that it has been subjected to critical review by other experts in the field concerned, and therefore you can normally trust it much more than you can trust information which comes straight from the originator. Some websites tackle this head-on, and have their own forms of refereeing and quality assurance. The most important thing is to *evaluate* the material yourself as best you can.

Despite reservations about the validity of information on the Internet, there are compensations. The information there is usually more *recent* than anything to be found in books or journals. In fast-developing fields this is a very important advantage. It can take at least several months, and sometimes a year or more, to get an academic or research paper through the various processes leading to publication in a journal. The best journals in most fields are in heavy demand and there is much pressure on researchers to achieve publication in reputable journals. Their research funding often depends upon successful publication. The journals often have waiting lists of papers and review articles. When researchers really want to gain credit for a new development, one of the quickest ways to do so, before someone else makes the same step somewhere else, is to get the idea up on the Internet. This means that some of the most important new ideas are to be found there. You may need to do a careful balancing act when making decisions about the comparative value of publications in respected traditional sources and new ideas on the Internet.

A final warning about using stuff from the Internet in your assessed coursework, however. Because it's so easy to 'Google' any topic and find a wealth of web-based information about it very quickly, this is exactly what is being done by lazy students as well as by diligent students like yourself working systematically towards being seen as the ones who are heading for a *good* degree. So what I'm getting at here is don't *just* use the Internet. Use it well by all means, but make *your* work stand out in that you've also tracked down and evaluated some sources that are harder to find than just on the Internet – and that takes us back to high-reputation journals, well-chosen books, and libraries.

Conclusions

Now that you've worked through this chapter, I hope you will have plenty of ideas about how to put your learning environment to work for you, including all the people around you, the various resources, and systems which you can use. We've now explored just about everything that can help you along the way to getting your good degree, ranging from your teaching–learning contexts, making good use of feedback, and putting your environment to work. Shortly we'll go on to making sure that you *show* what you know well, in coursework (Chapter 6) and in exams (Chapter 7), but first in Chapter 5 we'll explore a few things about *you* – for example, lifestyle choices, and a few other things which can make a difference to achieving your aim.

5

Looking after yourself

Getting involved • Becoming a student rep • Managing your paperwork • Some lifestyle choices • Working with computers • Managing your stress levels • Conclusions

In this chapter I would like simply to offer you some tips and wrinkles about a range of factors, some of which will have a bearing on your getting a good degree.

The first section concerns 'getting involved'. Career advisers strongly recommend involvement in extracurricular activities as a means of demonstrating your employability. One way of getting involved is by becoming a student rep at your university and I include suggestions as to how to go about this. If you are not one of these, and have no intention of becoming one, it is not necessary to read these suggestions. However, you should then look for other ways of showing your potential employability.

This is followed by some more general suggestions relating to committees and meetings. You may already be involved in committees of one kind or another, whether they are official university committees or ones relating to other areas of your social or recreational life. You are almost certain to become involved in committees and meetings later in your career anyway, so if you have the chance, develop useful skills relating to these while you're at university. Expertise and experience in such matters can be an invaluable element to include in your CV, or about which to talk to prospective employers at interviews.

Next, I offer some suggestions about managing your paperwork. This is not so much to do with the paperwork that you are using as part of your studying, but about all the *other* kinds of paperwork that you may be deluged with, especially if you are involved in committees.

The next section, on lifestyle choices, touches on a few things that may or may not contribute significantly to your progress towards a good degree. It is only possible in a book of this size to hint at some of the decisions you may need to make about such things as where you should live while studying, whether you should work part-time to finance your studies, and so on. Such issues can, of course, become all-pervading. In the context of getting a good degree, the most sensible advice is to *manage* these issues rather than letting them get out of control to the extent that they are managing you.

The next section is about working with computers and is aimed in particular at those who are relatively new to information technology. Your time at university is very likely to necessarily involve you getting your head round working with the new technologies, but if not, it could be worth your while to make a conscious decision that you're going to do this in any case. Computers and electronic communication, when used well, are tools rather than masters, and can serve you well after you have obtained your degree as well as on your way to it.

The final section is about managing your stress levels. You may not be at all stressed at the moment, but there is always the possibility that you could become so, especially during the more intense phases of working for your good degree. Either way, scan the suggestions that I offer to alert you to some of the ways that you can take control of any stresses you may be faced with.

Getting involved

There are many features which tend to distinguish students who earn good degrees from the majority of their colleagues. One such feature is getting involved in the academic and social life of your university. There are, of course, risks to take into account. Not everyone who gets involved gets a good degree! Indeed, there are always students who *could* have got a good degree if they *hadn't* got involved. It is all too possible for extracurricular work to get in the way of systematic studying. However, being able to manage both well is a hallmark of the sort of student who can win a good degree, and is also useful training and practice for working with other people in employment. If you wish to get involved, there are several decisions you should make, including:

- What sorts of activities do you wish to get involved in?
- Are they academic or social?
- How many such activities will it be sensible to consider?
- How well will you be able to get your balancing act right between studying and these activities?
- Will you be able to let go of these activities whenever you really need to do so – for example when getting ready for important exams?

There are all sorts of activities you could consider. They include:

- Becoming a student rep on university committees, such as programme boards, course committees, or various other groups where student representation is needed.
- Becoming involved in the operation of the students' union, perhaps as an officer of a club or society.
- Getting involved in local clubs and societies outside the university, perhaps as an officer.

Any or all of the above activities look good on your CV and show that you are the sort of person who can work with other people, handle responsibility, and has interests which extend beyond your own studying. Some of these activities help you to get to know better at least some of your lecturers. If they gain favourable impressions of you through these activities it is credit in the bank for you overall, as word tends to get around and if, for example, you ended up on a degree classification borderline, such credit could act in your favour. Much more important, however, is that getting involved in social or group contexts is excellent practice through which you can develop interpersonal and other skills which will serve you well throughout your career and life. And even more important, it can be great fun! Having your own ways of enjoying yourself can in itself help you to make your studies more efficient and focused.

In this section it is not possible to go into all the skills and competences which relate to getting involved effectively and successfully in committees, clubs, or societies. We will explore one particular example in some detail, and you can extend and extrapolate the principles for yourself. The example that we will explore is becoming a student rep.

Becoming a student rep

How are student reps chosen? Most universities have systems of student representation. Student reps may be involved in committees and boards on all sorts of topics, from the university senate or council to the committee which oversees the allocation of car parking permits! From your point of view, probably the most important and relevant roles you can consider are representing your particular course, module, or department, and student reps are often chosen quite haphazardly. It is not unusual for lecturers looking for student reps on university committees simply to ask for volunteers. If you're not there at the time, you've lost this chance. Sometimes students agree to undertake such duties because they don't quite know how to say, 'No thanks, I don't want to do this,' and they feel that they must accept nomination just to please the lecturers concerned. Alternatively, student unions sometimes operate processes of seeking out student reps more systematically, using hustings. Student unions sometimes also provide training opportunities for student reps. If you have such an opportunity, seize it! The training is likely to be good, and *free*. The training is also relevant to your future career, and could get you off to an excellent start when you get involved in activities in your company or organization.

There is also the possibility of gently putting yourself forward as someone who would be interested in being a student rep. If you enquire informally about this, and mention your interest to tutors or lecturers, you are quite likely to find yourself on the path towards participating.

Representing your fellow students

Here are some suggestions which should help you make the most of any opportunity you decide to take regarding being a student rep. Before you commit yourself to taking on the role, think hard about whether you are the right person to represent student views. As I have already mentioned, the duty is thrust upon the first student who shows interest – or who is too polite to refuse! It is best when all the students in a class have some time in which to choose who will represent them, maybe through a ballot or an election.

If you find yourself at your first formal meeting as a student rep, expect to feel somewhat in awe of the committee, at least at first. You may feel uncomfortable in a gathering of so many highly qualified academics, and this may tend to lead you to be an observer rather than a true participant in the processes of meetings. Be ready to be put 'on the spot'. You won't necessarily be able to speak at once on behalf of your classmates. You may be able to give your own personal view (which of course is valuable in its own right), but you may need to find out the opinion of your fellow students before reporting back to a future meeting of the committee or board.

Make the most of any opportunity to contribute to the agenda-forming process. When you are given time to supply suggestions for the agenda of a future meeting, you have the chance to discuss the matter with your fellow students. This not only helps you to be seen to be genuinely interested in representing your fellow students, but also helps your lecturers to see that you are willing and able to research their views and opinions. As part of your work as a student rep be prepared to take the responsibility for researching particular views of your classmates. It is important that this does not become burdensome for you. You can, for example, have more success at helping to get a good response rate to a questionnaire given to the class, especially if you get into the position of being entrusted to make your own preliminary analysis of the findings *before* giving in the completed questionnaires.

As a student rep, you will experience at first hand how formal committees work in your university. Expect to be treated as a full member of the committee. This means, for example, that you should expect to receive 'notice of meetings', agendas, and minutes in the same way as academic and administrative members of the committee. You may have to make sure that your contact address is available to those sending out the papers, or that you check regularly any avenues for internal university mail. You should also feel at liberty to show any of the documentation to fellow students, unless of course it is marked 'confidential'. Make sure that your comments and contributions at meetings are minuted accurately. Even if you make controversial comments, the fact that they *are* being minuted acts as an appropriate restraining process, and helps you to make sure that your comments will be seen as reasonable and fair. Also, this helps you to prove to the students you are representing that you have indeed followed through matters at the committee.

Explore any ways in which you may gain academic credit for your role. For example, being a student rep and keeping a log of your activities could be done as a project module in an independent studies pathway. Many student union branches are looking towards accreditation of the student representative role. Alternatively, consider finding ways of including your work as a student rep in any personal profile or record of achievement which you may be compiling alongside your studies. Don't become overburdened with duties and commitments. Remember that you are also studying, and it could be tragic if your studies suffered significantly as a result of the energies and time you put into representing fellow students.

Be careful about how you give feedback concerning your course or department. This is one of the most important roles of student representation. You may well be expected to report on everything that goes wrong in your experience as a student (including the views of your fellow students, which may be more critical than your own). This can all too easily put you into the position of seeming to be a troublemaker – not the best position to be in with people, some of whom may be your assessors. Try to give as much positive feedback as you can, alongside any critical feedback you need to give. When being critical, try always to have some constructive solutions to offer relating to problems that you are reporting to the committee.

Committees and meetings

In this section, rather than getting you to analyse your own way of contributing to committees, and making the most of your opportunities at meetings, I will offer you a selection of suggestions, from which you will need to choose the ones that are most relevant to your own situation.

Committee work and meetings can take many different forms, ranging from being a student rep on university committees, or a participant or officer at club and society meetings, to a host of other kinds of meetings. Most of the suggestions below are aimed at people who are relatively new to participation in committee work and who may find their first experiences of such work daunting, impenetrable, or confusing. In particular, if you're appointed to offices such as chair or secretary to a committee, some of the following suggestions may help you to get off to a good start and to systematically polish up your committee techniques, saving you time and energy in the process.

Meetings take time, and you've got other important things to do on your way to a good degree. Decide whether you are sure you need to attend a given meeting, and if you don't, tender your apologies in advance and in good time. Life is too busy to attend irrelevant meetings. If you find that you do not participate at a meeting, you probably should not have gone to it. If you find that you tender apologies for more than two or three meetings in succession, you should be thinking again about whether you *really* want to be involved in the committee. It is better to tender your resignation than to be seen as being absent time and time again.

Before meetings

Prepare for meetings systematically. This is especially important if you are new to a group as it helps you to get a feel for what is going on. It also helps you to feel clued-up, even if you have met the group several times before. Take the right paperwork with you to meetings. Find time before the meeting to read the paperwork – or at least to scan it – highlighting points where you may wish to make a contribution and jotting down key words which will help you to remember what you want to say. File your papers appropriately – this helps you to keep on top of the paperwork and enables you to find what you need for the next meeting without stress. A considerable amount of time can be wasted looking for the right papers, especially if the committee or meeting is unkind to trees! If you are intending to make a substantive contribution to a meeting, consider providing documentation in advance of the meeting. Do this for key issues you wish to raise, especially if you feel nervous about speaking your views. What you have to say is likely to be taken more seriously if it is available on paper. It also means that there is less chance of your points being left until 'any other business' when they are more likely to be ignored.

Try to submit any papers you are putting forward well in advance rather than have them tabled at the meeting. If people are presented with extensive reports at the meeting, such as tables of figures, they will not give them as much attention as when they are able to go through them in detail in advance. Also, if quick decisions are needed on the basis of your papers, circulating them in advance helps avoid the decisions being deferred on the request of some participants who may wish to spend more time with the papers. Make supporting papers short, precise, and readable. Try making an A4 summary if the information is detailed or contains support data or statistical information. Use bullet points rather than long sentences or paragraphs, and plenty of headings and subheadings to highlight the points you wish to make. Start each supporting paper with a short description of the issue or problem being addressed.

During meetings

1 *Work out who's who.* Make yourself a seating diagram so that you know who is saying what. This can be particularly useful at relatively formal committees. When names are not displayed on the table already, and if you are new to a committee, it can help you to pick up the threads of the different contexts and positions of contributors. Having people's names helps you to put names to faces in the future, and to connect what you've already heard about people to their behaviour and interests as seen at the meeting.

2 *Get noticed when you want to speak.* If you can't catch the eye of the chair, raise your hand. Normally a good chair is vigilant regarding who may wish to contribute, but no chair is infallible, so you may need to make your gesture visible. In some formal meetings, the convention of 'speaking through the chair' means that it is thought to be bad form to speak unless authorized by the chair to do so. If you are nervous about speaking, jot down your point or question before you speak. This helps to boost your confidence and means that if your nerve fails, you can still simply read out what you have written. Try to speak early in the meeting. If you can find a reason to interject in the first 15 minutes, even though it might be to make a fairly minor point, you will feel more comfortable about speaking later. If you leave it too long you might not feel brave enough to speak at all.

3 *Gauge the formality of the meeting.* Look and listen to those around you to discover whether first names are used, and whether conventions are treated casually or rules strictly imposed. You will be able to tell, from the way that people dress, the arrangement of furniture, and the status of the meeting, what is likely to be expected of you.

4 *Jot down your own notes at the meeting.* The minutes of a meeting may be minimal and focused on decisions rather than discussions and may not cover all the detail that you need to remember. Watch out for hidden agendas. An astute meetings-watcher can often discern all kinds of hidden currents and covert politics which may influence outcomes more significantly than the actual contributions to the meeting. You may need to keep your eyes and ears open, particularly for subtle nuances.

5 *Don't let conflict in meetings rattle you.* Often you will find that people who seem to be quite angry with each other at committee meetings often emerge from the meeting seemingly the best of friends. Remember that behaviour in meetings can often be strategic and theatrical. If you get bored in meetings, use your own techniques to stay awake. Give yourself permission to have 'out' thoughts, such as thinking about something entirely different – even your studies. (You may be well practised at this from your experience of less than brilliant lectures!) Then revert to making your own notes on the serious ideas.

6 *Know when to leave.* If a meeting turns out to be quite irrelevant to you, consider leaving politely. There is little point storming out – simply slip away quietly and with minimum disruption at a natural pause, so long as

the conventions of the meeting don't make this seem hopelessly dis-courteous. Alternatively, consider attending only parts of a meeting. This is especially possible when there is timed business, and you can judge when to arrive and depart from the meeting according to when the items you need to attend for are timed. However, it is a fair assumption to expect most timed business to overrun.

7 *Learn the jargon of meetings.* You will need to be able to distinguish between a vote that is passed '*nem. con.*', that is, without anyone disagreeing, as com-pared to a vote passed unanimously, that is, with everyone voting in favour (with no abstentions). Don't be afraid to ask questions if you don't under-stand something. People on the whole will be quite understanding of those new to the process. It is better to ask than to be left in the dark. At worst, it is better to risk looking silly for a few seconds than to remain in ignorance for a much longer time.

8 *Carefully note any action points that are down to you and act on them.* You can wait to see the minutes to check what exactly your action points are, but make sure that you can be seen to have taken action before the next meet-ing. If you're unsure about what you're expected to do, or don't think it will be feasible, make sure that you speak about it at the time during the meeting or approach the chair as soon as you see what the minutes have listed for you to do.

9 *Taking the chair.* Only accept this position if you are sure that you are going to be able to be present regularly at meetings and are willing to undertake the extra duties associated with the role. As chair you can do a lot to make the committee work effectively and can at the same time gather useful experience for later in your career. When chairing a meeting, ensure that the agenda has timings on it. People need to be able to plan when to start the next thing they will do after your meeting, so a realistic finishing time should be worked out and published. Also, separate agenda items should be timed appropriately, so that all can be discussed adequately and fairly in the time available, and so that it is clear to everyone when the time available for a particular item is about to be used up.

Managing your paperwork

There's quite a lot of paperwork involved simply in enrolling on a course and starting at a university. The paperwork doesn't stop there, however! You will continue to get all sorts of documents, handouts, course or module hand-books, as well as a plethora of information about anything else where your name and address are available to advertisers. Not many students have a large office in which to sort and file paperwork. One day you may have this luxury, but even then, good paperwork habits count! Millions of people keep tons of junk paper, often for many years. Develop your paperwork skills while you're at university and you will have another useful habit to take forward thereafter.

If you're already snowed under with papers, perform a crude sorting task on your existing accumulation of paperwork. Sort it out into three categories: (1) requiring action on your part; (2) worth keeping for the present time; (3) for the bin. Then prioritize your responses to incoming paperwork. Deal quickly with financial and university-related paperwork, and correspondence which you may be in danger of putting off until it becomes too embarrassing to deal with. It is always worth doing one non-urgent paperwork task *first*, then doing those replies or payments that must be done anyway. You will still make time to do the urgent tasks, because you have to do so. There will, however, then be *one less* task that could have become urgent. The strategy of always doing one non-urgent task first helps to ensure that fewer and fewer tasks actually become urgent, and this is a long-term one for being snowed under with paperwork.

Watch some experts at managing paperwork when you can: observe how secretarial and clerical staff tackle paperwork. If you are doing some work which generates a lot of paperwork (maybe as secretary to a committee), you may be surprised at how much you can learn from a skilled administrator. They keep files, not piles! Aim to handle each piece of paper as few times as possible. Try to avoid the situation of repeatedly sifting through piles of papers, looking for the particular documents you need. If you think how long you have spent on occasions looking for a particular piece of paper, you will know that the time needed to keep your papers in order is well spent.

Learn to love your wastepaper bin! How often have you kept something to read later, knowing full well that you will never actually look at it again except to remind yourself that you didn't want to look at it? Work out your own habits. If you know that you are not going to read something, don't keep it. Consider labelling the paperwork you decide to retain with small Post-its. These stand out easily from the papers themselves, and you can write on them short messages to remind you exactly what you are going to do with each of the papers, which prevent you from having to read them all trying to work this out again. You can make your own colour codes with the Post-its, maybe to remind you of the 'urgent' or the 'important' as opposed to the 'routine'. Use plastic wallets to ensure that papers which *need* to be kept together stay together. Paperclips are not so good for this: front sheets can become detached and you may then spend ages working out what the rest of the papers actually are!

Save paper. For non-urgent dissemination to a small group of people, such as members of a student club, try circulating a single copy of a document with a 'pass on to . . .' list, rather than sending everyone a copy – people who want their own copy can spend their own time making one! Make sure that the single copy is destined to end up in a sensible place at the end of its circulation, perhaps back to you, so you know everyone has seen it. Also, consider using alternatives to paper. If you've access to a free phone, this may be quicker and more efficient than written replies. Can you use email? Electronic communication is quicker, less protocol-bound, avoids paper, and saves photocopy costs. Also, don't neglect good old fashioned notice boards.

Some lifestyle choices

In this section of the chapter I would like you to think about some of the choices that you may need to make, alongside studying for your degree. Studying is only one part of your life, even though at the present time it may be the most important thing in your mind. Other important things you may have already made, or need to make, decisions about include:

- where to live: at home, in a hall of residence, in shared accommodation, and so on.
- Diet, drink, and drugs.
- Getting a part-time job to fund your studies and your lifestyle.
- Developing your interpersonal skills.
- Relationships.

Many of these are issues where you will need to make, and live with, your own personal choices. There are no 'right' answers, but I hope that the following discussion will help you towards reaching decisions which will work for you.

Where to live?

You may already have made this decision and be satisfied with it. However, if you are thinking of reconsidering where you live while at university, here are a few thoughts to bear in mind. Each of the possible choices bring with them their own advantages and disadvantages.

Living in a hall of residence

The advantages include:

- Heating, lighting, and many other aspects of living are dealt with for you.
- There may be fast Internet access and direct links to university computing servers.
- You may like to be in the sort of student community that a hall offers you.
- You can make friends fairly easily.
- Catering may be included or may at least be conveniently located.
- Travelling time may be minimal, allowing you to avoid wasting time getting to and from college.

The disadvantages include:

- You may find that having so many students around you is too much of a distraction, and that work-avoidance opportunities increase!
- Halls can be very noisy, and if you need solitude, peace, and quiet to work effectively, your work output could be impeded.
- Accommodation may only be available during term-time, and you may need to make alternative arrangements for any out-of-term times when you wish to be close to the university.

Shared accommodation

Many students choose to live in shared houses or flats. Sometimes, groups of students find ways to *purchase* accommodation and sell it on later, maybe at a profit. Otherwise, most students rent. The advantages of shared accommodation include:

- You will have more choice of whom your immediate neighbours are than in a hall of residence.
- You have more chance of collectively controlling the environment, so that you can all get your heads down to work when you need to.
- You may have a wider choice regarding catering, and whether you self-cater or eat out.
- You will normally have more freedom to have friends stay over and sleep on floors, for example.

The disadvantages include:

- It can be disruptive, traumatic, and expensive if you fall out with your housemates or flatmates and need to move on.
- Travel to and from university may be more expensive and more time consuming than at a hall of residence.
- You are likely to have to take on your share of routine housekeeping and maintenance, and this can take time, and can sometimes cause conflict if everyone is not contributing equally.
- The areas which you can afford to live in might be noisy, scruffy, or even downright dangerous!

Living at home

Many students go to university without leaving home. In many parts of the world, government financial policies seem to encourage students to go to the university nearest their home, with no assistance towards travel or accommodation costs away from home. The advantages of studying at home include:

- You are likely to have better studying facilities, more space, and less worries about the costs of heating, lighting, and so on.
- You may well already have Internet access, and computing and printing equipment of your own.
- You could have the benefits of encouragement and support from family members.
- Your accommodation is not subject to university terms, short-term leases, and so on.

The disadvantages include:

- You may not be able to really get your head down and work hard when you need to because of your family's expectations of talking to you.
- You may feel under pressure, with people continually asking you, 'How's it going?' and enquiring about your marks and grades all the time!
- Travel to and from campus could be time consuming and inconvenient.
- You may not easily be able to enter fully into the social side of student life at your university.

Diet, drink, and drugs

Food for thought

It is, of course, wise to eat sensibly. A balanced diet helps you to be fit and well, and avoids you going down with repeated minor ailments and infections. A healthy body helps you to think well too. That said, the eating habits of the human species vary enormously across the world, and whether you're vegetarian, vegan, or omnivorous, you are likely to be able to get a good degree on it. Students often change their dietary habits considerably after leaving home and going to university. Such changes can be brought about by financial reasons, or through cultural and social influences. You may have to make decisions to balance how your expenditure goes between food and other things. There is the apocryphal evidence of one student who decided to spend his money on an electric guitar and a sack of oats. Oats can be a major component of a possible staple diet, but this student developed scurvy as a result of the lack of vital vitamins in an oat-cuisine diet! Most people eating reasonably balanced diets don't need extra vitamins, but such supplements are perfectly safe, and can be quite necessary if your diet is seriously deficient in anything important. One piece of advice is not to make sudden or major changes to your diet at a time when you are wanting to make sure that your mind and body work together towards getting you your good degree. It isn't the time to go on a strict diet, or to become vegan. Sudden changes tend to bring repercussions. There is all the rest of your life for you to try out completely different dietary habits, should you wish to do so.

Drink

In some cultures, drinking alcohol seems to be part of student life. Alcohol, in all its various forms, remains what scientists call a *toxic* substance. In other words, it is a poison! It is also somewhat addictive, meaning that if you get used to having it you could have difficulty doing without it. For large numbers of people (not least students), it is a poison that they enjoy. Other people regard it as something to be avoided at all costs, and some religions ban its use. There are two types of symptom of alcoholic poisoning: acute and chronic, either of which can be dangerous if too severe.

Intermittent over-usage causes *acute* symptoms: short-term effects, caused fairly immediately by consumption of alcohol. They include getting drunk, thinking you can sing better than you really can, and believing that the story that someone has just told you is tremendously funny, and that you will remember it tomorrow! There is usually a hangover to follow. Such symptoms, if not too serious, usually wear off after a day or two, if there is no further exposure to the toxin.

Chronic symptoms of alcohol poisoning are the effects of regular, longer-term use of the toxin, and include serious liver damage and brain damage. Alcohol is in fact a depressant rather than a stimulant, even though it relaxes inhibitions and gives the feeling of being a stimulant. The medical profession tends to believe that some alcohol is actually better than none at all. It is claimed that a moderate intake of red wine is believed to be beneficial by helping to prevent heart disease (and I cheerfully adopt this claim myself). However, the doctors I know tend to enjoy red wine, so the claim may not be unbiased. If use of alcohol is against your religion or ethics, there are plenty of other ways of looking after your heart, including sensible exercise or sporting activity (which is against *my* religion!).

Probably the most significant tension between alcohol and studying is the time which can be spent happily going about its consumption in social environments, coupled to the further time taken to recover from enjoying its effects. While affected by the short-term symptoms, any life problems and study problems may feel less important (but of course are still there). For some time after being affected by the enjoyable symptoms, the efficiency of both brain and body are impaired. If you've got a lot of work to do, this can mean that backlogs are generated, and the temptation is to steer away from worrying about the backlogs by using some more alcohol, in the company of further backlog-escapers.

Alcoholic poisoning can result in death, which is most often caused by the intake of large quantities of strong drinks (usually spirits). If you are worried about yourself, or one of your friends who is impossible to rouse and has become unconscious or seems to have stopped breathing, call an ambulance immediately. Alcoholic poisoning is serious and should not be ignored. It is, of course, much better avoided, but sometimes 'friends' think it is funny to spike drinks without realizing the potentially fatal consequences. There are also, from time to time, alcohol-related deaths caused by inhaling vomit after high alcohol intake, because the sufferer is too drunk to notice what is happening. If you are worried about a friend, stay with them (make them sleep on your floor if necessary). If you are worried about yourself, seek help.

Alcohol is not inexpensive. If you can afford some, this may not be a problem. The problems come when people become addicted to it and use their resources to purchase alcohol at the expense of a healthy diet.

One way some students balance their wish to enjoy social drinking *and* time for effective studying is to study well into the evening, then head together for the pub or Union getting there (say) half-an-hour before closing time. At least then quantities consumed tend to be moderate, though there seems always to be somewhere else to go to where a celebration of some kind is taking place afterwards, and when pressures of work are strong this can cause problems. Also, late nights are not particularly compatible with full participation in early morning lectures, practicals, or tutorials. Our species does need sleep – we're not computers.

Drugs

There is vigorous argument about the relative effects of mind-altering or mood-altering agents. Some weeds are much more addictive than alcohol – notably nicotine. The health risks of smoking tobacco are well aired! The risk of serious addiction is often the most notable hazard. Also, there is the expense factor. Governments seem to remain blinded to their responsibilities to promote healthy living by the tax revenues they can accrue from users of legal drugs like tobacco.

Many students use illegal substances of one kind or another, which carry varying levels of risk. Much of what has been said about alcohol applies also to the use of drugs and there is also the possibility of criminal charges. It is probably wise to wish to remain in control of your brain as far as you can while working towards a good degree, and to avoid the sorts of complications that can accompany getting dependent on anything from which re-establishing your independence may be a battle.

Getting a part-time job

Many students, perhaps most, need to have at least a part-time job to help them finance their way through working for a degree. Some educationalists argue that you may be *more* likely to get a good degree if you have a part-time job rather than none, though there's a crossover: if your part-time job takes too much of your time and energy, your degree is bound to be put at risk. If you have (or are seeking) a part-time job, it is worth thinking about what *sort* of job might serve you best, and why. It is also worth keeping in mind that when you apply for full-time jobs to commence after getting your degree it is useful to be able to convince prospective employers that you have already been able to hold down a part-time job of one kind or another. This at least tells them that you are able, for example, to get out of bed in the morning! Various kinds of part-time job, along with some factors you might consider, are listed below.

Relevant jobs

These are part-time (or vacation) jobs which are at least partly relevant to your fields of study, and/or to the career pathways you are considering investigating. The advantages of such jobs are that they can help you to deepen your university learning and can show you how some of the things you are studying actually work in the real world. Such jobs may be considerably better paid, even at part-time rates, than the irrelevant jobs mentioned below. Disadvantages include that in such jobs you are probably not having a rest from your studies. Such jobs may in their own way be stressful and tiring.

Irrelevant jobs

Many students get part-time jobs simply to earn them some money to finance their student lifestyles, and choose jobs that are quite unrelated to their studies. Such jobs include working in restaurants, shops, and bars. They may be undemanding and unstressful (though undemanding jobs can have their own kinds of stress, associated with boredom or feeling unfulfilled). The purpose may be simply to earn money, but such jobs tend to be low paid, and to earn *enough* money can take a long time – one effect of this can then be exhaustion.

Irrelevant jobs that you make relevant

One story concerns a student who spent many hours stacking shelves in a large chain store, but was able to use this job as an opportunity to write a case study for his university course on how the store's management systems worked. In some ways, this job brought many of the benefits of a work placement, but without some of the stresses associated with a *real* work placement.

Vacation jobs

These can be relevant or irrelevant, stressful or routine, part-time or full-time. Stress levels are less important as such jobs are normally restricted to parts of the year where you are not intent on doing major work on your studies in any case. The primary object may be to make enough money to see you through the next term or semester. Alternatively, you may wish to use vacation work to build up your portfolio of work experience, and to develop systematically skills and knowledge which you think will be useful in your likely career path. Vacation jobs in particular can be worth listing on your CV, so that prospective employers see evidence that you have done other things besides being a university student.

Developing your interpersonal skills

Interpersonal skills include your ability to work well in teams, leadership skills, and effective communication skills. In several parts of this book I have reminded you that interpersonal skills are highly valued by employers, and that it is useful for you not only to develop them while at university, but to accumulate some *evidence* that you can apply them successfully. Interpersonal skills development may already be part of your curriculum on your degree course, and be tackled through group work, work placements, field trips, or other college-based course activities. Not all degree programmes, however, place emphasis on such skills. If yours doesn't, you may be well advised to take on this responsibility for yourself. Some of the ways you could do this are outlined briefly below.

- Use part-time or vacation work to develop your skills. Such jobs can be very useful ways of practising working with other people, being a member of a team, communicating with people, taking on responsibility and leadership roles, and so on.
- Read about interpersonal skills development. Even if you don't have the opportunity to develop interpersonal skills while studying for your degree, you will still have the opportunity to read all about them! Your university library will have many sources worth consulting. You may be able to look at books and manuals suggesting tasks and activities which are useful in helping to develop these skills. There will be computer-based learning packages which will allow you to test out your present levels of these skills and to diagnose areas for improvement.
- Watch and observe. Interpersonal skills are at play all around us. Simply watching human behaviour is in its own right part of a training in such skills. Watch your fellow students, watch your lecturers, watch the admin and support staff at your university. You can learn all sorts of things that are worth emulating, and worth avoiding, just by being observant as you go about your normal life.

Relationships

There are no 'right' answers here! Students who haven't got satisfying and deep relationships in their lives often think that their progress towards a good degree can only be improved if this yawning chasm in their existence is bridged. Students who have relationships and families filling their lives sometimes think that if only they hadn't got them, their progress towards a good degree would be certain and assured. The nature of deep relationships is that they can seem to constitute the whole of one's world, and this of course is how our species continues to survive and evolve in the world, so it's no use pretending that it is a minor or easily controlled side of life. The only person to reach wise decisions about relationships is yourself. One benefit you may have while at university is the fact that there may be people around you with whom to talk to about relationships should you need help in putting them into perspective. Counselling help is likely to be available if you need it, and your fellow students themselves may be a vital support resource. If you do experience serious problems, such as a long-term partnership break-up, it's worth letting your tutor know so that your situation can be regarded as an extenuating circumstance if your work suffers subsequently.

Working with computers

Be proactively willing to keep up with technology. The rate of development of computer-based technologies continues to accelerate. Gone are the days when books and papers were the only learning resources that you were expected to handle. Most students seem better able to cope with these than many of their lecturers. There is increasing recognition that degree students need to be competent with computers – and indeed most of them already are. There is talk of making such competence a prerequisite for admission onto degree programmes in the future. However capable you are with the information technology equipment available to you at the moment, give yourself time to check up what's coming online, and keep yourself at the forefront of developments. Remember that it's all too easy to *play* rather than learn. Be careful to distinguish between studying with computers and having fun with them, and ration your time for playing.

Look for ways of getting yourself up to speed with computers, word-processing packages, electronic communication, and computer-based learning packages. There are several ways in which you can do this, alongside your degree studies. These include the following possibilities:

- Check out the short courses run by your own university's computer centre or information technology service. Such centres often offer a programme of short courses for anyone from the university, and there may not be any charge for student attendance (but you may need to book your place in good time). Such courses can be ideal for getting going with particular word-processing packages, computer-aided drawing packages and a wide variety of other aspects of electronic communication, such as computer conferencing, using electronic mail lists, and making good use of the Internet.
- If there are no suitable courses for you at your own university it is well worth investigating whether any local colleges offer similar programmes. Many colleges offer open courses in the evenings or even at weekends, and these

can be an excellent way to get some practice in with computers. You may have to pay to attend these, but the fees are not likely to be exorbitant.

- You may be able to take advantage of courses and provision at *other* universities, for example near home during vacations. Most universities offer arrangements of reciprocal user-rights in each other's library. There aren't usually reciprocal *borrowing* rights for obvious reasons, but you may well be able to go into just about any university's library, by arrangement, and make use of the equipment, training programmes, and software available there.
- Some temporary employment agencies provide free training opportunities for anyone registering with them for part-time or full-time work. They often offer diagnostic test programmes, which help you to find out which of the various training programmes may be most relevant to the sorts of employment that you may be intending to pursue, either part-time while working for your degree, or full-time thereafter. Such agencies often have a wide range of expensive computer-based training packages, and you can get the benefit of these free by signing up with such an agency.
- If you are working part-time in any case, make the most of any training provision that may be offered by your employer.
- Major public libraries often have computer equipment and training packages for use by all comers. You may need to book your time slots to use these packages, but they can provide free training opportunities, and there may well be library staff or other users around who can help you if you need assistance.
- If you are already skilled at using the Internet you will be able to track down all sorts of interactive web-based training packages which will help you develop your skills using particular computer-based processes, and broaden your experience of making the Internet work usefully for you. The danger of playing with such packages when you really need to be doing some coursework or some systematic revision remains present!

People who seem to have a natural gift regarding working and playing with computers are sometimes called (and even call themselves) 'nerds' (though I prefer the term 'mouse-trained'!) If you're not such a student, it can be somewhat traumatic making your first acquaintance with electronic technologies; the following suggestions should help you to minimize some of the difficulties.

1 *Don't get blinded by science.* It's easy to get discouraged when someone demonstrates a new piece of equipment to you, and to feel, 'I'll never remember all these things at once!' Don't even expect to learn how to use something from a demonstration of someone else using it – expect only to learn a bit about what it does and how it works: learning is by doing, and making mistakes. The best way to get into using a new machine or a new program is to try using it. It usually doesn't matter too much whether you use it correctly right from the start, so build in some informal practice until you feel ready to take the plunge. Keep your own personal 'idiot's file'. If you

keep forgetting commands and actions, write them down for yourself and keep them handy. This will be more use than having to plough through the instruction book every time.

2 *Don't be afraid to ask.* There's always someone who has already got the hang of a new computer-based package (and if you're that someone you don't need these tips!). Ask such a person to 'talk me through getting the thing to do so-and-so please' and make sure they make *you* do it rather than show you how they would do it. Don't underestimate your fellow students! While some students will need all the help they can get from you to get tuned in to computer-based packages, there will always be some students who seem to have been born with modems instead of ears. Such students can help less experienced users.

3 *Keep backup copies of everything you do.* Disks can corrupt, and computers can erase their memories. If you're preparing anything important on computer, save it to more than one memory stick or disk, regularly. We've all had occasions when two hours of brilliant work got entirely lost due to a power cut or computer failure. It is very boring indeed to do it all again, and it's never quite as brilliant as that lost first attempt! It seems the only way that we learn to save regularly is to lose something important once! Keep your backup disks somewhere else. Think of the situation where a computer was stolen, together with all the backup disks which were in a locked box next to the machine! If you have a computer of your own, keep your backup files somewhere quite different.

4 *Keep your files organized.* Remember to archive or delete unnecessary or out of date files. If you use computers regularly, it's worth thinking about setting yourself a slot every week where you do such housekeeping operations with your information. It helps to know exactly what is on which disk or drive. In particular, find ways of making sure that you don't forget the file names of important documents that you saved to disk. The time you may otherwise waste looking for a particular file among a mass of redundant information justifies such housekeeping. Consider including a footer in your files with the file name. This may seem simple, but it can save hours of searching and trying to remember what you called a particular file, if you can find it in an old printout.

5 *Don't always assume it's your fault when the system crashes.* It's more than likely that it's nothing to do with you, even though you may be in the front line as far as people who are inconvenienced are concerned. Don't be afraid to use the help line. Your university probably already paid for such help when the software or hardware was purchased. Also, the cause may be a common problem with a readily available solution at the end of the phone. Few problems are a global 'first'! If you are not authorized to use such help lines, try to find out who in your institution can do this for you or with you. Remember that you are very unlikely indeed to break a computer, and it is often possible to retrieve something that you have lost (although it may take almost as long to find out how to retrieve it as it took to write it in the first place).

6 *Don't forget your health and safety.* If you are using a computer for several hours a day, it's important that you use equipment that is ergonomically appropriate, with an anti-reflective screen on the monitor. At college, your institution should be looking after this for you, but if you have your own machine as well, you need to make sure that you don't damage your well-being by using it in an uncomfortable way.

Managing your stress levels

In society in general, more people seem to be suffering from stress than ever before. The statistics about days lost from work confirm this. Partly this is because the pace of life seems to increase continuously, but it is also partly because medical research has linked stress to all sorts of other symptoms. Some stresses can be avoided, but others can't and have to be tackled as and when they arise. Being a student has its own stresses. Not least of these is the business of trying to gain a good degree, and all the work that is entailed in the process. On top of such causes of stress are those to do with relationships, family, and friends.

Tips for managing your stress levels

1 *Don't ignore stress.* There are no prizes for struggling to the point of collapse: indeed, this is the last thing you should be doing. As the symptoms of stress become apparent to you, such as sleep disturbances, eating problems, weight gain or loss, headaches, or just finding you are on an increasingly short fuse, try to identify the causes of your stress and do something about it. You may not be able to remove all the causes of stress, but you may be able to reduce some of them. You may also be able to develop your own stress management techniques so that you become better able to cope with stress.

2 *Work out exactly what seems to stress you.* When you've got time to do some gentle analysis, work out what it is exactly about a task, or about a person, that actually seems to cause you stress. Then you may feel that not everything about it or them stresses you, just one or two identified things, and that is easier to cope with. Also try a negative brainstorm – imagine three ways that the stress could be made even worse. Doing this often gives useful clues to how the stress could in fact be reduced by doing the opposite of the stress-increasing actions.

3 *Make lists, to save you cluttering your mind.* For example, at the start of a day make a list of the top things you want to try to achieve that day (not that year!). Often, you'll be surprised how, once you can see all the items, you're better able to get stuck into any one of them, secure that you haven't got to

keep remembering everything on the list any more. Next, prioritize your tasks. Try to sort your work into jobs that are urgent or not and important or not. Do urgent, important things first, and also do some important but non-urgent things. You will have a great glow of achievement about having got some of them out of the way. Review carefully the jobs you think are neither important nor urgent, and ditch them, or save them for when you have nothing better to do!

4 *Take a break!* Often our panics over time management are caused not by how much we have to do, but rather by concern over whether we feel we have sufficient time to do it in. Try to take a real break from time to time, so as to help you get your workload into proportion. A little holiday or a whole weekend without college work occasionally can make you better able to cope with the onslaught on your return.

5 *Employ work avoidance tactics purposefully!* For example, if there's a job that you're a bit stressed about, do something entirely different – something short – first. This gives your mind time to get prepared for the more daunting task. Or, have some fun! Look for ways in which you can de-stress yourself by doing things that make you happy. Spoil yourself. Think about the things that give you pleasure, like reading, listening to your favourite music, going to concerts, or having a day of total sloth. Regard these as part of a programme of active stress management rather than as a guilt-inducing interference with your work. You deserve some time to call your own and you shouldn't regard it as a luxury. Make sure that you have a life outside college. Family and friends still deserve your attention, even if your study schedule is very busy, and we all need to learn to keep a sense of proportion in our lives. Try not to neglect hobbies and interests, even if you sleep through the film.

6 *Anger is allowed – but not for long.* It isn't surprising that people under stress often feel full of rage, which is often not specifically directed. People often become very frustrated when they feel powerless, so it may be worth taking stock of what is, and what is not, within your control. Anger, once generated, can be spread in many directions, and the most harmful of these is inwards. All the same, it is unwise as well as unprofessional to vent your rage on others, especially innocent bystanders who are caught in the crossfire. Find ways to let off steam that are not destructive to yourself and others. Taking some vigorous, healthy exercise helps many people to dissipate stress-related tensions. However, try not to personalize a situation into hatred and blame. It is easy to fall into the trap of seeing all your stress as being caused by an individual or group of people who have it in for you. Of course this *may* be the case but usually high-stress situations are caused by cock-up rather than conspiracy!

7 *Write stress out of your system.* Key it into your computer. Some people find it very helpful to write about the issues that stress them and make them angry. This can take the form of a diary in which you record your feelings and analyse the situation, or letters you would like to send to the people

who are causing you stress (don't *send* them – this causes more stress!), or other forms of escapist or study-related writing to take your mind off the current situation. Be very careful, however, about the ways in which you use your writing. Try to avoid firing off missives in anger that you might regret at a later stage.

8 *Don't lie awake worrying about not being asleep!* Sleep disturbance is one of the most common features of stress and worrying about it makes it worse. Try to ensure that you are warm and comfortable at bedtime, avoid working for at least an hour before you retire, and use music or reading to help get you into a relaxed state. If sleep doesn't come, try to use the rest period to recoup some energy, and try not to go over and over in your mind what is troubling you. Many people fail to recognize that they don't actually *need* as much sleep as they may wish to have. Make the most of catnaps and snoozes when you can and try not to let anxiety about lack of sleep exacerbate the problem. Taking exercise and cutting down on your caffeine intake (some soft drinks contain at least as much as tea or coffee) can also help. If you find that you're still under the weather after trying most of the ideas above, don't be afraid to go to your doctor. The worst excesses of stress can be helped by short-term medication. People are often unwilling to resort to a visit to their GP for matters of stress when they wouldn't hesitate to seek help for a physical ailment. Don't let such feelings get in the way of finding the kind of support you need.

9 *Develop your relaxation capacity.* There are innumerable methods that can be used to help you unwind, including deep breathing, massage, aromatherapy, and meditation. It might be worth your while to explore the techniques that sound most attractive to you, and try to use them to help you cope with stress. Alternatively use exercise as a relaxant: work your stress out in the gym or the swimming pool. It may feel like the last thing on earth you want to do at the end of a stressful day, but lots of people find that physical exercise helps them relax. Take someone's dog for long walks, take up golf, play a mean game of squash, or just do aerobics at home to help your body to become as tired physically as your mind is mentally. Find out what kinds of exercise work best for you and try to use them as a bridge between your studying life and your own time. The time you spend exercising will be a sound investment in helping you keep on top.

10 *Don't do anything big hastily.* If things are really tough for you, try to avoid making important life changes at the same time. It is best to make important decisions with far-reaching consequences when you're feeling totally in control of your stress levels, rather than floundering around making changes without knowing what the consequences will be. Audit your intake of stimulants. For those whose culture allows alcohol, a little can be felt to be a wonderful relaxant, but excessive intakes can be problematic. It's natural to drink a lot of beverages containing caffeine when trying to get through a lot of work, but it can interfere with your metabolism and sleep patterns. Eating rich food too late at night and smoking too much

can also get in the way of being calm. Moderation is boring but a good policy for those under stress.

11 *Accept the right to feel stressed.* Don't pretend it's something that should never happen to you, or that it's a weakness on your part. It is perfectly normal human behaviour to get stressed under various circumstances. Indeed, it can be argued that if we have too little stress we are in danger of sinking into lassitude and boredom. A complete absence of stress is not our goal – it is better to look at ways of coping with *some* stress. Acknowledging that one is feeling stressed is often a useful first step towards countering the causes of the stress. Try to adopt a long-term perspective. If you are feeling stressed today, the chances are that in a year's time (or longer) you could look back and question why on earth you were letting things get you down. A problem is only a problem when you don't know what the solution (or resolution) is going to be.

12 *Counselling can save your life!* Just about all higher education institutions employ counsellors – to help staff as well as students. It helps any of us to talk about our problems. Actually voicing what is stressing you to a fellow student, a friend, or the person you are closest to, can sometimes improve the situation. Bottling it all up through some misplaced sense of fortitude can be dangerous. Sometimes there's no substitute for talking to a trained counsellor, whose expert help can be invaluable in times of great stress. These people understand students and their problems, and won't just tell you to pull yourself together! Don't forget, however, that a problem shared with the *wrong* people can be a problem doubled! Stressed people meeting in groups can reinforce each other's stress by constantly rehearsing their problems. If you find yourself in a group of people suffering from similar causes of stress, encourage the group to agree a moratorium from time to time on chewing over the same old issues.

Conclusions

This chapter has ranged far and wide around many things. At least some of them may have little to do with your own life, but I hope that you have found at least something helpful from this chapter to take forward into building and maintaining your life as a student, and making sure that your lifestyle is compatible with your aim of getting that good degree.

In the remainder of this book, we'll get back to the core business of getting credit for what you know (and more importantly for what you *do*) in assessment contexts. We'll split the exploration into two parts – in the next chapter concentrating on coursework assessment and in the final chapter, on exams.

6

Going for gold in assessed coursework

Essays • Reports • Online assessment • Peer assessment
• Self-assessment • Assessed group work • Practical work • Research
projects • Final year dissertations • Presentations • Assessed seminars •
Vivas (oral examinations) • Work placements • Conclusions

Your good degree is one where the various parts which add up to the overall award have been *judged* to be good. In other words, to get a good degree, your *work* has to be seen to be good. Some of the credit (perhaps most in some courses) is associated with your exam performance, but your coursework performance counts and can get you noticed as a student who is heading for a good degree. In this chapter we will explore a variety of the *assessed* coursework components, or elements, which may contribute to the overall quality and classification of your degree. We will look in turn at:

- Essays.
- Reports.
- Online assessment.
- Peer assessment.
- Self-assessment.
- Assessed group work.
- Practical work.
- Research projects.
- Final year dissertations.
- Presentations.

- Assessed seminars.
- Vivas.
- Work placements.

You may not have all of these on your degree programme. You may have some of these which are on your course, but which are not assessed and don't actually count towards getting a good degree. How much attention you devote to any assessed work should naturally depend to some extent on how much it is likely to contribute towards your overall degree performance. However, assessed coursework of any kind is not usually there just for assessment, but to help enrich and focus your learning. Therefore, even if a particular element of coursework is not assessed and does not seem to count, it may well be important in helping you to develop knowledge, skills, and attributes which pay dividends in other assessed components of your course, not least in final exams. Before we start looking at individual kinds of coursework, pause and reflect on your current view of the relevant importance of each of the types listed above, in the degree programme *you* are studying, and complete the task that follows.

Task: relative importance of types of assessed coursework

Use the table below to map out which types of coursework seem to be important in your own degree programme.

Type of coursework	Very important	Quite important	Not important or not relevant
Essays.			
Reports.			
Online assessment.			
Peer assessment.			
Self-assessment.			
Group work.			
Practical work.			
Research projects.			
Final year dissertations.			
Presentations.			

Type of coursework	Very important	Quite important	Not important or not relevant
Assessed seminars.			
Vivas.			
Work placements.			

Next, think about how familiar (or unfamiliar) you are at present with approaching each of those you ticked as very important or quite important, and complete the following task.

Task: how familiar are you with different kinds of coursework?

Use the table below to map out how familiar (or otherwise) you are with the types that you selected as very or quite important in the previous task.

Type of coursework	I'm familiar with doing this	I have some experience of doing this	I have not yet met this
Preparing essays.			
Writing reports.			
Engaging in online assessment.			
Doing peer assessment.			
Doing self-assessment.			
Doing group work.			
Tackling assessed practical work.			
Doing research projects.			
Writing final year dissertations.			
Giving presentations.			
Delivering assessed seminars.			
Preparing for and giving vivas.			
Undertaking work placements.			

In this chapter we will explore in turn each of these possible components of assessed coursework. There may be further assessed components in your own course, and many of the suggestions made in this chapter should extend to these.

My discussion of 'essays' is the most detailed one, and this is not just because essays are widely used as coursework assessment elements, but because essay writing is also relevant to exams. I have included a lot of detail in the section on 'essays' relating to working up draft materials, saving drafts, and other matters which relate every bit as much to writing reports and dissertations, and other kinds of assessed work. So even if your course doesn't contain assessed essays, it is worth you looking through this section to check up on things that may link to your own study contexts.

Some of these coursework elements are linked to discussions in other parts of the book. For example, work placements are part of the 'work-based learning' teaching–learning situation mentioned in Chapter 2, and work placement supervisors are among your human resources discussed in Chapter 4. In the present chapter we are concentrating on how to gain *credit* from each kind of assessed coursework, cumulatively to lead you towards being awarded a good degree.

Essays

Good habits when preparing and developing essays include:

- Starting work on them well in advance of deadlines.
- Planning the structure as well as researching the content.
- Doing two-thirds of the work before putting pen to paper (or fingers to keyboard) for the final draft.
- Writing fluently, with clear cohesive argument.
- Making sure that the essay starts strongly, and lives up to its promise.
- Coming to a definite, clear conclusion, summing up your response to the original question or title.

In many disciplines, essays play an important part in the overall picture of assessed coursework, so it's worth making sure that you use them to maximize your opportunity to show that you are worthy of a good degree. To be on your course in the first place, and to be consciously working for a good degree, it's unlikely that you are bad at essays! Therefore in this section I don't propose to start from scratch regarding essay writing technique, but will assume that all you need to do is to polish up parts of your existing technique after looking through the suggestions in this section. If essay writing is a major part of your own degree discipline, I suggest that you may find it really useful to look at some of the books that go into a lot of detail about it, for example Creme and

Lea (2003) and others listed in the References and further reading section at the end of this book.

In the discussion that follows I will break down the process of writing a good essay (i.e., one that scores the marks or grades you want) into a series of logical, time-efficient steps. Your personal way of going about putting together an essay may well be somewhat different, but you might like to think about whether there are any parts of my recipe for success that you could adapt or add to your own technique.

Don't forget, however, that in many disciplines, exam questions require you to write essays (but without access to a wide range of reference material, and against the clock). Therefore, many of the skills you can develop in coursework essay writing will also serve you well in such exams.

Look carefully at the title or question

All the marks allocated in examiners' marking schemes tend to be for things that relate directly to the title or question *as set*. Assessors don't like essays that run off on tangents nor, where there is a word limit set, do they like ones that run well over length. Look carefully at the most important words and phrases in the briefing, such as compare, contrast, describe, explain, discuss, evaluate, justify, prove that, evaluate, and so on. Also look at any further descriptors that give you clues about what will be looked for by those assessing your work. Such words include 'critically'. There's a lot of difference between the task of 'discussing' something and '*critically discussing*' it. Underline or highlight all the important words in the question or title, and if necessary look up the meanings of any about which you are not quite clear. Some of these words are likely to have specific meanings in the context of your own subjects or disciplines, and you may be wise to ask a few other people in your field of study how they interpret such words.

Turn the title into lists of short, sharp questions (just a few words will do for each question, as long as you know what you mean by them) as follows:

1 Important questions that your essay should include the answers to, where you already know the answers.
2 Important questions that your essay should include the answers to, where you don't yet know the answers.
3 Further less-important questions of either of the kinds above, which you may use if you have time, energy, or need some extra words.
4 A few questions which are quite different: individual, lateral-thinking kinds of questions, from which you may decide to select one or two, to score those marks that are reserved for essays which cover the question as set *and* give something a little unusual, or special, or distinguished – in other words, plan from the outset of each essay that yours is going to be a worthy indicator of someone who is heading for a *good* degree.

Notice how the 'w' question-words and phrases spawn useful essay building questions. These include:

- Who?
- What?
- How?
- Where?
- When?
- Why?
- So what?

Note also how useful it can be to add 'else' to deepen the questions and extend the agenda – 'why *else*?', 'what *else*?', and so on.

Don't stint yourself on the questions you think up. You don't have to address *all* of them in your essay, but the wider your choice of questions, the more likely it is that you will be able to choose to address the most interesting and important ones.

Make an egg diagram of your questions

Shown in Figure 6.1:

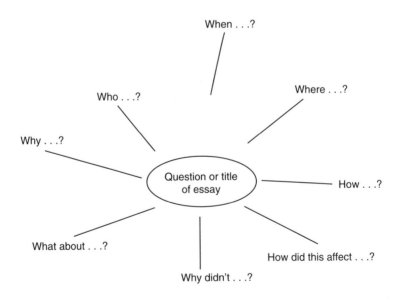

FIGURE 6.1 Laying an egg to hatch some ideas to start planning an essay!

Start researching the answers to some of your questions

One way of doing this is to jot down key words and phrases about the answers that you find out onto an egg diagram such as that shown in Figure 6.1. At this stage you will also think of several additional questions, which it will be worth addressing in your essay. Add these to your diagram (see Figure 6.2), along with key words about the answers that you will give to them. Also, as you research your topic, it is worth keeping a note of each source that you use in tracking down answers to your questions, so that when you come to add references to your final essay, you won't have to go looking for things all over again to find out exactly how to refer to them.

Start planning how you will structure your essay

This too can be done on your egg diagram. Decide which of your original questions (or ones that you added in at the previous stage) would make the best starting point for your essay. Put a '1' beside this element of your diagram. Then look at which is the most logical point to move on to next, and put a '2' beside your key words. Continue navigating a coherent, logical track through the ideas you have collected. Don't go all the way in one direction, however.

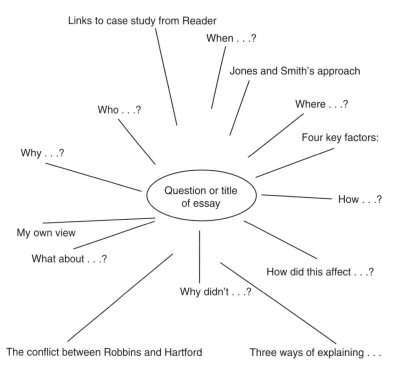

FIGURE 6.2 Hatching some more detail on to the egg diagram!

It can be useful to decide where you really want to *finish* quite early in your planning, and call this 'X' (for exit) on your diagram. You may then work backwards from this, looking at the best way to lead into your conclusions, and call this 'X–1' on your diagram. Then perhaps decide which point or idea leads best into 'X–1' and label this 'X–2' and so on. Your starting and finishing points will soon be heading towards each other.

Then look at what you have in your diagram that may not have been covered in your logical sequence from start to finish. Is each such component really necessary and relevant? If not, delete it or save it for reserve. Sometimes it will link to another area you have already numbered and come between, for example, idea 4 and idea 5, in which case you can call it '4a'.

Sometimes, as you make your links, it will occur to you that you need some additional material to lead from one thing to the next, and you may well at such stages add extra spokes, questions, and keywords to your diagram.

The diagram may by now be looking much more complicated than that shown in Figure 6.3, but it will be becoming a useful map to pin above your desk as you start assembling the bits and pieces which will make up your first draft essay.

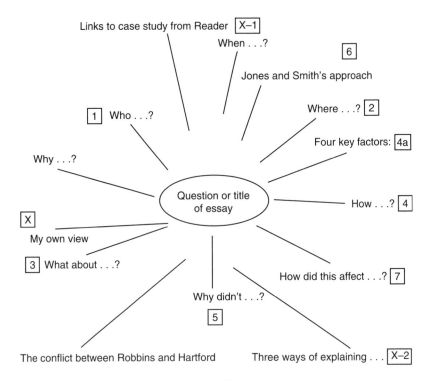

FIGURE 6.3 Sorting the ideas into a feasible or logical order

Start writing draft paragraphs

You can start anywhere on your diagram. However, it is best *not* to start right at the beginning. Your introduction is too important to write straight away! You can only write your introduction *really well* when you know what will be in the body of your essay, *and* what your conclusions are. Then you are in a position to write an introduction to what you actually did, rather than one which is full of hope which may not be delivered.

Pick on one of your numbered ideas, and (if you're putting your draft together in handwriting) on a separate sheet of paper (or piece of card) write down two or three sentences which will be the basis of a paragraph about that idea. The first sentence should provide the gist of what is to come, and successive sentences should elaborate, explain, justify, expand on, or argue with that first sentence, depending on the nature of the paragraph, and how it will fit into your overall essay. A paragraph should consist of one main idea, usually introduced by the most important of its sentences – the first one. A paragraph should not be too long – you don't want your reader, in assessing mode, to lose the will to live before reaching the end of your paragraph. How your assessor feels at the end of each paragraph has at least some link to how many marks that paragraph will earn you.

Continue writing draft paragraphs until you have covered all your main ideas in at least a sketchy form. If a paragraph looks as if it is becoming too long, see whether you may be justified in splitting it into two or three separate paragraphs, and annotate your diagram to show this subdivision and to help you decide which order will be best for the separate parts of the idea involved.

Most assessed coursework nowadays is required to be submitted electronically. Even if you are asked to submit a paper copy of your work, it's increasingly probable that you'll be asked to supply it as an attachment to an email (which is also useful as confirmation of the date you submitted it). Most universities now use plagiarism detection software on electronically submitted coursework. You may indeed receive training as a student on how you can use this software to check your referencing and sources. This software essentially compares *your* work with everything that has been submitted through the software system in the past, including a wide range of electronic journal source materials, and (not least) millions of other people's essays, reports, dissertations, and so on. The software normally can detect where a section has been downloaded from the web and slipped into a student's work. Direct quotation of other people's work is fine, when it is done according to the rules, and sources are fully and correctly cited and referenced.

If you are writing on a word processor you can build up your separate paragraphs all in one file, for example by putting your draft paragraph 'titles' in order and filling in sentences under each title. The 'titles' may not go into your final essay at all, or may become the basis of the first sentence of each paragraph. You can still change the order of your essay, by cutting and pasting when necessary.

Alternatively, you can open up a new file for each paragraph and work on each separately, saving each new version separately (for example as 4.0, 4.1, 4.2, and so on). This helps you keep track of which is the most recent attempt at each paragraph and allows you to continue to have control of the actual order in which you will assemble the pieces of your essay by inserting files.

Save, save, and save again – your work and your sanity!

Everyone who writes electronically has tales to tell of losing material by carelessness, power-cuts, computer crashes, and many other calamitous occurrences. There are few things worse than having to sit and try to recapture the brilliant bit of writing that you've just lost-for-ever by doing the wrong things with the technology – or by the technology simply crashing. One of the most irritating of the ways of losing many minutes (sometimes hours) of hard-crafted writing is when an attachment is opened via a server on the web, and even when saved repeatedly to the same destination, is gone for ever as soon as the computer is logged-off from (or loses contact with) the server. It's ever so important to make sure that work is being saved to somewhere real – a hard disk, a memory stick, a floppy disk, or suchlike. It's even better practice to save everything to more than one destination, and if working online to send successive versions to someone (or yourself) as email attachments, so that you can backtrack to a recent version when things go wrong and the machine goes down or offline. Software will often ask you whether you wish to 'save changes?' If you choose 'no', you risk losing the last episode of your work. If you choose 'yes', you risk losing the *previous* version of your work for ever! It's catch 22. The best thing is always to select 'save as' and choose a new name for each draft – e.g. section 2.1, then 2.2, then 2.3, and it's not unusual to get to 2.34 or more. Every time you do something significant, *especially* when you've just deleted a chunk of your draft, save it as something else. That means if you want to go back and re-include the bit you deleted – your options are still open.

Also beware every time you see the prompt 'replace existing file?', especially when backing up work on memory sticks, hard disks, or floppies. Many is the writer (including myself!) who has accidentally replaced a later version of a file with an earlier draft – irretrievably losing the work which went into the later one. There is nothing more frustrating than sitting for an hour or more desperately trying to recapture the undoubted genius which disappeared into the ether when some work was irretrievably lost. Somehow, however hard one tries, one never feels that one has written it as well as in the version which vanished. And it's such an entire waste of time and energy – demoralizing in the extreme.

All this saving, especially when you're working in parallel on several different sections of your work, can result in problems of 'versioning' – but the software can tell you the date and time when each file was last saved. However, it does no harm to include in the filenames you choose additional information to remind you of the date – this can help when searching days or months later for the particular file you're wanting.

If you follow this advice about saving, by the time your essay is ready to submit you may have tens or hundreds of files relating to draft versions and fragments. These can all be put into one folder, preferably with the same name as the essay title followed by 'drafts', and then saved to a CD or floppy disk or two, then deleted from the working memory of your computer and your memory sticks (having checked that they open correctly from their saved locations).

Write your conclusions carefully

Remember that the last impression you make on your reader is very important, and may have a significant influence on the mark or grade that you are awarded. Make sure that your conclusion is totally relevant to the title or briefing, and try to make it special. Think of what will be regarded as above a run-of-the-mill ending. You will probably want to continue to edit your conclusions but it is worth getting them down in words as soon as you can, and well before writing your final version.

Now draft out your introduction

This, after all, is the first thing that will be seen by whoever is assessing your essay. First impressions are really important. Use whatever ways you can to make your introduction seem particularly good, setting up expectations for a really good essay. If your assessors have been led to expect a brilliant essay, they are more likely to appreciate one when they get it. Most importantly, your essay should live up to the promise shown by your introduction; what better way to guarantee this than to write your introduction when you *know* what your essay is going to deliver, and how it is going to conclude? Don't promise in the introduction anything that you won't be getting round to in the essay. You can still choose to save some surprises for the body of your essay, but even then it is worth flagging at the outset the basis upon which such surprises may rest.

Put together a first draft of the whole essay

This can be as rough and ready as you wish. It is much, much easier to edit a draft than to write from scratch, so it's important to get something down, however tentative, on paper or on screen. This is then something that you can get down to editing and polishing. For example, you could cut and paste your separate pieces of paper into a first draft, allowing you to see how well each section leads into the next. While putting your draft together, expect to wish to alter the beginnings and endings of each section to make them more coherent and better linked. If you're working on a word processor this is the time to print out your first draft so you can sit back and *read* how fluently or otherwise it hangs together. Check that your word count is right, if you've been given a word limit, or a suggested range of length. If you've got far too much, start thinking about which sections are best to shorten or omit altogether. Look at which strands of your overall argument are least important or least interesting.

Put it away for a couple of days – a week if possible

One of the problems with writing an essay (and many other longer forms of written work) is that one gets too close to it, and when you read it you tend to see what you *meant* to write and not always what you actually *wrote*. Reading it afresh after a while can give you a much more realistic picture of how well it flows. You may also then notice gaps, inconsistencies, jumps, and so on, which are relatively easy to amend once you've spotted them.

Get feedback on your drafts

If the only eyes to see your essay are yours and those of your assessors, you're at a distinct disadvantage. The only feedback you will then get will be from your assessor, and that will be too late for your purposes. Make at least one copy of your draft so that you can get feedback from more than one person, making as many copies as you need, but still keeping one without anyone's comments written on it. Almost anyone can give you some useful feedback. Not all feedback will be authoritative, but you don't need *only* authoritative feedback. You also need to find out how your essay reads to people who don't know much more about your subject than you do, and to people who know nothing at all about your subject. Even they can give you useful feedback on how well your ideas are getting across. Feedback from fellow students can be particularly valuable, but of course you have to balance your risks: you don't want to give away all your ideas to someone else who may use them in competition with you. Feedback from students who aren't doing the same essay but who are studying the same subject (or have already studied it) is really valuable. Ask people to scribble all over your copies of your draft. In particular, ask them to jot down any questions that your work brings to their minds. Have you missed out anything important? Have you missed out any necessary explanations or background details? Have you missed considering any source materials that they know about? What do they like most about your draft? What do they find the most irritating aspect of your draft? What grading would *they* award it at this stage? When possible, see if they will also talk you through your work, and capture as much as you can of the matters arising from their comments as they question you about it. Resist at all costs being defensive. If you try to justify what you have done you are likely to stem the flow of feedback from people. It is much better to let everyone have their say, soaking up as much information about what they think of your work as you can. You can make decisions *later* about which feedback is worth taking action on and which you can safely reject or ignore.

Don't forget, however, the dangers of plagiarism (or *perceived* plagiarism). If you build-in sentences and phrases which you gathered through feedback from other people you may not always be certain where these elements actually originated.

Redraft – and redraft

This is, of course, much easier when you are working with a word processor. As I urged you earlier, keep saving, save each new attempt as a separate file, and save it in more than one place: keep backup copies on separate memory sticks, floppy disks as well as on a hard disk if you've got one. Computers break down. Disks corrupt. Keep your copies in different places. Don't join the growing band of students who lose all copies of their work, or whose computer is stolen along with the pile of disks beside it! If you're particularly nervous, print out a version of each important draft, so that if all goes wrong you have at least got the option of typing it in again, or scanning it in. Continue getting feedback, but without being too much of a nuisance to the same people. You will want to use the people who give you the *best* feedback again and again, so be sparing with their time, and show gratitude for their help.

Listen to what you write!

Sounds strange? You'll be surprised at how much you can improve your writing by listening to it. Get people to read out bits of your writing to you. Often, you'll find yourself thinking, 'That's not quite what I meant!', and you've still got the opportunity to change your words so that your meaning comes across loud and clear. Sometimes if your readers struggle as they try to read out one of your longer sentences, your assessor might have faced the same struggle regarding what you were trying to say. If whoever is assessing your work can't work out what you meant, you simply don't get the marks for it! If your readers run out of breath in the middle of one of your sentences, chances are that the sentence is much too long, and your assessor may have lost the will to live before getting to the end of that sentence when marking your work. Although you may *think* that you can 'read things out to yourself' you will still tend to read what you *meant* – not necessarily what you actually *wrote*. Whoever is marking your work only has the latter of these. That's why other people reading your work to you is so useful. When *they* can't tell what you mean, they'll usually ask you – the best possible feedback regarding making what you write clearer and better.

Prepare your final version

Be particularly careful to follow any guidance or briefings about how the work is to be submitted. When work is to be submitted electronically, there are usually rules about page set-up – whether the text is to be single or double-spaced, the size of margins, which font is to be used, the size of the font, and so on. When paper-based submissions are asked for, you may be asked to print your essay out double-spaced, and with a fairly substantial margin so that feedback comments can be written on it by your assessors. Even if you are hand-writing your essay, it is best to leave margins. There may well already be a margin at the left-hand side of your paper. It can be worth adding another small margin at the right-hand side too, not least so that assessors can insert their numerical scores or grade letters as they assess your work. It can be worth leaving a gap of a line or two between each paragraph, to make room for short, immediate feedback comments, even when you may get feedback from tutors as a continuous email, note, or letter, or on an assignment return sheet. Besides, these small amounts of free space are really useful if *you* think of the occasional further important point you wish to add right up until the time of submission.

Hand it in on time and at the right place

It is best to hand your work in slightly early, rather than at the last moment on the submission date. Don't hand it in *too* early, even if it's finished, as you may then have the frustration of thinking too late about some additional important points you could have added. Many universities have a system of giving students some kind of receipt for submitted work. It is important to hand your work in yourself, unless you absolutely can't get to the submission point. There are countless tales of students who entrusted their completed masterpieces to fellow students to hand in for them, but something dreadful stopped this from happening! If your work isn't received on time at the right place, you normally lose all of the marks you could have earned – and this could so easily damage your mission regarding that good degree.

Increasingly, electronic submission is taking over from paper-based hand-in. An advantage is that the computer software normally keeps records of the day, hour, minute, and second the work was submitted, and can be programmed to send you an autoreply confirming that your message has been received. This, however, does not necessarily mean that your attached files have got there in a readable form. Tempting as it is to delay sending your electronic submission till minutes before the closing deadline (just as your lecturers get tempted to do in their electronically sent bids for research funding, or applications for new jobs, and so on), I suggest work around 24 hours ahead of any such deadlines. The university's server could be down, the phone lines could be down, the power at your end could go down, and so on and so on! Deadlines are about when your work is *received* – not when you tried (and failed) to send it.

Essay writing is a key skill

We've gone into quite a lot of detail about the business of essay writing. There is some criticism that essays are over-used in higher education, and that in many subjects graduates are hardly likely to need to write essays in their day-to-day lives. However, being able to communicate well, and fluently, in writing is a key skill that you are likely to need in one way or another throughout your life and career. In particular, it is well worth becoming able to be your own editor, and to *develop* a piece of writing from your first ideas to the final, polished product. In the shorter term, all the skills involved in writing coursework essays also extend to writing essays under exam conditions, and can contribute directly to leading you towards that good degree. In short, it boils down to, 'Don't just write hard, write smart!'.

An aside about deadlines

Coursework (essays or whatever else) normally comes with deadlines. Many lecturers will tell you there's a strong relationship between students' promptness at meeting assessment deadlines and the quality of their work. The first work to be handed in is often the best, and the last the worst. However, students often report that

> 'Assessment deadlines always seem to come at the same time. The assignment we leave till last is always going to be a last-minute piece of work.'

For a start, assessment deadlines should *not* always come at the same time; many institutions have assessment timetables in place to try to avoid this. But if it happens to you, you've got to accommodate it one way or another. One way of doing this is to plan your work so that enough time is given to the work with the last assessment deadline, even if this means that some of the earlier pieces of work don't quite get the time and attention that you would otherwise have given them. This allows your performance in the last of the assessment tasks – the one where you're under most pressure – to be *seen* to be good. In its own way, this is not so much a problem for you, but an opportunity for you to demonstrate that you're the sort of student who can handle several things at the same time, and still manage to give your best when under pressure of time and volume of work. That, in itself, is one of the characteristics of the sort of student who is destined for a *good* degree.

Reports

Good habits when writing reports include:

- Adhering closely to the particular structure required in your discipline.
- Writing a short, well worded abstract or summary, summing up what's in the report.
- Writing for different audiences appropriately.
- Explaining unexpected or unanticipated findings.
- Ending each report in a solid, firm way – not just letting it fizzle out.
- Not having a backlog of reports to write up.

In many disciplines, reports are more important than essays, and in numerous professions you can expect to be required to write reports for a range of purposes, whereas you're unlikely to need to write any essays once you've got your degree (unless of course you continue to postgraduate study, but where it could be argued that preparing academic papers for submission for publication is rather more akin to writing reports than writing essays, but with some overlap). As in the case of essays, it is increasingly probable that reports will be required to be submitted electronically nowadays, and that plagiarism detection software may be used to check that a report is 'all your own work', and that references to the literature are accurately cited.

There is a lot in common between the practices of writing essays well and putting together reports in a skilled and fluent manner. I won't repeat the steps I suggested for writing essays here, other than to say that planning a report can be done in a very similar way to planning an essay, and it is just as useful to have other people's feedback on draft versions of your reports.

With reports, structure tends to be even more important than it is for essays. In most disciplines there are conventions about how a report should be set out. There are also conventions about the tone and style that is acceptable for reports. For example, you may well be expected to present a report in a third-person passive style, such as 'it was found that such-and-such happened' rather than 'I tried adjusting this, and finding out what happened to that'. Some lecturers are much more fussy than others about the tone and style, and it's worth finding out as much as you can about what the lecturers who will be assessing your reports consider to be good style.

An essay has one main intended 'audience': in the context of assessed coursework that is the person who is assessing it. Reports, however, can have different intended audiences. These include:

1 *The person who is assessing the report!* This is in many respects the most important audience when you are writing a report with the goal of getting a really good mark or grade.
2 *A panel or committee who may make a decision on the basis of your report.* For

example, you could be asked to write a report in the form of a proposal for a research project, or the design of a survey or experiment, and so on. In such cases, the tone and style that would be most appropriate would be addressed to several people rather than one assessor, even if the report was to be assessed in the normal way.

3 *An editor.* Some reports are intended for publication, in in-house publications, journals, or magazines relating to the field of study. A report that is designed to be read by a wide or diverse audience is necessarily written in a rather different way from one which will only be read by people who know a lot about the subject already.

4 *A work placement supervisor.* Such a person may expect a report style quite different from those required by university tutors.

Reports are most often used for writing up the findings from practical, studio, field, or laboratory work. Such reports vary considerably in length and structure. You may well be required to write 'full' or 'long-form' reports from time to time, which are complete and self-sufficient accounts of the design of the practical work, including perhaps such elements as:

- A well-chosen, concise title (maybe with subtitle) to give a clear first impression of exactly *what* the report will be about.
- The intended outcomes of the practical work, phrased as aims or objectives.
- A rationale for the design of the practical work.
- Details of the experimental procedure.
- A summary of any related theory.
- Records of observations and measurements made during the practical work.
- Computations or statistical analysis of the findings and interpretation of the meaning of the data.
- Analysis of the error limits of the various measurables, leading to an estimate of the precision of the main findings.
- Comparisons of the findings with existing data from the research literature.
- Conclusions.
- Recommendations for the redesign of the practical work or further research.

The order in which these elements may be required depends a lot on the nature of the practical work, the discipline area involved, and not least on the particular ethos of report writing in your own university department, and the expectations and preferences of those who will be assessing your reports. Different lecturers across the subjects you are studying may have quite different ideas of what makes a 'good' report, and you will need to find out as much as you can about their expectations. Badger them for a full briefing, if they don't provide it of their own accord.

Full reports take a lot of time to prepare. They are also time consuming to assess, so in many universities there is an increasing move towards using full reports somewhat sparingly, and asking students to write 'short form' or structured reports for at least some of the practical work they undertake. Some of the principal elements of a full report will still usually be required, but less emphasis is then placed on the relatively routine elements such as reporting details of experimental procedure or methodology, and briefings usually indicate which combination of the following aspects are required:

- Records of observations and measurements made during the practical work.
- Computations or statistical analysis of the findings and interpretation of the meaning of the data.
- Analysis of the error limits of the various measurables, leading to an estimate of the precision of the main findings.
- Comparisons of the findings with existing data from the research literature.
- Conclusions.
- Recommendations for the redesign of the practical work or further research.

What makes the difference between a really *good* report and an ordinary one?

Part of it is routine: presentation, structure, firm conclusions, and so on. But part of it is that touch of flair or originality, such as one or more of the following:

- Going one step further than expected in comparing the findings with evidence from the literature.
- Including full discussion of the results that *don't* fit with predictions or expectations.
- Providing ideas for redesign of the same piece of work for anyone attempting to repeat it or improve on it.
- Adding useful suggestions about further work that could be done to follow up the findings from the practical work reported.
- *Not* blaming any discrepancies between what was found and what was expected on poor equipment, lack of time, or other variables outside the control of the experimenter.

When should reports be written?

Within a week of completing the work is a useful (and tough) maxim. This of course does not mean that you can't start writing your reports as soon as you start the work on which they are going to be based, especially if personal computers are available in the labs or studios in which you are doing the work. You can draft out almost from the start such elements as:

- The intended outcomes of the practical work, phrased as aims or objectives.
- The rationale for the design of the practical work.
- Details of the experimental procedure.
- A summary of any related theory.

You may well wish to revise and polish these later, in the light of your own findings and analysis. However, it is much quicker to revise and polish something than to write it from scratch. In practice, with most practical, experimental, or investigative work there are times during the observations and measurements when there is nothing better that can be done than such routine writing.

What about measurements, observations and data?

This is another reason for trying to write reports straight away: it is not just awkward if you lose or misplace your data, but it is wasteful of time and energy. It is well worth recording observations as neatly and fully as you can *during* the practical work, rather than jotting things down on scraps of paper, intending to transpose them neatly 'soon'! In fact, scraps of paper are probably the worst possible vehicle for raw data and observations. It is much better to have something more solid, such as a robust hard backed book. Pages don't get lost accidentally from rough books in the way that they escape from ring-binders. It doesn't matter if the data is captured haphazardly and untidily, as long as it is all *there* for later transposition and analysis. A useful habit is to put the date and time against each entry. This can pay dividends in all sorts of ways. For example, if some scientific measurements which depend on environmental conditions happen to be made on a day when the atmospheric pressure is abnormally high or low, the time and date are a means of backtracking to find out whether the conditions could have affected the observations.

Another possibility is to record measurements directly on a computer, or online. When doing this, it goes without saying that it is particularly important to keep saving the data to different locations – for example emailing it to yourself as an attachment, saving it to a memory stick, CD or floppy disk, and so on. All the warnings about how easy it is to accidentally lose electronic data mentioned in the section on 'essays' continue to apply.

Why is a backlog of report writing so terrible?

There are several powerful reasons for *not* having a backlog. These include:

- It is in fact much *quicker* to write up things such as experimental method while you remember exactly what you actually did – or indeed in gaps while you are actually doing it. You can write quickly about what is still in your mind. You can remember details of what you saw much better on the first day or two after seeing things. Most staff who assess reports can tell you tales of students who wrote about things that were mentioned in the methodology briefings for a piece of work, but which no one actually ever did; these are the students who write up the reports using the briefings as a substitute for remembering what actually happened. These reports don't score top marks!
- Backlogs tend to become log-jams; they are cumulative. Once you get

behind with report writing, the danger is that the backlog becomes your reason for *not* writing the present practical work up straight away, and so on.

- Backlogs spill over into time that you can't afford. If you're still catching up with a backlog in your report writing when everyone else has already started systematic revision for imminent exams, for example, you may end up passing the practical work and failing the exams.
- Staff who assess reports are usually impressed by punctuality. The first few reports to be submitted for assessment usually end up as the ones with the best marks. Staff come to expect this, and anticipate that early reports will be good ones, from the students who seem destined to be working towards getting a good degree. Make sure you're noticed in this positive way.

Online assessment

Online assessment is a fast-growing area in many universities. I've already mentioned that it is increasingly likely that essays and reports are required to be submitted online for assessment, either by sending them electronically to a server, or presenting them on floppy disks, CDs, or memory sticks (sometimes along with a printout).

However, online assessment is rarely *just* about submitting traditional assessments electronically. It also increasingly includes:

- Computer-based or web-based multiple choice tests, where you select the 'best' option in each of a series of questions which also include common 'wrong' answers as distractors.
- Online short answer electronic tests, where you key into the system your own responses to a series of short, specific questions.
- Formative online exercises (often including multiple choice formats) where you sit at a computer and make choices, then get on-screen feedback about each and every choice you make, including congratulatory words when you pick the best option first time, and helpful explanations every time you pick a distractor, explaining what is wrong with that particular choice.
- Computer-based simulation programmes where, for example, you can manipulate data to see the effects of changing it (for example you could play with the economics of a country by changing interest rates and spending).
- Participation in intranet-based discussion boards using virtual learning environments (Blackboard and Web-CT are common ones in higher education, though many universities have developed their own systems). Your contributions may well be assessed by tutors as elements which count towards your degree. The quality and frequency of your contributions

may count. Even when the discussion boards are only used formatively, they represent a major opportunity for you to learn by putting onto the board your own thoughts and work, and learning from seeing everyone else's work there too – helping you to check that you are indeed on track to be one of those students whose work will earn the good degree you're aiming for.

Some of this online assessment is formative – in other words, it's primarily to help you deepen your learning and no scores are used formally as part of your overall assessment. At other times, however, online assessment can indeed be summative and contribute to your overall degree, so it's well worth knowing which is which.

Good habits regarding online assessment include:

- Taking full advantage straightaway of each and every opportunity for formative online assessment so that you find out quickly and regularly how your learning is going.
- Developing the speed and accuracy of your skills at working with computers and e-systems through your use of online assessment opportunities, increasing your competence to undertake any summative online assessment.
- *Repeating* formative online assessments, so that you check that you are improving your learning continuously, and finding out which mistakes or wrong choices you are in most danger of repeating.
- Not just leaving your learning behind on the computer. Instead, it is really useful to make notes for your own future use about things that tripped you up, so that it doesn't happen again.
- Practising regularly with all formative online assessment materials available to you, as rehearsal opportunities to prepare you well for any summative online assessments which will contribute towards your overall degree.

Notwithstanding all the ways in which formative and summative online assessment can be used to embrace forms of assessment which are quite different from essays and reports, it is increasingly likely that when you submit these traditional products of your work electronically that you will get feedback on your work sent back to you electronically, for example:

- Emails from a tutor assessing your work, direct to you about the strengths and weaknesses of your work.
- Notes from tutors posted onto a discussion board, showing general trends in the work of your class, and commenting on and responding to frequently occurring mistakes and problems.
- Your own work sent back to you by tutors with discussion comments inserted directly into it (most frequently using the 'track changes' features of word-processing software such as Microsoft Word).

- Tutors using electronic equivalents of 'front sheets' to give you feedback about how your work meets the assessment criteria, or demonstrates your achievement of the learning outcomes, with these being sent back to you in emails or as attachments to emails.

At present, in many universities, the overall view of online assessment is that it is 'something different' or 'something new'. However, as online assessment continues to 'grow up' in the next few years, it is certain that it will be every bit as 'mainstream' as essays, exams, and reports, and will be integrated quite seamlessly into the overall assessment and feedback procedures used in higher education. After all, students today are 'digital natives', (this probably includes you?) and have mostly grown up with online technologies, and indeed are usually well ahead of many of their lecturers (and other university staff) who even when they are enthusiastic about technology are often in fact 'digital immigrants' (including me), having moved to online environments from more traditional things such as paper and slides. Before long, the digital natives will also be university lecturers, and the tide will have turned irreversibly – and online learning will have grown up.

Peer assessment

Peer assessment is increasingly used in higher education in many parts of the world, where students assess each others' work in ways similar to tutor assessment. The growth in the use of peer assessment is partly due to increasing class sizes resulting from policies to widen participation in higher education, resulting in the assessment load being simply too much to be done by tutors. However, it has become increasingly realized that peer assessment is actually very good for students – you have the opportunity to deepen your learning considerably by getting your head inside the assessment culture of your university, so that in tutor-assessed work (including exams) you know much more about what is being looked for. Peer assessment also gives you the chance to learn from others' triumphs and mistakes.

Good habits when doing peer assessment include:

- Being really willing and keen to learn from assessing fellow students' work.
- Getting your head thoroughly round the assessment criteria being applied.
- Looking systematically for your peers' evidence of achievement of the assessment criteria.
- Making objective judgements.
- Being open to the judgements of your peers when they assess you own work.

Peer assessment can seem quite frightening! If fellow students are peer assessing your work, or if you are about to assess their work, you may feel various emotions including one or more of:

- 'What do *they* know about it?'
- 'Are they so good that they can assess *my* work?'
- 'Will they try to put themselves one up by putting my work down?'
- 'Surely it's the lecturers' job to do assessment.'
- 'I don't see how students can assess things as fairly as lecturers would.'
- 'I don't want the responsibility of assessing other students' work!'
- 'I don't want to put myself in the position of maybe losing friends.'

Such emotions are all the more likely if the peer assessment is to count towards something that is part of the overall assessment profile leading to the quality of your degree. However, there are very significant benefits for *you* both in acting as a peer assessor and in having your own work assessed by fellow students.

What's in it for you? The benefits include:

- You find out a lot more about the nature of the assessment criteria which may be used by *lecturers* on your work, both coursework and exam answers.
- You deepen your own understanding of subject matter by making judgements on how well other students have met the peer-assessment criteria.
- You may further deepen your understanding by explaining to fellow students *why* you made particular judgements on their work, while applying the assessment criteria.
- You can get a lot of feedback *from* fellow students about your own work – probably more than would have been possible from busy lecturers.

So how can you yourself *do* peer assessing really well? The most important thing is to resist just making spot judgements, and to base each decision as firmly as you possibly can on three factors:

1 The evidence you are assessing (not what you *think* it is meant to mean, but what you *see* in front of you).
2 The criteria you are using to make the assessment.
3 How you will be able to *explain* your assessment judgements to whoever did the work – in other words, the *feedback* you could offer them about their work.

Usually, these criteria will be either given to you or formulated by the group of students with the help of a tutor to ensure that they are realistic, appropriate, and above all can be applied. It's not enough to just *think* that you know what is meant by the criteria used for peer assessment. For it all to work, everyone involved has to *know* how to interpret and apply the criteria. This means talking about the criteria, and when in doubt asking other people how they would judge particular aspects of the evidence that you may be peer assessing.

Peer assessment is particularly useful in helping you to get your head round the nature of the assessment culture used on your course. Peer assessment is necessarily public and open: if you are over-critical when you peer assess a fellow student's work, you are likely to find out about it. The fellow student may complain to you or may seek arbitration from a tutor. If you are under-critical, you may find a tutor who is moderating the quality of peer assessment breathing down your neck. You've got to get it as objective as you can.

When you've had some practice at peer assessing, and then do similar tasks in formally assessed situations such as tutor-assessed coursework or exams, you will find that you have a much firmer idea about what tutors are looking for in *good* answers. You will also be better informed about the things that can go wrong, such as mistakes or misconceptions you will remember seeing in fellow students' work when you were peer assessing.

Self-assessment

Good habits when doing self-assessment include:

- Using your own *evidence* to estimate the quality of your learning and the products of this learning.
- Devising and applying appropriate assessment criteria to your work.
- Evaluating your own performance accurately.
- Seeking, and being receptive to, feedback on your self-assessment.
- Working out for yourself what you need to do to improve your learning.
- Deciding how best to *show* what you know in future assessments including exams.

Going for gold in self-assessment may seem a strange concept! If you are required to self-assess aspects of your own work, what is to stop you giving yourself 'gold' right from the start? In practice, awarding yourself unreasonably high grades or scores is not a useful ploy. For example, if an assessor checking the validity and reliability of your self-assessment discovers you to be too lenient or accommodating about your own work, you may be in for some downward adjustments.

Nor is it sensible to indulge in excessive humility! If you are unduly critical of your own efforts, you may escape from suspicion of giving yourself scores or grades that are too high, but at the same time you are demonstrating that you're not very good at self-assessment. In a nutshell, the main targets to aim for in self-assessment include:

Questions to get you self-assessing your work	Your self-assessment comments
4 If I had the chance to do this assignment again from scratch, how (if at all) might I decide to go about it differently?	
5 How difficult (or easy) did I find this assignment?	
6 What was the most important thing that I learned about the subject through doing this assignment?	
7 What was the most important thing that I learned about *myself* while doing this assignment?	
8 What do I think are the most important things my assessor will be looking for in this assignment?	

Assessed group work

In Chapter 2 we thought about good group-work habits for *successful* learning, but now we want to think about *assessed* group work. The habits are not dissimilar! Good habits when doing *assessed* group work include:

- Coping well with any problems that emerge in the group.
- Recognizing and accommodating people's different abilities.
- Playing to individual strengths.
- Keeping the team output in mind and avoiding personal nit-picking.
- Using the team as a resource.

It is worth becoming good at group work anyway, not just when it happens to be assessed. Life is a group-work business, unless you like being really quite lonely. Employers rate group-work skills very highly: they want people who can work together and get on with each other, rather than lone stars. As degree qualifications are gradually made more 'readable' by employers, there is increasing recognition that just having a *good* degree classification is not sufficient for employers, but that they also need to be able to tell a lot more about what sort of *people* the successful graduates are. This is a strong reason not only for using more assessed group work on degree programmes, but also for making the results public by including ratings for group work alongside ratings for individual achievement on degree profiles. Even if your degree programme does not yet separate things in such ways, it does you a lot of good to have some tangible evidence of your own that you are successful at group work. You can include such evidence in your own portfolio of your achievements, mention it in your CV, and refer to this evidence or demonstrate it when you are seeking employment.

Coping with problems is an important part of successful group work. There are many benefits when people work together, but, human nature being what it is, problems are inescapable. With independent, private work, there may be no one but yourself to blame when things go wrong, and that makes life simpler! In the case of group work, it is always possible that anything that goes wrong (or doesn't get started) is someone else's fault. Sometimes it may be *your* fault. When anything is someone's fault (or yours), there is a tendency for blame to be apportioned. When people start blaming each other, group work is impeded, and a lot of time and energy can be dissipated uselessly in working out whose fault it all is. When something goes wrong in group work, the best approach is that the *group* has a problem, rather than an individual in the group *is* a problem. Working out group solutions to such problems is a useful process, and is good practice for the rest of your life anyway.

There are many different approaches to problem solving. One common step is to work out exactly what the nature of the problem is, and this is best done in group-work contexts by frank and open discussion by everyone involved. The next step can be to work out several alternative ways of overcoming the problem, looking at who can do what to solve it, and not stopping with the solution that places responsibility regarding solving the problem at the member of the group whose 'fault' it seems to be. It is useful to brainstorm solutions to each identified problem, and then to step back and look at the relative advantages and drawbacks of each possible solution in turn. Another way to find solutions to problems is to do a negative brainstorm, and to work out two or three ways that the problem could be made worse! Then it is possible to look at how some of these ways could be put into reverse, to make the problem better.

Members of a group are by definition different people. Each has different strengths and weaknesses. An effective group takes this on board, plays to the strengths of everyone in the group, and also acts in ways which minimize the effects of the identified weaknesses belonging to each member. When allocating who does what in group work, there are some contradictory processes involved and a balance has to be agreed between factors such as:

- Do you allocate each task according to who is likely to be *best* at it, or in terms of who might gain the most benefit from having a go at it?
- Do you split up the overall workload so that each part of the work is attempted by one person, or do you choose some of the tasks for everyone to have a try at and then bring your efforts together?

One of the main barriers to effective group work is nit-picking. It is easy to fall into this, especially when one member of the group is dissatisfied with the amount of effort that someone else has put into a task, or when different members have conflicting ideas about how to approach a task. Nit-picking tends to stop people from trying to contribute, and it is best to set some ground rules for the conduct of the group to minimize the effects of such behaviours. Ground rules work best when they have been decided on and agreed by the members of a particular group, who then feel ownership of them and are likely to try to stick to them.

Some starting thoughts for ground rules for effective group work are as follows:

- Meetings of the group will be short and frequent, rather than long and occasional (but may continue in a social dimension when members wish this to happen).
- Punctual arrival for the start of each meeting will be expected.
- Apologies for non-attendance will be made in time to cancel any meeting where not enough representation is going to happen.
- Someone (rotating round group members) will keep brief records of the outcome of each group meeting and circulate copies of these to everyone, promptly.
- Each meeting will be for a specific purpose, known in advance.
- Members will not criticize other members' views, unless they can make suggestions about a better way of doing things.
- The primary purpose of the work of the group will be that the group as a whole succeeds as well as is possible.
- An aim of the group will be to share out routine or boring tasks so that no one ends up lumbered with substantial amounts of dull work.
- A running estimate of each member's relative contributions to the group will be kept and work allocations will be adjusted to keep this as balanced as possible.

But, you may be thinking, 'It's all very well to be thinking here about how can I make sure group work actually *works* effectively. But how is group work actually *assessed?*'. There are several possibilities, and one of the things your group needs to do is to find out which will be used, and adjust the group's work accordingly. Possibilities include:

1 The *product* of the group work is assessed by a tutor, not the actual working of the group. The product could be a presentation, or a report, or both, or many other things. In this case, it's important to focus the group on producing a good product.
2 The *processes* of the group work are assessed, by the members of the group, or by a tutor who works out from asking the group about it whether the group worked well. This is harder to achieve, but clearly it becomes more important to make sure that all group members contribute as equally as possible to the work of the group.

3 The learning arising from the work of the group is assessed in another way, such as in an exam question. This is fair in that each individual's learning is assessed, and anyone who didn't pull their weight in the group is unlikely to do as well as productive group members. However, the assessment then is more on how well you can *write* about what you learned in the group, and not necessarily about how good you were at being a good member of the group.

4 A combination of two or more of the possibilities above!

You can see from the list above that it is important, in the context of assessed group work, for the group to find out exactly how the assessment is going to work, and tune in the way the group functions accordingly.

Practical work

In most subjects where practical work counts towards your degree, what is *actually* assessed is usually the documentation which arises from the practical work – reports, for example, and we've already looked at how to go for gold in report writing, and the good habits which indicate such work. That said, in some disciplines, practical work itself is assessed as well. This can be done by various means, including:

- Someone (usually a tutor) *observing* your actual practical work, and making judgements on its quality.
- Products *other than* a report being assessed, for example the purity of a compound being prepared in a chemistry practical exercise, or a computing program which you designed being tested out.
- A practical exam, where you perform practical things in conditions where assessment of the products is possible, and where observations on your practical skills can be recorded as well.
- Oral exams, where you are quizzed about your practical work to see, not least, that you know what you're doing and why you're doing it the way you are.
- You being required to give a presentation on your practical work to reflect what you learned from doing it, and to probe whether you knew what you were doing!

There is wide variation in how practical work is assessed. The first thing you may need to find out is whether or not practical work is actually measured and counted in the overall context of work towards your degree, or whether it is only products (such as reports) which count – or indeed whether practical work is just regarded as 'the icing on the cake' and does not directly count towards getting the good degree you're working towards.

All that said, it remains very valuable for you to be *seen to be good at* any practical work, where such work is part of your course. The people who *see* this are likely to include tutors and examiners who may be assessing your written work and exams. It's about making the right impressions, being seen once again as the sort of student who is going to be worth a *good* degree.

Research projects

Reasons for including research projects in degree programmes include:

- To give students the opportunity to study something in depth.
- To help determine which students are really worthy of a *good* degree.
- To bring teaching and research together.
- To introduce to students research methods and concepts.
- To help students to develop an awareness that there are limits to 'confident knowledge'.
- To give students the opportunity to develop a wide range of personal, transferable skills.
- To allow students to accumulate visible evidence of their research achievements.

You can see from the list above that if project work is included in your degree, it is likely to be regarded as a very important element. In other words, project work may well be an aspect of your degree where you have the opportunity to shine, and be seen to be a candidate who warrants the award of a good degree.

Good habits when doing research projects include:

- Planning well ahead.
- Getting feedback, all the way, from anyone and everyone who can provide it.
- Expecting problems, and using them as learning opportunities.
- Writing up your work effectively – good beginnings, coherent 'middles', solid endings – just as for essays and reports.
- Effective time management – for example not leaving writing up until it is too late.

A research project is normally an extended piece of work, done towards the end of a course. It is usually the most specialized and in-depth element of your entire studies for your degree. A typical definition of a research project is 'a piece of research or other extended study, carried out in the final level of study, involving the acquisition and critical assessment of new information and usually resulting in a printed report' (Luck 1998: 134). A research project may well lead in to a dissertation or extended report, and perhaps also to an assessed presentation. In most degree programmes where a project is involved, the project element has at least to be passed to gain a degree, and excellence in the project is more or less essential if you're aiming for a good degree. Elsewhere in this chapter we have explored some of the ways to make sure that writing up your work is done effectively and efficiently, and how best to give a good presentation about the results of your project. In this section, however, we will look at the business of organizing *doing* your project.

Some hazards of project work

There are several significant dangers associated with project work. For example:

- It tends to take a long time and one danger is that it is easy for you to fall behind schedule.
- It has to be accommodated alongside other demands, not least keeping on top of each subject for which there may be a forthcoming examination.
- It can be a lonely pursuit. There may not be any fellow students working on a project at all similar to your own. When you encounter problems with your project work, you are likely to have to solve them under your own steam.
- It is usually highly individual. There may be relatively few people who are in a good position to give you authoritative feedback on how your project work is progressing.
- It is often the main area of degree study where you are given the opportunity to demonstrate your creativity, self-organization, and determination. Therefore, you can feel under pressure to use project work to prove that you deserve a *good* degree.
- Getting due credit for project work depends on not only *doing* the work well, but on *writing it up* well, and on schedule. It can take much longer than you expect to write it up!

Luck (1998) analysed the skills acquired by students doing research projects at Nottingham University, and presented them in a table under four headings: process skills, presentational skills, management skills, and personal skills (see Table 6.1). The table gives you a broad idea of all the different things that you should try to bring to bear on doing your own project particularly well.

Looking at Table 6.1, you will probably see that many of the skills could be located in other columns from the ones shown, or in more than one column. However, there is little doubt that all the skills in the table are indeed developed through work on various kinds of research project.

TABLE 6.1 Research project skills

Process skills	Presentational skills	Management skills	Personal skills
Problem formulation	Language	Project planning	Independence
Assessing information	Data presentation	Setting objectives	Self-confidence
Sifting evidence	Oral	Project	Self-reliance
Problem solving	communication	management	Self-discipline
Library searching	Report writing	Progress review	Self-enquiry
Use of literature	Word processing	Time management	
Data analysis	Desktop	Working to	
Developing arguments	publishing	deadlines	
Attention to detail		Working with	
Numeracy		others	
Literacy		Person	
Computing skills		management	
Laboratory skills		Coping with stress	
Safety			
Good laboratory			
practice			

Source: Luck 1988

Task: grading the skills

Go back through the table above, and put '**' beside each of the *top five* skills that you reckon your project will depend upon, and '*' beside each of the *next top five*. Next put 'X' beside any skills that are quite irrelevant to the sort of research project that you may be involved with. Then look through the rest of the relevant material in this section (and indeed in the chapter as a whole) and look out particularly for suggestions that will help you improve and develop the skills that you have identified as particularly important – those top five.

It is beyond the scope of this book to try to offer you advice on how you can optimize all the skills listed in Table 6.1. However, to be aiming for a good degree, and to be already at university, you will already have developed many if not most of them. Doing really well in your research project depends on finding out which of these skills may need that extra boost to get you there. The following suggestions for organizing your project work can help you to make best use of it as part of your overall strategy for getting a good degree.

Find out exactly what your project is worth. How much does it count for in the overall assessment scheme leading to your degree? If, for example, a project equates to a third of a year's assessment credit, it is reasonable to suppose that you may be expected to devote about a third of your time during that year to it. If it only counts for a sixth of the credit for the year, you would be ill-advised to spend a third of your time on it, however involved in it you might get!

Think carefully about any choices you are given regarding project work. You may be asked to select from a menu of outline projects, or you may be expected to think up a project of your own. Don't think too long, however, as you need to get started on your project work as soon as you reasonably can. If you have the freedom to choose a supervisor for your project, do some research into who is likely to be the most effective supervisor for you. Various factors are worth considering, including:

- Do you think you will get on well with the person concerned?
- Will he or she be relatively easy to track down for meetings with you?
- Has your intended supervisor supervised projects before, and if so, were the outcomes successful?
- What do people who have already been supervised by the person concerned think of the support that they received?
- Does the person concerned know enough about the particular topic that you are going to work on to give you authoritative guidance?
- Does the person concerned know *too much* about the subject, with the danger that you may be pushed beyond reasonable limits in the context of the time and energy you have available for the project?

How to eat an elephant!

Of all the work which may contribute to your degree, a project tends to be the biggest single element. The best way to eat an elephant, indeed the only way, is one bite at a time! The same goes for projects. Find out the size and shape of the elephant. Work out, and agree with your project supervisor, the outline aims and objectives of your project. The overall aim should be broad enough to allow you some room for manoeuvre: not everything works out exactly as planned in project work – that's why it is called project work! The objectives should be a list of reasonable tasks that you set for yourself. Work out in advance an estimate of the *evidence* you will need to collect as you tackle each objective, so that you will know whether you are going in at the right depth in your work on your project. For each objective, plan a timescale, including when you will *start* work on that particular objective; when you hope to *finish* work on that stage; and at one or more point in between where you will *review* your progress (and with whom) on that objective. Try to schedule your planned work on the successive objectives so that you are not starting or finishing too many things at the same time. Don't spend so much time planning, however, that you don't get started. You can start *something* almost as soon as you know the approximate topic of your project.

Don't be put off by the size of the elephant. Beware of not getting started! Break the work you will do to achieve each of your objectives into manageable tasks, and try to do something relating to your project every day, even if only for a few minutes. Because a project feels big, it is very easy to keep putting off starting it, and to do all sorts of other tasks (however useful they are) as project-avoidance strategies. If you manage to put off starting work on it for too long, it really *will* be a big task.

Monitor how you are digesting the elephant. Get help and feedback all along the way. Some of this you can expect from your supervisor, but beware of becoming a nuisance to them. If your supervisor feels that he or she has done too much work on *your* project, there may be a tendency to deduct some credit from you when it is completed. Get help from anyone else whose feedback could be valuable. For example, library staff may be able to offer useful suggestions about sources you should look at, including ones that you may not have found for yourself. Fellow students may also be able to help, by giving you feedback on your plans and efforts in return for you doing the same to help them. When anyone gives you feedback about something you have done, listen to what they have to say. Don't defend your position or they will stop saying as much. Make your own mind up about the value of each element of feedback you receive in due course, but thank everyone who offers help, even when your considered decision is not to use it.

Put together a very early first draft. It's never too soon to build a skeleton around which you will gradually flesh out all the important detail. With an extended piece of writing, your fourteenth draft will be a lot better than your second draft. You will never get to the fourteenth draft unless you have completed a first draft really early in your timescale. Drafting and polishing is far easier and more efficient using a word processor than by hand. Much of that vital difference that will make for a *good* project report, dissertation, or presentation comes from the time you spend polishing rather than creating.

Anticipate problems. Project work is an ideal training ground for research. Research *is* research because you are venturing into the unknown. Research sometimes involves spending three weeks finding out *how* to do something which will only take an hour or two to actually complete. In project work, don't expect everything to turn out the way you would expect it to straight away. Regard each problem as a learning opportunity. A problem, by definition, is something that there isn't an easy or ready answer to. That often means that it's something where the answer will be valuable, once you find it. Don't, however, keep on and on tackling the difficulties, and end up spending so much time fighting the problems that you haven't left yourself time to do the straightforward parts. When working with something difficult, it pays to keep at it, but also to do a little bit of the easier work before each attempt at the tricky bit you're having problems with. That way, you make steady progress with the straightforward parts alongside your attempts at the hard parts, and even if some of the hard parts don't work out, you're still making steady progress.

Don't throw anything away. Sometimes, with research-type work, it is not possible to distinguish what is valuable from what is rubbish, at least at first. When you think something that you have tried has not worked out, hang onto your data and observations. You may later discover something that makes sense of them.

Beyond your good degree

As we've seen, project work is very like research. When you get your good degree, you may well want to go on to postgraduate study and research for Masters-level qualifications or a Doctorate. The skills you develop in your undergraduate project work will serve you well then. But more important, the skills you *demonstrate* in your undergraduate project work are likely to be noticed by significant people around you, including tutors who may want to have you as one of their postgraduate students. Investing wisely in your current project work may indeed be paving your way to your *next* degree too.

Final year dissertations

Good habits when writing final year dissertations include:

- Managing your time effectively.
- Reviewing the field well, and early.
- Getting really good at citing others' work correctly.
- Being really particular to get your references exactly right in your bibliography!
- Seeking, getting, and *using* a great deal of feedback on your drafts, all the way to your final draft.
- Knowing when to stop working on the dissertation.
- Valuing originality.

If you are expected to complete a dissertation in your final year, it is likely that it will contribute substantially towards the assessment profile of your degree. Excelling in your dissertation may have a strong bearing on ending up with a good degree. A dissertation may be the way you are required to put together the results of a project, and most of the suggestions about success-fully tackling project work also apply to working towards a dissertation. In some ways, a dissertation is rather like an extended essay or a very full report, so many of the suggestions about essays and reports in this chapter are also relevant, particularly the importance of the dissertation starting well, then living up to the expectations set by the opening, and having strong conclusions.

What's different about a dissertation? For a start, it's likely to be much longer than the usual assessed essays or reports you will have written on your course. A dissertation is likely to be expected to run from anything between 5000 to 60,000 words. That's a big range, making it all the more important to find out as much as you can about the required size before you start work on it. It therefore takes all the more planning, and is not something that you can do quickly the week before the submission deadline is due. A dissertation could also be your passport to a good postgraduate opportunity. Working for higher degrees such as Masters or PhDs usually involves putting together a thesis of some kind, which is just a bigger and better dissertation. Your dissertation may be the most relevant piece of evidence you can furnish to persuade your potential higher-degree supervisors that you've got a lot going for you as a research prospect. So there are at least two good reasons for making sure that you go for gold in your dissertation.

You will need to manage your time well. This means balancing the time you spend on your dissertation with any other study-related activities which you will be doing at the same time. You may also be preparing for exams, and have other coursework which counts towards your degree to prepare and submit. As with projects, the danger of not getting started is an obvious one. It's very, very easy to put off starting work on something so big as a dissertation. This hazard causes many *not* to get a good degree – or not to get a degree *at all!*

Think of what you may say to yourself:

- 'This is *really* important, so I'll get all these other things I have to do clean out of the way and then I'll make a concerted effort at getting this dissertation really cracked.'
- 'I'll need to spend at least a month planning my dissertation before I can do anything really useful towards putting it together.'
- 'I just don't know how to put together a dissertation and I'm scared of starting. Maybe I don't really want that good degree!'
- 'I'm not ready to start work on my dissertation – I've not finished the reading I need to do.'

All of the above are in fact ADWATs – Advanced Dissertation Writing Avoidance Tactics! All of them are bad starting points, particularly the last one! You will *never* finish your reading – there is always more that could be read. If you wait for 'finishing your reading', you will *never* start your writing. The fact that a dissertation is indeed important does *not* mean that you can't start useful work on it until you've cleared away all the other things on your agenda. While it's wise to put a lot of effort into planning a dissertation, this effort does not need to be done solidly before starting *real* work towards it. In fact, the planning should be an ongoing feature, not just a start-up one. Being scared of starting is healthy enough, but like most big jobs, putting together your dissertation is a lot less scary once you've started.

An essential element of any dissertation is your review of what has already been published on the field of your work. It is never too early to start work on this review. In fact, the quality of this review is at least as important as the overall quality of your dissertation. Researchers need to be able to demonstrate their competence at reviewing the available literature on a topic. Your dissertation review may be useful evidence to prove that you will make a good researcher.

To write an excellent review you will need:

1 The most *authoritative* sources. Reading around will help you to find out which authors' work is referred to most commonly by other leading authors in the field.
2 The most *up to date* references. Once you have found out who the leading authors in the field are, you're in a good position to use searches to track down whether they have recently written something new, which is not yet on the shelves of your library.
3 *Accurate* references. This means the right volume number for journal issues, the right page numbers for things you may quote from authors' work, the right year of publication, and the correct way to refer to the journal or book publisher.
4 *Confidence* that you have not missed anything important that may be known to your assessors. If you know who will be assessing your dissertation (especially the names of any external assessors who may be involved), it is worth checking whether they themselves have written anything relating to the field that you are reviewing. External assessors are normally rather pleased to see their work mentioned, and can be quite cross if it's not! You don't have to agree with their point of view, however, as long as you argue your case well.

It's worth building up your database of references right from day one. As soon as you know what your dissertation will be about, start systematically combing the literature for relevant sources. Use all the help you may be able to get from people like library staff, who may have more knowledge than you thought about who's who in the field you're going to be working in. Use your tutors wisely. Don't get labelled as someone who can't find things for yourself, but, for example, mention something you've found and listen for their reactions to it.

Build your database in a robust way. For example, use index cards to gather your data about the most relevant sources, along with notes of things you may wish to quote or refer to in detail. Alternatively, use a computerized package to build up your bibliographic database. If you do this, however, take careful precautions against losing your database. Always save copies on separate CDs or floppy disks in different places.

As soon as you can, start putting together the skeleton of your review section. You don't have to wait until you've interpreted your own ideas, data, or findings. It is never too early to start mapping the territory. The review section of your dissertation is the part that will have the most drafts. It will probably be the last thing you will adjust, not long before the submission date, as you make sure that it includes references to the absolute latest, important, or interesting things to have emerged in the literature.

Writing a review is a demanding task, and it can be quite a boring one! It may be much more interesting to write about *your* findings, *your* ideas, *your* interpretations, and *your* conclusions. Indeed, all of these are necessary in your dissertation, but as they are more interesting to do, there is less danger that they won't get done. This is yet another reason why writing your review section should be done a little at a time but very regularly, and right from the beginning of your work on the dissertation.

A dissertation is never *finished*, it is just abandoned at the least damaging point!

Know when to stop. A dissertation is finite. Marks are not awarded according to the weight in kilograms. Marks are awarded for quality rather than quantity (provided of course that the quantity is reasonable). A dissertation is rather like a non-fiction book – it is never actually finished. There will always be more things you could add to it. There will always be further polish and refinement you could bring to it. There will always be some things that are wrong in it! There will still be some typos or grammatical glitches in it. Spending too long on all the minor details invokes the law of diminishing returns. You may only get a fraction of a mark more for that last two weeks' worth of editorial overhaul. You've probably got much more important things to do in those two weeks – things that will bring in other valuable contributions towards your getting that good degree. So stop, and hand it in. Don't look back. Once it's handed in, it's out of your hands. Don't then worry about it: it's not worth it! This seems obvious, but so many students continue to worry about things that are out of their hands.

Presentations

Good habits when giving presentations include:

- Preparing.
- Practising, seeking feedback.
- Polishing, building on feedback.
- Prioritizing: selecting the most relevant and valuable information to include in your presentation.
- Performing: showing how well you can communicate your ideas.

Giving a presentation can be quite a daunting task, especially if you've not done one before. It's all the more daunting if you know that it is going to be assessed and will count towards the quality of your degree. However, it is useful practise for more than just your degree. Skills at giving presentations are quite hard won, yet very useful. The same skills help you to give better interviews. They may help you show yourself at your best in a forthcoming viva (oral exam), which might be important in the final decision about what class of degree you achieve. If you move towards an academic career, some practice at giving presentations paves the way towards being able to give lectures. If you are heading towards research, your reputation is likely to be enhanced considerably if you can give polished presentations about your work at conferences and meetings.

A group presentation may feel more comfortable than a solo one. For a start, you have less time under the spotlight. You also have the chance to learn a lot from watching your fellow students' strengths and weaknesses. You can pick things to try to emulate yourself, and you can also observe things which you decide to avoid at all costs in your own parts of the presentation! That said, even for your bit of a group presentation, for the minutes you're up front, it's all up to you, even if there are able colleagues waiting in the wings to step in if you really get into difficulties. The following discussion should help you to plan, practise, polish, and perfect your presentation technique, so that you perform well on the day.

Find out what it's worth. I've said this a number of times in this chapter, but it continues to be a factor worth considering. There's not much point spending half of your time working up a brilliant presentation if it only counts for a few marks in the overall assessment scheme of your degree, and if there are other important things you need to be doing with that time. That said, a presentation is a very public affair. If you do it really well, word gets around that you are a really worthy candidate, and this may bring its own dividends, and could be part of the icing on the cake towards getting your good degree. The 'halo effect' comes in when, if you're known to be a good candidate through one particular example of your work, tutors and assessors may *expect* other things that you do to be equally distinguished, and may be more ready to award good grades for these too. Furthermore, the time you spend developing your technique is not wasted, as your presentation skills are likely to continue to serve you well after you graduate. So though it's not wise to spend *too* much time preparing your presentation, it's worth spending a bit more time than may at first seem logical.

Find out as much as you can about the assessment criteria. These are often quite public, and may have been negotiated with the group of students preparing to give presentations. When you know what is being looked for in a *good* presentation, you're in a strong position to set out all along to give a good one. If, however, there isn't any information about the criteria, you will need to think about what sorts of criteria those who assess your presentation are likely to use, whether consciously or subconsciously. A few such criteria are suggested below: make your own mind up about which of them may be relevant to the sort of presentation that *you* will be giving, and add more criteria along the same lines as and when they occur to you. The criteria given here are not intended to be in any particular order, nor of equal importance:

- Promising, interesting start.
- Aims of presentation clearly stated near the beginning.
- Confident, authoritative manner.
- Good eye contact with audience, adding to credibility.
- Evidence of thorough research.
- Knows what he or she is talking about.
- No embarrassing silences or pauses.
- Clearly audible.
- Visual aids useful, appropriate, and well-handled.
- Handout material (if used) helpful and professional-looking.
- Clear, cogent summary.
- Recap of the aims.
- Questions handled confidently and well.
- Not flustered by difficult questions.
- Time-keeping good.

Preparing your presentation

It's much, much easier to give a presentation on something you know quite a lot about than on something which you're struggling to get your head round. This does not mean that you have to know everything there is to know about the subject, but it does mean that you need to know a lot about what you are going to *say* about the subject. It's obviously useful to start your preparation early, so that you have more time to become really familiar with the material you will use in your presentation.

Think about whether or not you are going to read your presentation from a script. To distinguish yourself as a high-flier, you may be well advised to only have a script as an intermediate stage in your preparation, and to practise sufficiently that you can deliver your presentation without it. You can, of course, still use other cues. Indeed, even experienced presenters like to have something to fall back on for those moments when what they intended to say next disappears entirely from their heads. Some people write main headings or questions down as an agenda. It can be useful to have these in quite big bold writing or large print, so that you can see them as and when you may need them without having to peer down at your notes. Some presenters put such main points on small cards and gradually work through the cards during their presentation. Think about how you will support your presentation. It can reduce your anxiety levels a lot if you have ways of taking the gaze of your audience away from you and towards a screen or handouts.

Make it visually attractive and professional

Prepare your visual aids carefully. Most people use PowerPoint slides to accompany their presentations nowadays. I've adapted the suggestions below on using PowerPoint from advice I prepared for new lecturers at Leeds Metropolitan University (Race 2006b).

Prepare paper copies of all of your slides, say two per page, and lay these out in front of you if possible at the start of your presentation. Write clearly the numbers of the slides on your paper copies. When giving your presentation, you can go to any slide at any time, and in any order, simply by keying in '5' then 'enter' to go to slide 5, '23' for slide 23, and so on. This is particularly useful when someone asks a question and you may want to go back to an earlier slide, or for when time is running out and you want to skip ahead to a later slide, and so on. It gives you full control of which slides you show when, without having to clumsily run backwards or forwards though slides you're not actually going to use on that occasion.

Ten tips for good slides:

1 Don't put too much on any slide. A few questions, headlines, or bullet points are better than solid paragraphs. Detailed information is best left to handout materials.

2 Use large fonts, to ensure that everything can be read from the back of the room. Check this out – or get a colleague to run quickly through your slides with you sitting at the back yourself.

3 Check which colours work well. Some text colours (notably orange and red) don't come across clearly at the back of the room. The software allows you to have dark text against light backgrounds and vice versa. However, light text against dark backgrounds works rather badly if you can't dim the lighting in the lecture room (for example if there are windows without good blinds).

4 Try to fill only the top half or two-thirds of any slide. Members of your audience may have to peer around each other's heads to see anything right at the bottom of a slide – you can tell by when they move their heads as you reveal a 'last bullet point' on a slide.

5 Use pictures, cartoons, and graphs when they help to bring your subject to life.

6 Don't include detailed graphs, tables, or flowcharts if the detail would not be clearly visible at the back of the room. Such detail is better in handout materials than on-screen in the presentation room.

7 Don't include 'slide numbers' on slides (the software allows automatic numbering if that's what you wanted). Not including slide numbers gives you the freedom to pick-and-mix your slides, without your audience realizing that you're skipping some of them!

8 Don't cause 'death by bullet point'. It gets tedious for the audience if successive bullet points always come one at a time in exactly the same predictable way.

9 Learn from other people's use of slides. Whenever possible sit in on others' lectures and presentations, and also conference presentations, and see what works well for others – and what doesn't.

10 Remember to switch the slides right off – and know how to get them back easily. There are few things worse than a slide staying up on screen too long after it has been used – for example when you've moved on to talk about something else or are answering a question from your audience – it then just becomes a distraction. An easy way of switching your slides off when using PowerPoint is to press 'B' on the keyboard – 'B' for black. When you want your slide back, all you need to do is press 'B' again – 'B' for back. This is far safer than risking switching off the data projector with its remote control – some machines take minutes to warm up again if switched off.

One problem with going for technology to support your presentation is that you can't be sure it will all work on the day. You will need to make sure that you can get to the room you are going to present in at least half an hour before your presentation, to get the equipment working, adjust the lighting, draw the blinds if necessary, and so on. If the room is heavily timetabled, this might not be possible, and there's little worse for anxiety levels than having to try and set up in just a minute or two while your audience waits and watches you!

Practice makes perfect

Once your preparation is well advanced, you need to be moving into the 'practice' stage. If you haven't given many presentations before, or if you are rather nervous, do as much practising as you possibly can. Initially, it's a good idea to practise on your own. Time yourself. There is usually a fixed time allocation for a presentation, such as 20 minutes plus 10 minutes for questions. Remember, too, that what takes you 20 minutes in the relaxed comfort of privacy may take all of 10 minutes when you're keyed up with a real audience! Include in your presentation some optional extras, which you can slip in if you find yourself running ahead of schedule, and practise these extras too. Also, work out some parts of your presentation that you can smoothly and unnoticeably miss out, should you find yourself short of time (such as because of a late start, or because half of your audience walked in after you had started and you had to repeat the aims of your presentation once more). As you continue practising, gradually reduce your dependency on your notes or prompts. Continue, however, to have them available.

Feedback helps

Next, start practising with the chance to get some feedback. Give part or all of your presentation to anyone you can muster! Fellow students may be willing to participate. When a group of students all are preparing for presentations, it is extremely useful to everyone concerned to help each other by being an audience and giving feedback. Everyone's standard improves as they see things that others do well, and also things to avoid. If you're brave, you might take up any chance to give a run through of your presentation with someone pointing a video camera at you. You can learn a great deal about your style from watching the recording, but don't be too put off by it. You are almost certain to be your own worst critic as you watch yourself presenting. You will notice your own mannerisms and hesitations much more acutely than will other people. Use all of the feedback you can get about your performance to add further polish to your presentation.

Get used to responding well to questions

It is really worth practising handling questions. In many ways, this is the most important part of your presentation. For example, if you give a brilliant presentation, and then get flustered when answering questions, people's principal memories will be of your getting flustered and they will forget how good your presentation was. In assessed presentations, the marks or grades you will achieve depend quite a lot on overall impression, and you need to make your last impression a good one. You also need to make your first impression serve you well, so practising and polishing beginnings and endings is even more important the practising middles.

How can you develop skills at handling questions? The best way is obvious: by answering lots of people's questions in your practice sessions. There are, however, some further tactics that can help you when you're faced with a tough question. For a start, if you really don't know the answer, it's best not to try to pretend that you do. You may wish to pass such a question back to the questioner or the audience as a whole and ask if they would like to contribute some views on the answers to the question. Another useful tactic is to repeat people's questions before trying to answer them. This is useful on three counts. First, not everyone might have heard the question, so repeating it helps them. Second, repeating a question back to the questioner often helps to clarify exactly what the question was intended to mean – the questioner may chip in with some further detail of what the question was *really* getting at. Third, it gives you at least a few seconds to start thinking about how you are going to answer the question. It's surprising how fast our brains can work in such circumstances.

Assessed seminars

Good habits when delivering assessed seminars include:

- Showing that you've done your preparation.
- Maximizing the participation of others.

- Coming prepared to contribute, even when you're not leading the seminar.
- Asking relevant questions at other students' seminars.
- Offering divergent viewpoints.
- Arguing the case well.

Your degree programme may or may not involve assessed seminars. If it does, the assessment may be wholly associated with presentations that students make to seminar groups. Giving assessed presentations is covered in the previous section. However, there are other possibilities regarding the assessment of seminar work. One possibility is that it isn't assessed at all. This simplifies matters, but you should not take it to mean that seminars aren't important: tutors can't help but notice *which* students contribute actively and well to seminars, and this may well influence the marks or grades they award for other areas of your work. A further possibility is that some credit is allocated to each student for seminar work, usually on the basis of attendance, participation, and contribution. The suggestions below are intended to help you put such seminars to best use as a step towards gaining the credit that leads to your good degree.

The first, if obvious, step is to be there at seminars. If everyone decides not to attend, there won't be any participation, and the seminar programme won't be serving any real purpose. Once there, how do you convince tutors that your contribution is worth the award of good marks? *Not* by being so voluble and irrepressible that no other students have the chance to contribute. You may regard it as the job of the tutor or seminar leader to maximize the involvement of the students present, but each participant can help towards this. If *you* give the impression of being 'good value' at each seminar, and help to get a relevant, lively debate going every now and then, you are more likely to earn good grades.

Being there is not enough in its own right. You need to attend each seminar having done at least some preparation for it. Even if someone else is leading the seminar, find out what it's about, and do a little research or reading of your own before turning up for it. Tutors can see all too easily who *hasn't* done any preparation. Even without saying anything, students who don't know anything about the topic of the seminar show it on their faces. If you've already got some ideas about the topic, you will look more interested and alert, and you will score more marks even before you contribute yourself.

Asking questions is important at seminars. That's part of the purpose of seminar programmes. So, how could a tutor possibly assess each student on the basis of the questions they ask? Two ways come to mind: quantity and quality. The quality of the questions you ask at seminars is actually much more important than the quantity. Someone who asks too many questions usually ends up irritating rather than impressing. So it boils down to how *good* your questions are. However, if your questions are *too* good, you may be seen as a bit of a pain, showing up everyone else. It's a fine balance to strike.

Seminars are occasions when it can pay to offer alternative, divergent viewpoints. This is usually seen as a worthy activity, and a demonstration of some of the skills that distinguish a student who is heading for a good degree from the rest. Also, seminars are occasions when it's normally good to argue. This does not mean opposing everything that everyone else says or thinks, however. It's important that when you take up an argument, you've thought about it already and have something to defend or propose.

How can I speak up at seminars if I'm a shy person?

Participating actively in seminars is quite difficult for shy people. Boiling down the problems, one is 'getting started to say something' and another is 'saying something sensible when started'. But even when you're preparing to make a contribution, don't stop listening to what others are saying. It is worth remembering, however, that the students who jump in without much thought don't always actually end up saying anything that is particular valuable, and that it is often the quieter student who has been listening carefully who often comes in with something that is really important. The following three suggestions may help you to contribute effectively:

- Jot something down which will be the skeleton of your contribution. Even a Post-it is enough to jot down two or three points – or, better still, questions – which you can elaborate on. It does wonders for your confidence if you have something to stop you becoming tongue-tied and to remind you of your second point when you've made your first one.
- Get noticed as someone who is waiting to add something to the debate. The very fact that you may have been seen to be noting down something often helps to alert whoever is chairing the seminar that you have something to contribute. Above all, avoid 'butting in' while a fellow student is still talking, and wait for a suitable short silence when you can attract the attention and get yourself invited to contribute.
- Don't feel that because you have *thought* of a contribution, you definitely have to go ahead and make it at all costs. Sometimes, what you thought of might already have been covered by someone else just before you were about to join in – no point repeating it. Many is the tale of the contributors who have been so busy preparing what they were going to say, that they never even noticed that someone else had, in fact, just said it! – not the way to be noticed as a student who is heading for a good degree. Sometimes, you may have second thoughts about the relative importance of your contribution, particularly if someone else has just said something really pertinent to the debate. Deciding when *not* to make a contribution is just as wise as making the most of your real opportunities to contribute. Of course, don't just decide not to contribute at all!

Most of the techniques involved in 'going for gold' in assessed seminars depend on you using your wits and tuning in to what seems to be liked by the staff facilitating the seminars. Use these occasions to make your impression as someone who is heading for a good degree, and who is an asset to such group situations as seminars.

Vivas (oral examinations)

Good habits when preparing for and giving vivas include:

- Keeping your cool.
- Knowing your own work well.
- Coping on your feet with questions.
- Managing silence well.

A viva (or viva voce, meaning 'live voice', to give it its full name) is an oral examination, or a face-to-face interview with one or more tutor, where the purposes can include one or more of the following:

- To decide whether candidates on a borderline deserve to be placed above or below the borderline.
- To confirm the standard that is equated with achieving a *good* degree.
- To check whether people who *seem* to be placed for a good degree really deserve one.
- To interrogate candidates about certain aspects of the work they demonstrated in other assessments.
- To verify that candidates did indeed do the work they handed in for other assessments.

A viva may feel like a kind of 'trial by ordeal'! You are confronted by people who should know a lot more than you do about most of the questions they are going to ask you. It is like an interview, but it's not the sort of interview where all you've got to lose is a job opportunity that you may or may not have really wanted in the first place. At a viva, you may have the opportunity to lose getting your good degree. The worst thing to do in preparation for your viva is just to hope that it will be all right on the day. You may *deserve* for it to go well, but it's important to take some steps to maximize the likelihood that nothing will go wrong.

Practice helps. Research students, preparing for rather more frightening vivas, such as having a viva for a PhD, often set each other mock vivas and role-play difficult, tetchy external examiners until they feel confident regarding answering any reasonable (or unreasonable) question on their work. There's nothing to stop you working with some fellow students and giving each other practice vivas. The main benefit is that you get used to the feeling of being asked questions and to the sound of your own voice as you answer them.

You also find out more about which questions you enjoy answering, and which you are least comfortable about. This is useful, as when you get a 'good' question in your real viva, you can then make the most of your opportunity to answer it well, and maybe use up some of the time that otherwise could have involved less-good questions.

Make a list of all the possible questions you might expect to be asked. This will probably be at least ten times longer than the *actual* list of questions you are faced with, so don't be frightened at the enormity of your list. Practise answering questions from your list, alone and aloud. When you find questions where you need to research the answers, skip them for the moment, but look up what you need to know in due course. Get other people to quiz you against your list of questions. Anyone will do – you don't need fellow students who know the answers. *You* will know when you fudge an answer and that's all that matters. Use friends, relatives – anyone who is willing to fire your questions at you.

As you prepare for your viva, look particularly at the things you know that you did least well in your course, particularly the final exams. Examiners at vivas often try to give candidates a further chance to remediate things that may have gone wrong. If you know you made a mess of an exam question, work out how you should have answered it, just in case the topic comes up in your viva.

Having paid some attention to the possible weakness areas, next look back at the principal things that you know you did really well. If the viva is based on a dissertation, remind yourself of the most interesting or important conclusions you reached. If the viva follows up some exams, think back to some of the best answers that you wrote. You are quite likely to be asked to expand on some of the things you did well. This is partly to give you the chance to relax and show yourself at your best on subject territory that should be familiar to you. It may also be partly to make sure that the things you did brilliantly weren't just freak occurrences, or that it really was *you* who did them.

You may not know whether or not you are going to be called for a viva. You may be asked to be ready, just in case. There are many reasons for such uncertainty: there may only be enough time to conduct so many vivas; the external examiner may select the candidates who are to have vivas; the selection may be all about borderlines or it may be entirely random. Don't read anything sinister or celebratory into whether or not you are selected for a viva. Just be ready to use it, if it happens, as an opportunity perhaps to *improve* the quality of your degree.

Now for some suggestions about how to make the most of your viva once you're in there. For a start, don't invent answers to any questions where you really have no idea. By all means guess, but *call* your answer a guess, don't pretend you know. The examiners may be asking *all* the candidates a particularly searching question, just to see how they react.

Don't annoy your questioners. Listen carefully. Wait for them to finish their questions before you start answering. Watch their body language. Listen to the tone of their voices. Tune in to the vibrations you feel as you start to answer. You can often tell whether you're going along the right track just by watching the effects your words have on the person or people listening to you. Allow them to chip in if they want to – they're in charge of this event – and don't interrupt them. Let them talk if they want to: every second that *they* talk is one second less for you to have to answer questions!

Try to minimize silences. Silence at a viva (or any interview) is usually bad news. Remember, though, that what seems to you like an interminable silence in a viva is usually quite brief. If you feel the silence is going on for too long, offer some further explanation of the last thing you were talking about, if it seems appropriate to do so.

Demonstrate confidence. Smile (but not unnervingly!). You may ask, 'How can I demonstrate confidence when I'm scared stiff? How can I actually smile?!' This is where you may need to develop your acting talents. Ask any public performer who radiates the essence of confidence – actors, newsreaders, even politicians. They are often incredibly nervous, their pulse rate often well raised, their blood pressure often elevated, despite how calm they appear. They have, however, *learned* to behave like a calm, confident, and poised person. Moreover, they've become so practised at this that they don't have to work hard trying to look at ease. Why is it important to look as confident as you can at your viva? Mainly because how you appear will be remembered by your interviewers after your viva, when they are deciding what their verdict is going to be. If you have come across as confident and credible, they are likely to believe in you overall, even if some of the things you said were incorrect.

Work placements

You may or may not have work placements as part of your degree. If you do, this section should help you to use them to improve further your chances of getting a good degree. If your degree doesn't include work placements, some of the suggestions in this section may still be useful to you in the context of your first job, or even a vacation appointment.

Good habits when undertaking work placements include:

- Entering fully into them.
- Using them to try out what has been learned on the course.
- Keeping good records of your learning and achievements.
- Not coming across at the workplace as an arrogant git!

Work placement environments are usually very different from university environments. A university is the environment created by a community working together on learning, research and scholarship. A business, public service, or industrial environment each has its own characteristics. You may feel like a fish out of water at first in your work placement (or indeed in your first appointment after graduating). You may *look* like a fish out of water. That is not a crime. But to *behave* like a fish out of water is more serious. It is important to enter into the spirit of any work placement you experience.

Even if you regard many of the things you are asked to do as routine or boring, don't give the impression that they are 'beneath your dignity or professional integrity': that is a sure way to lose friends. Don't forget that *someone* will be assessing the success of your work placement. Whether or not this directly influences the quality of your degree, such records are important evidence for future employers and the flavour of your work placement performance will almost certainly find its way into references from your tutors when you apply for jobs.

Work placements are intended to be reasonably relevant to degree course content. The extent and nature of such relevance cannot always be the same, however. Any work placement will necessarily involve students in topics, skills, and situations which are far too specialized to have been covered in a degree course, even though the underlying theories and principles may have been taught. Work placements can be time consuming to arrange, and where student numbers are large, the match between some students' work placement experience and degree topics may only be slight. If you find yourself in such a situation, it will be largely up to you to look for opportunities to bring some of your learning to bear in the environment in which you find yourself. You may need to negotiate with your work placement supervisor, and/or the tutor at your university who holds overall responsibility for your placement, so that you can make the most of your placement. It is important *not* just to object to the situation you find yourself in, but to look for ways that you can be of more value to the company or organization you're in, and negotiate these with the people concerned.

One of the things that students notice first about the world of work, particularly if they have not already held vacation jobs, is that working days tend to be longer than college days! You may feel quite exhausted at the end of a day or a week. Your real work, however, is not over when you return home after a day on work placement. Sooner or later, you need to get down to keeping records of what you have done, what you have learned, and what ideas have occurred to you as a result of your work experience. You need to build such records into tangible evidence, which you can show to your college-based tutor from time to time, and which you can use in discussions with your work-based supervisor. It may seem daunting to have all of this to do on top of a full work schedule, but it is in your own interest to excel at compiling and arranging your portfolio of evidence.

Evidence gathered during a work placement may serve you well in forthcoming job applications as a visible demonstration of how you can apply yourself to new situations. Moreover, gaining for yourself a good track record in the overall context of your work placement is yet another weapon in your armoury in the campaign to make sure that your degree is going to be a good one. Staff at your university department will know soon enough if your work experience turns out well (or badly), and this can colour their impressions and expectations of you as a person, and of your performance as a student. If, for example, there was some area of your practical work that was not too brilliant, but you more than made up for it in real-life work placement surroundings, the latter may be given due prominence in working out your overall performance.

To sum up, work placements can be hard work, but you need to turn them into *smart* work too. Some of the work may be far less demanding intellectually than some of the tougher parts of your syllabus, but that does not mean that it is less valuable. The smart thing to do is to *make* it valuable to you, and to those around you.

Conclusions

This may have been the chapter that can best help you to make the difference between getting an ordinary degree and a good one. Parts of it will probably have been irrelevant to your own particular degree, but other parts may have got you thinking about opportunities, through coursework assessment, to show that you're not just ordinary, but deserve to be considered to be a student aiming much higher.

Notwithstanding the importance of coursework, in most degree systems, exams count. In some, exams count a lot. Even if your coursework is first-rate, you will most probably still have to provide convincing evidence that you can demonstrate 'good degree' performance under exam conditions. To have got this far, you're probably pretty good at exams. But you may have to be that bit better at exams than 'pretty good', one time more, to achieve your ambition. Just one more time, as after your final exams it's unlikely that you'll ever again in your life have to prove yourself under exam conditions – at least not with such high stakes involved. It's well worthwhile not just resting on your previous tactics for revision and exams, but making that extra effort, one last time, to really excel at the 'exams game'.

That's why there's one more chapter in this book – about exams and revision. After getting this far with how best to approach all your teaching–learning contexts, and making the most of all the resources around you, it would be tragic if at the last hurdle your revision and exam techniques proved to be the fatal flaw which prevented your overall performance as being judged to be indicative of someone who deserved that good degree. That's where, I hope, the final chapter in this book will serve you well. Read on – and adjust your techniques where adjustment will serve you well.

7

Aiming high in revision and exams

Revision strategies • Exams – the days of reckoning • Preparing for a viva • Conclusions

How many exams have you already done in your life? You may feel that you have done so many that you have nothing to learn about how to go about preparing for exams, and how to perform during them so as to pass them. However, the nature of your next exams may be somewhat different, and their importance may be more crucial. This time, the quality of your overall degree may depend significantly on your revision strategies and on your exam technique. You may have just one shot at getting a *good* degree. The quality of your degree will be important for the rest of your career, even if you go on to get higher degrees later. If you're studying in a country where there's a degree classifications system, there's no second chance to have a first or 2:1 on your CV! Even if you feel you've got revision and exams really cracked, and that they pose no problems for you, it is worth checking through this chapter, and ticking off all the sensible things you already do. In this chapter, I'll start with some thoughts about revision, then we'll look at exactly what is measured by different kinds of exams as a basis for planning how best to revise. We'll end by looking at some of the things you can do *during* exams to get those extra few marks which could make that vital difference and secure for you your good degree.

Revision strategies

What do we mean by revision?

Revision is probably the wrong word. Revision could be taken to mean 'looking again', and the learning pay-off of *just* looking again at lecture notes, textbooks, handouts, practical reports, tutorial exercises, and any other course material is not tremendously high – it can indeed be surprisingly low. There are other words in common usage, including 'swotting' and 'cramming', neither of which sound really attractive or motivating. What you really should be doing when 'revising' includes:

- Getting a grip on what has been learned successfully.
- Finding out which parts you have not yet learned successfully, and getting a grip on these too.
- Finding out what has slipped your mind, and working out ways of keeping it in your mind.
- Preparing to *show* that you've got a grip on what you have learned.
- Finding ways to prove that you are better at all of these things than most of your fellow students.
- Practising those things that you will need to be practised in when you have to *prove* that you've learned things well.
- Getting up to speed at communicating your knowledge in the ways that you will need to do so when being tested on it.

Therefore, revision is much more than looking again at your resource materials, and *good* revision, as we will see later in this chapter, is about writing and talking rather than reading. I will still refer to it as 'revision' however, as this remains the most commonly accepted umbrella term for all the processes which lead towards your opportunity to prove that you deserve a good degree.

Why is revision important?

In many degree courses, examination results count more than the products of all the other kinds of assessment put together. While it is often the ways that you distinguish yourself in other kinds of assessment that make you stand out to your assessors as someone who deserves a good degree, you still need to make sure that your examination performance is also distinguished. Your examination performance depends significantly on how much revision you have done. It depends even more on the quality of your revision, and that is where you may need to do some planning to make sure that the ways that you spend your time revising are the most productive uses of your time and energy. The ideas in this chapter should help you make wise decisions about *how* you revise, *when* you start, and how you *measure* the efficiency of your revision.

Balancing revision and coursework – have you started serious revision yet?

One of the problems with most courses is that the teaching sessions continue until the exams are really quite imminent. There will always be coursework which needs attention. New topics continue to be introduced. It is dangerously easy to keep on paying attention to coursework, while the exams draw nearer and nearer. This means that, for many students, serious revision gets started far too late. There are several good reasons for starting systematic revision as soon as possible, and this means *today* for you (if you have not already started), as part of your strategy for getting your good degree. Begin, however, by doing the next task and then reading the discussion that follows.

Task: reasons or excuses?

If you have started systematic revision already, well done! If so, you don't need to do this task. If not, rate yourself regarding the following reasons for not yet having started serious revision, indicating where you stand in each case. Tick whichever column fits you best.

Reason	Very like me	Quite like me	Not at all like me
1 I've got too much coursework still to do.			
2 I'm still getting new material.			
3 If I learn it now, I'll just forget it all again.			
4 No one else seems to be revising yet, why should I?			
5 I know I should start now, but I can't face it yet.			
6 I don't want my friends to see me as a swot!			
7 Come on, I need a life, I can't work all the time.			
8 I've always been able to revise quickly.			
9 I don't know what to revise yet.			

Discussion: reasons or excuses?

Just about all the 'reasons' given in the task above actually turn out to be *excuses*. If you've ticked any of them as applying to you, please read the following comments about them, and see whether you're guilty of finding ways to convince your own mind that you don't have to start yet!

1   *I've got too much coursework still to do.* If this is one of your reasons for not having started revision, think carefully about the relative balance between coursework and exams in the overall assessment of your course. While coursework does indeed count, exams usually count more. While coursework gives you many chances to demonstrate that you are a candidate who deserves a good degree, exams remain the times when you really need to prove that you have earned one. If you have a substantial amount of coursework on your agenda, it is still sensible to start some systematic revision straight away. This does not mean abandoning the coursework, but perhaps spending a little less time on it than you may have done to make room for some revision time.

2   *I'm still getting new material.* Yes, you probably are. You will probably continue to get new material well towards your exams. One reason for this is that your lecturers and tutors can't just stop work for weeks on end to allow students time to get their act together for forthcoming exams. Another reason is that lecturers often find it quite hard to get through their portions of the curriculum in the time they have available to them. They usually know so much that they rarely feel they have shared with you all that they would like to cover. Of course, it's not *they* who have to get through the curriculum: it's *you*! Sometimes, courses are timetabled to end well before exams, so that students can spend time on revision. However, even if this time is available to you, remember that you're aiming for a *good* degree and you need to be able to distinguish yourself from most of the students who start their revision at the last moment. This is all the more reason for getting started on your revision well before anyone else!

3   *If I learn it now, I'll just forget it all again.* Well done if this is *not* one of your reasons for not starting revision yet. Many students put off the moment of starting serious revision with this as an excuse. It is true to say that we do indeed forget things that we have learned. However, it is much *quicker* to relearn something that you have learned once and then forgotten. It is quicker still to relearn something that you have forgotten twice. And so on. And every time you relearn something, you become less likely to forget it. You also make deeper sense of it each time and increase your understanding. So it turns out that the likelihood of forgetting things is all the more reason to start learning them early, leaving yourself plenty of opportunity to find out *what* you forget and to do something about it. The things that are most easily forgotten are often the trickier concepts and

ideas, and these are where you need to be proving that you're ahead of most of your fellow students. The act of finding out that you have forgotten these important parts is a useful process in alerting you to the things on which you will need to spend most time.

4   *No one else seems to be revising yet, why should I?* What a favourite excuse for not starting revision this one is! It is very tempting to put off the evil moment until other people are starting to revise. But are *they* making a wise decision? Remember that you are intending to distinguish yourself from most of your fellow students. One of the best ways to make sure that your exam performance will do this is to set out right from the start to put more into your revision than most people around you.

5   *I know I should start now, but I can't face it yet.* If this was one of your reasons for not having started revision yet, you already know that it is an excuse rather than a reason. Your ultimate success, especially with unseen written exams, depends more on the quality and quantity of revision that you do than on any other single factor. Revision, and especially *early* revision, is an investment in your own success. No one is likely to take much notice of the fact that you start revising early. Even if they do, nothing much will happen besides the possibility of some people regarding you as slightly odd – but it's *your* future, not theirs.

6   *I don't want my friends to see me as a swot!* If this was 'like you', you may have to make a decision between popularity and success. If fellow students are aware of the fact that you are ahead of them in revision, they're quite likely to mock you, not least because of their own guilty consciences. Also, don't forget that it can actually be very difficult to *tell* whether anyone else has started systematic revision. Many students exercise their time management skills so that they make a good start on revision without it showing. Your friends may well have started too!

7   *Come on, I need a life, I can't work all the time.* This is a sensible statement. It is not, however, a good reason for not starting revision really early. It comes back to task management as well as time management. Revision is one of the most important tasks on your list. It may not yet be an *urgent* task, but that does not diminish its importance. As a student aiming high, your best route to having a life is to be on top of your work, so that you can really enjoy all the other things that make up your life, with an easy conscience and without the stress of thinking that you should be working at your studies for more of the time. There's another, less happy, way at looking at this one. That is to ask yourself whether you really 'need a life' *now*, compared to the rest of your life. Working diligently now is likely to increase your chances regarding the rest of your life being of higher quality than it might otherwise be. Your best bet is to strike your own sensible balance between having a life now, and having a good one later. You can indeed do both. Your ability to balance work and play is one of the things of which a good degree turns out to be an indicator.

8 *I've always been able to revise quickly.* You are fortunate if you have always been able to revise quickly, and you may well be able to continue this habit towards getting your good degree. However, there is always danger in complacency, and complacency is *not* a performance indicator associated with getting a good degree. Don't underestimate the possibility of your *next* spell of revision being a lot more demanding than ever before. Even if you have, in the past, found it quite easy to get to grips with large amounts of study material in a short time before exams, that may be the last occasion when you will be so fortunate. Don't leave it to chance; *this* time choose to give yourself plenty of time to revise, and that means starting early.

9 *I don't know what to revise yet.* This 'reason' may seem quite reasonable but, like most of the others, it is just an excuse in disguise. It is certainly possible that at the moment you are not sure what to revise, but very unlikely that there is *nothing* you can revise. Even if you spend some time getting to grips with some aspects of your subject that turn out not to be particularly important, that is not a disaster in any sense. All knowledge is valuable, even if it is not directly concerned with getting marks. It is better to have learned four things, then find out that you only need two of them, than to learn nothing and have those two still to learn.

What different sorts of exam are there?

Most exams are occasions where you have a given time, in a fixed location, to write out your answers to someone else's questions. Such exams are called 'time constrained unseen written exams'. In other words, you don't know what the questions are until you get there, and you write your answers to them there and then, on a fixed timescale.

Although time constrained unseen written exams may well dominate your own exam agenda, there are other possibilities, and it's worth looking at the alternatives before going into more detail about how to prepare for exams, because the best ways to prepare depend on what sort of exam you have. The sorts of formal exam that are in use in universities in general include:

- Time constrained unseen written exams (as described above).
- Time unconstrained unseen written exams (where you can take longer if you want to or need to).
- Time constrained *seen* written exams (where you know in advance some or all of the questions).
- Open book or open note exams (these can be time constrained or time unconstrained. You may be allowed to take in with you *any* reference material that you think fit, or alternatively you may only be supplied with

given sources of reference, and will then have to do the best you can using these sources to answer the questions).

- Take away exams (where you're given the questions or task briefings at a given time and hand in your answers at another given time, which may be a few hours later or even some days later).
- Short answer exams (usually time constrained, and unseen, where you write short answers to structured questions in the exam room, either on paper or via a keyboard into a computer assessment system).
- Multiple choice exams (may be time constrained or time unconstrained, where you pick one or more options from those provided for each question, and enter your choice directly into a computer system or onto a computer-readable card).
- In-tray exercise exams (where you have to make sense of a dossier or 'in-tray' of various items of data and information given to you at the start of the exam, and then answer questions which are issued at various stages during the exam to test how well you can handle the information as you apply it to the new situations that the questions address).
- OSCEs – Objective Structured Clinical Exams for medical students (or equivalent exams in some other disciplines, where you walk around to different 'exam stations', perhaps interpreting some X-ray plates at one, looking through case notes at another and reaching a diagnosis, talking to a patient (actually, an actor) at another, and so on – real-life simulations of things doctors actually do in their professional practice).

What does each kind of exam actually measure?

Each kind of exam measures some things that are different, and some things that are similar. Let's start by looking at time constrained unseen written exams. See if you can rate what these tend to measure. Try the next task, based on your existing experience of such exams, and also on the nature of your present studies at university. Then read the discussion that follows.

Factors measured by written exams?	Measured very well	Measured to some extent	Not really measured
1 How much you know about your subject.			
2 How much you *don't* know about your subject.			
3 The *quantity* of revision that you have done.			

Factors measured by written exams?	Measured very well	Measured to some extent	Not really measured
4 The *quality* of revision that you have done.			
5 How intelligent you are.			
6 How much work you've done the night before.			
7 How well you keep your cool.			
8 How good your memory is.			
9 How good you are at question spotting.			
10 How fast you think.			
11 How fast you write.			
12 How legible your handwriting is.			
13 How good you are at answering exam questions.			
14 How carefully you read the questions.			
15 How wisely you choose the questions that you attempt.			
16 How well you manage your time *during* exams.			
17 How well you keep exactly to the questions in your answers.			
18 How well you set out your answers to the questions.			
19 How skilled you are at solving problems.			
20 How carefully you read your answers after writing them.			
21 How well you edit/improve your answers after reading them.			

Discussion: what do time constrained unseen written exams measure?

The factors in the task above are by no means the *only* ones which may be measured by time constrained unseen written exams. We are looking at these factors at this point in the chapter not only to point forwards towards good exam technique, but more importantly to give indicators about what sorts of *revision* are most appropriate in your preparations for time constrained unseen written exams, to pave the way towards you being able to use such exams to prove that you really do deserve a good degree.

1 *How much you know about your subject.* Exams give *some* measure of how much you know about your subject. However, the correlation is not particularly good! Any written exam does not take very much time, even if it seems as though it goes on for ages. During an unseen written exam, you are only going to have time to write down a small fraction of what you know about the subject. To be more precise, you are going to be measured on what you know about the *questions* that happen to be on the paper on that particular day. This *may* reflect your overall mastery of the subject, but needn't necessarily do so.

2 *How much you* don't *know about your subject.* Exams do indeed tend to be a measure of what you don't know about the particular *questions* that you happen to answer on the day. This may or may not be an indicator of what you don't know about the subject in total.

3 *The* quantity *of revision that you have done.* Exams do tend to measure the quantity of revision that you have done, unless of course you knew the topic so well that you did not need to do any revision to prepare you for the exams. However, quantity of revision is not enough. There are many things in this list of factors that are more important than quantity.

4 *The* quality *of revision that you have done.* Traditional unseen written exams can be a good measure of the quality of your revision. High quality revision is that which equips you to have the best possible chance of coping with the uncertainties of an exam, including the questions that may or may not come up in the paper, and how well you are able to tackle those questions on the day. Good quality revision focuses not just on knowing things, but on being skilled at putting them across in writing, against the clock.

5 *How intelligent you are.* This is a controversial one! Exams may well be *intended* to measure intelligence, but it is questionable whether they actually manage to measure this. They measure all sorts of things that are *indicators* of intelligence, not least how intelligently you plan your revision. In the final analysis, intelligence as measured by exams is as much to do with *technique, organization*, and *planning* as it is to do with innate intelligence.

6 *How much work you've done the night before.* You can probably remember exams which *did* seem to test this. You may well recall sitting in an exam room and writing fluently about something that you only learned at the last minute. When we think, however, about *degree* exams, things should have moved on a long way from this position. It would not be very sensible if the quality of your degree was *only* about how much cramming you could do at the eleventh hour. In fact, the situation tends to be the reverse of this. If you do too much work during the day or night before an exam, you may well *know* the subject rather well, but could be too *exhausted* to write really good answers! So your actual exam performance could be inversely proportional to how much work you did the night before.

7 *How well you keep your cool.* There is no doubt about this one: exams *are* a measure of how well you keep your cool. This is one of the arguments for having exams. Employers need people who can keep their cool under stressful situations. You may well ask, 'Why measure this factor so often?' As long as assessment systems in higher education over use traditional exams, as they have done for decades, we do seem to be measuring this too repetitively. However, you can do something about developing your skills at keeping your cool. Keeping calm and composed is not just something that does (or does not) come naturally to you. It depends a lot on how well prepared you are for the exam. It is easier to remain calm if you *know* that you've got everything you need inside your brain to do an exam really well, and that it is just a matter of getting on and *doing* it well. To know this, however, you need to have had the right sorts of practice during your revision so that you are not just keeping your cool in a new situation, but doing something that you have done many times before.

8 *How good your memory is.* Time constrained unseen written exams are indeed a test of memory. They may well be *intended* to measure more important things than memory, and they may indeed measure several other skills besides memory, but there is no getting away from it: having the right things well filed in your memory is a great help in such exams. Again, this has a lot to do with revision, and in particular how practised you have become at *recalling* things that are in your memory. It's not just a case of having things stored away in your head, it's more to do with being able to get at them as and when you need them, under the somewhat stressful situation of a silent room, and the relentless advances made by the clock! In fact, it boils down to how well you've *trained* your memory to deliver what you need, and that leads us back to the common factor of practice.

9 *How good you are at question spotting.* Unseen written exams do indeed reward those candidates who were fortunate enough to guess the nature of at least some of the questions, and who have then followed this up by

becoming well practised at answering these questions. However, if you don't spot enough of the right questions, and practise answering the *wrong* questions, you have a problem! The situation becomes much better if you've spotted a large number of possible questions, so large that you've spotted just about everything that comes up on the paper. That, however, is not really question spotting, and is just sensible revision of the broad area of the topics to be tested. Some of the worst disasters bright students experience come about because they guess wrongly.

10   *How fast you think.* Unseen written exams (and indeed many other forms of exam) depend at least in part on how fast you can think. However, they depend more on how well you can turn your thoughts into answers on paper. We can all think a great deal faster than we can write, so speed of thinking is not the only factor involved. How fast you can think about your answers to the questions that you encounter in an exam depends on how *often* you have marshalled similar thoughts. In other words, the right sort of speed of thinking can be polished up by practise during revision. This means that your revision processes should include activities that give you practise at thinking, and not just be limited to practise at writing down your thoughts.

11   *How fast you write.* Most exam candidates feel that unseen written exams (when time constrained, obviously) involve at least some dependence on speed of handwriting. This is seen to be reflected by the number of candidates who are still busy writing when time is up. Many candidates exclaim, 'I could have done considerably better if only I had had an extra thirty minutes'. However, it's not all down to speed of writing. At least part of the equation is *selectivity* in writing. If you are a relatively slow writer, it is all the more important that everything you write is directly contributing towards earning marks from the examiners. You need to write smart rather than just fast, and time at the beginning of the exam used for planning, not writing, is always well spent.

12   *How legible your handwriting is.* Exams are not intended to measure this. After all, something so basic as legibility should hardly be any part of the agenda for making degree-level decisions. However, legibility is a factor that is bound to have some effect on the marks given by examiners, even if they are trying not to be influenced by it. If they have real difficulty reading your handwriting they may miss or pass over areas where they would normally have awarded you marks. If your writing is really easy to read, examiners will be able to mark your script more quickly, and that tends to put them in a better mood, and *that* may be reflected when they make final decisions about how many marks you have earned for an answer. If your handwriting is difficult to read (mine is probably much worse than yours!), you may have to make a careful compromise between speed and legibility, so that you write reasonably fast, but slowly enough

to be decidedly legible. Remember that big, bad handwriting is easier to read than small, bad handwriting. Also, try out different writing implements and see which suits you best. If you have genuine difficulties, such as dyslexia, it is worth discussing these with your tutor and, for example, finding out whether your university makes special provision for such candidates by allowing them extra time in exams.

13 *How good you are at answering exam questions*. This factor is spot on. Particularly with time constrained unseen written exams, the *main* thing that is actually measured is how well you answer the questions. This in turn depends on how well practised you have become at answering such questions, and how much you have improved your precision at doing so, and your speed at getting your answers down on paper. This has very significant implications for your revision strategy.

14 *How carefully you read the questions*. Just about all kinds of exam measure this, not least unseen written ones. Most examiners can confirm that more marks are lost by candidates not actually answering the question as asked, than by candidates not knowing how to answer the questions. This means that you need to read the questions really well, and that in turn means slowly, deliberately, and more than once. Work out for yourself exactly what each question is really asking you to do. Look for the key words in the question. When organizing your revision it is useful to make your own glossary of the meanings, as related to your subject discipline, of such words as:

- Explain
- Describe
- Discuss
- Compare
- Contrast
- Compare and contrast
- Evaluate
- Decide
- Explore
- Account for
- Prove
- Derive
- Show that
- Review

It is well worth jotting down what you *think* these words mean, checking your answers with those of fellow students, and then cross-checking with tutors. These words can have quite different shades of meaning in different subjects and disciplines, so dictionary definitions are only a start. This is also why I didn't attempt to share with you my own views of the meanings of these words.

15   *How wisely you choose the questions that you attempt.* When there is a choice of questions, a lot can depend on choosing the questions that will prove best for you. This partly depends on reading *all* the questions really well before you make your choices. It is very frustrating to struggle for a while answering a particular question only to find out later that there was a different question to which you would have been able to provide a much better answer. Many exam candidates make false starts to questions, then have second thoughts and move on. As long as it is clear to the examiners that the false starts are exactly that and are not to be marked, the only penalty for this is the time that is lost in making the false starts, but that is quite a serious penalty in its own right. The implications for your revision and preparation are that you need plenty of practice at *deciding* which questions are winners, which are losers, and which are 'in between' and worth doing after you've tackled all the winners.

16   *How well you manage your time* during *exams.* Time constrained exams (of all kinds, not just unseen written ones) measure time management to a much greater extent than is realized by many candidates. This does not just mean dividing the available time up equally between the number of equal questions that you may need to attempt. It also means planning time to read, edit, and improve your answers, and allowing time at the start of the exam to read all the questions thoroughly and decide which to tackle.

17   *How well you keep exactly to the questions in your answers.* Many candidates *start* to answer a question in a well focused way, but 15 minutes later have drifted so far off the question that they are not scoring any marks at all! Have you ever looked back at the question mid-way through your answer, and said to yourself, 'Is that what the question was? Has someone changed it since I started writing my answer?!' The only way to avoid such drifting is to keep looking at the question. If all exam candidates could be programmed to check, at ten minute intervals, that they were still answering the question, the danger of running off at tangents would be just about eliminated. Sometimes when candidates go off on a tangent, everything that they actually write is correct or even inspired, but they gain no marks for any of it because it is not directly relevant to the question as set.

18   *How well you set out your answers to the questions.* This is not the main factor tested by unseen written exams. However, like legibility, layout and structure play their parts in setting the expectations of the examiner. It is certainly worth making sure that the way you go about setting out your answers will not put the examiner in a bad mood, or you could lose some of those 'benefit of the doubt' decision marks. If your layout lost you such a decision five times in the same exam, that could mean five marks, and that could just about be the difference between a good degree and an

ordinary one! Always be extravagant with exam paper rather than cramping your layout, as it makes space for your last-minute amendments and additions.

19 *How skilled you are at solving problems.* Some exams measure exactly this. Particularly in disciplines such as science, maths, engineering, and in specific parts of many other disciplines, many exam questions measure your skill to solve problems, often against the clock. Problems often involve calculations or computations, and are different from many other forms of exam question in that there is usually a 'right' answer, or at least an answer which will score most or *all* of the available marks. Few candidates score 20/20 for any essay-type answer; no such answer can ever be regarded as 'perfect'. With a calculation, it is indeed possible to get it entirely right, and this usually means getting 20/20. Ability to solve problems depends only a little on knowing how to solve the problem, and a great deal on how often you've solved very similar problems. The implications for revision in these subjects are obvious. To get your good degree, if some or all of your exams involve problem solving, you simply need to be faster and more accurate at coming to the correct solutions to the problems than are your fellow students.

20 *How carefully you read your answers after writing them.* In all forms of written exam this counts a lot. Actually, it's not the *reading* of your own answers that counts directly in getting you extra marks, but what you *do* as a result of reading your work. However, you can't do anything with what you have written unless you go to the trouble of reading it, so the reading itself is absolutely necessary to get the extra marks that are waiting for you.

21 *How well you edit/improve your answers after reading them.* As hinted at in point 20, it is just about always possible to get some extra marks by editing and improving your own answers. When you read something you have already written, you will often notice mistakes, or places where your meaning does not come across as clearly as you wished, and so on. You will also find that since the time when you wrote your answers, further thoughts about the questions have crept into your mind. Many of these further thoughts are so relevant that they are worth marks. You can only get these extra marks if you turn these extra thoughts into additions to your written answers. The implications of this for revision include giving yourself plenty of practice at editing and adjusting things that you have written. This can include past pieces of coursework and practice answers to exam questions that you have written out.

Summary: revising for time constrained unseen written exams

As you will have seen from the 21 possibilities discussed above concerning what unseen written exams actually *measure,* it boils down to building appropriate practice into revision. Such exams measure, more than anything else, how practised and confident you are at the business of writing answers in the circumstances involved. Preparing for such exams is *not* just a matter of getting to grips with your subject to the maximum extent possible, in the hope that on the day you will be well primed to cope with whatever you see in front of you. It is, of course, wise to be as well prepared for anything as you can be, but the technique side of things is just as important. There are plenty of candidates who *deserve* to get a good degree on the basis of what they know about the subject when they walk into an exam, but who don't get one because they aren't sufficiently prepared to prove that they deserve one, in the ways that the exam demands.

We've spent some time now looking at what is measured by one kind of exam. Next we'll look at some of the different things that may be measured by those other types of exam, with a view to deciding what differences in revision strategy are indicated. If you know that you haven't (and won't ever have on your course) any of these other kinds of exam, you could skip the next section unless you're interested.

What is different about all those *other* kinds of exam?

As well as time constrained unseen written exams, you may remember that there are several other possibilities. Many of these measure knowledge and skills in similar ways, but it is worth noting some of the more important differences, so you can decide how to adjust your revision tactics to make yourself as prepared as you can be for what these exams actually measure. After each subheading is a short explanation of what is meant by each type of exam, to help you to decide which kinds you may need to accommodate in your revision tactics.

Time unconstrained unseen written exams

These allow you to take longer if you want or need to. When you know you are preparing for this sort of exam, you can relax a bit regarding speed. This means that it is not so crucial to be able to think quickly and write focused answers quickly, or solve problems quickly, and more important to be able to do these things *well* than at speed. In your revision, you can then plan to practise spending more time on structuring your answers. This can include making really good introductions to essay-type answers, and ensuring that the assessors of such answers will be impressed by the way you come to firm, clear conclusions.

Time constrained seen written exams

Here, you know in advance some or all of the questions, or a case study is given out in advance. Preparation for such exams is quite different in some ways. For example, you may know very well *what* you want to write in your exam answers. You may only know this for some of the questions, however, especially if there is one or more compulsory question that you have not already seen. One of the most significant dangers with seen written exams is that candidates prepare answers that take too long to write down. This can mean that they end up not answering all the questions, getting very good marks for some of them and exactly zero for any that they didn't answer! This is not a good strategy for getting the marks that will earn your good degree, so it is worth practising to ensure that even in the exam situation you can comfortably write all you intend to write for the answers that you have prepared. Not having to stop and think is a way of making sure that you put your time to best effect, and you can indeed practise not having to stop and think. Do your thinking ahead of the exam, but also practise getting your thinking down in writing, so that you know very well how long it is going to take you to express your answers.

Open book or open note exams

These can be time constrained or time unconstrained. You may be allowed to take in with you *any* reference material that you think fit, or alternatively you may only be supplied with *given* sources of reference, and will then have to do the best you can using these sources to answer the questions. Open note exams allow you to take in all your notes, but no published material.

Open book and open note exams are now being used more widely. This is not least because of growing recognition that traditional unseen written exams don't necessarily reward the candidates whose knowledge and understanding is best, but rather those candidates whose exam technique is best. Also, more people now accept that unseen written exams are somewhat artificial, and that open book or open note exams are better at resembling real-life situations. In an open book or open note exam, if the questions have been well designed, you will *not* be required to write out large tracts of the material that is already in your open books or notes! You will be required to *find* relevant material in your sources, to make decisions based on the material available to you, and to do things with information from your sources.

Take away exams

Here, you're given the questions or task briefings at a given time, and hand in your answers at another given time, which may be a few hours later, or even some days later. You can go onto the web to search for information or data. This kind of exam is still relatively rare, but if you know that you are going to face one there is a lot you can do to be better prepared on the day. For a start, you don't need to learn and remember quite as much of the material, though it can help you to save time looking up source material if you remember most of the important aspects, and remember exactly where you can find the details that you may need to answer your exam questions. Although take away exams don't involve the stress of sitting in a quiet exam room, they involve different kinds of stress. For example, *all* your fellow students may be chasing the same reference materials in the library at the same time, or using all the available access to the Internet. One way of becoming good at take away exams is (like most things) to practise. Take away papers are very much like other coursework that you undertake – with some added stress!

Short answer exams

These are usually time constrained, and unseen, where you write short answers to structured questions in the exam room. In some ways, short answer exams are less frightening than full answer ones. Not so much will depend upon your written communication skills. You won't be working so hard to write convincing introductions or robust conclusions. However, it is possible for a short answer exam to interrogate you on a much broader cross-section of the syllabus than a full answer exam, when you only write about a few elements of the syllabus. There is less opportunity for you to hedge your bets regarding any parts of the syllabus you might decide to miss out of your revision. Speed can be important in short answer exams, as there may be a large number of short questions to answer. Short answer exams also test how well you write appropriate short answers: if they're too short you will lose out, and if they're too long you could penalize yourself in terms of time, and not manage to answer all the questions.

Multiple choice exams

These may be time constrained or time unconstrained, where you pick one or more options from those provided for each question, and enter your choice either on a computer-readable card or directly into a computer terminal. Multiple choice exams are very similar to short answer exams: the main difference is that your 'answers' are very short indeed and involve just making your choice about which (one or more) options are the best (or correct) ones for each question. Multiple choice exams involve a great deal of thinking, and speed of thinking becomes very important. It is also useful to get the right kind of practice so that your technique becomes well developed. The best kind of practice is actually *answering* multiple choice questions, and this may mean composing for yourself hundreds of possible questions in this format so that you can give yourself random speed tests. If you are collaborating with a few fellow students to help you to prepare for multiple choice exams, it can be really productive to compile together a significant 'bank' of questions and to quiz each other with them.

In-tray exercise exams

With this type of exam, you have to make sense of various items in a dossier of data and information given to you at the start, and then answer questions which are issued at various stages during the exam to test how well you can handle the information that you have in order to apply it to the new situations that the questions address. Essentially, in-tray exercise exams measure four things:

1 How well you can assimilate the data and information presented to you at the start of the exam.
2 How successfully you can organize this data, so that you can find anything in it at short notice.
3 How well you can then respond to the unexpected changes or questions that are issued during the exam.
4 How clearly and relevantly you can write down your answers to the questions.

Building these processes into your revision practice is the best way to develop these skills. It is extremely useful if you can lay your hands on past examinations of this kind, but this is not always easy as the information presented at the start of such exams is often collected in at the end, along with candidates' answers to the questions posed during the exam. You may need to invent your own exams of this kind to practise on. This can be made much more productive by collaborating with some likeminded fellow students with the common aim that each of you becomes better at handling unanticipated questions and tasks on the basis of given information.

OSCEs – Objective Structured Clinical Exams

These are essentially practical exams where you work your way round a series of assessed activities, practising the kinds of skills you are intended to have developed. They are used in medical education, as already mentioned, but equivalent types of exam have been devised for a number of different professions too. In general terms, this kind of exam measures how up-to-speed you are at the various things you should be able to do in your profession, as well as your decision making skills, and your ability to quickly interpret information and plan what to do on the basis of your interpretation.

Keeping your cool during revision

It is worthwhile to remain calm and composed while revising. This is easier said than done, for three reasons:

1 If you're a bit anxious about the prospect of forthcoming exams, each act of revision reminds you of your anxiety.
2 It is natural to find revision a somewhat slow process and then to start being anxious about all the rest of the revision that is still to be done, becoming concerned that it won't all get done in time and feeling that the dates of the days of reckoning are rushing towards you.

3 When revising, you may often find out things that you've forgotten and things that you discover you had not actually understood in the first place, and this gets you wondering how much else you must have forgotten, and how little you may have actually understood about anything!

Each of these three factors can add to a feeling of being stressed as you revise. Yet to revise really efficiently (and enjoyably) it is best to reduce your stress levels. Probably the best way of keeping your cool during revision is to accept any of the above factors as natural and inevitable, and to decide to confront them.

It is natural to be a bit tense about the days of reckoning. It is therefore quite permissible to feel some of this anxiety every time you do anything which is directly concerned with your preparations for such days. It is important not to try to escape this anxiety, such as by *not* doing any revision! You would become more anxious if you knew that you were evading the task. The best way of avoiding anxiety in revision is to keep busy and productive, so that you feel you are making real headway in your preparations for the unknown.

It is useful to find out anything that you had forgotten. This alerts you to the fact that it had slipped your grasp at least once. This usually means it is quite tricky, or quite important. It does not take nearly as long to regain something that has slipped as it took to learn it in the first place. The more often you regain some ground, the more firmly you hold on to it. It is also useful to find out things that you had not understood first time round. This is a sign that you are deepening your understanding as you revise, and is only to be expected.

Probably the most significant cause of stress while revising is that you feel you are only dealing with a little bit of the total picture at any given time, and the enormity of the rest of the picture keeps crowding into your mind and distracting you from the part you are studying at the moment. This is worth fighting. You may need to remind yourself that you can only polish one tiny part of your knowledge, skills, and understanding at any given moment. It is worth forgetting everything else at the time, and concentrating on making the task of the moment successful and productive. This is best done when you know that you have a strategy for getting to grips with the whole picture, and that everything else is going to be accommodated safely and securely in due course.

Which revision processes have high learning pay-off?

In this section we will look at the *efficiency* of some of the principal processes that you can build into your revision strategy. Successful revision is *not* about spending every moment you've got in your life feverishly working on your studies. Success depends much more on how much learning pay-off you derive from each activity you do during your revision. You've almost certainly revised in many different ways in the past, and in the next task you can start deciding which of these ways is most effective, efficient, and focused.

Task: the learning pay-off of different revision activities

What do you feel is the learning pay-off of the following 11 different revision activities? Tick the columns according to your own experience, then read the discussion that follows to see if there are any surprises for you. Not all possibilities will be relevant to revising *your* subjects, however, so just put a line through the columns opposite any that don't apply to you, at least for the moment (you may decide that they *could* apply after reading the discussion).

Revision activities	Learning pay-off		
	High	Medium	Low
1 Reading your lecture notes, handouts, books, and articles over and over again.			
2 Making summaries of your source materials as you read them.			
3 Writing important things out over and over again.			
4 Practising writing out full essay answers.			
5 Making essay plans for essay question possibilities.			
6 Practising writing out answers to old exam questions.			
7 Working out hundreds of short, sharp questions of your own, and practising writing out answers to these.			
8 Practising *speaking* the answers to past questions, and to short, sharp questions that you have written for yourself.			
9 Practising *thinking* through how you would answer questions.			
10 Practising solving problems.			
11 Getting fellow students to quiz you and quizzing them.			

Discussion: the learning pay-off of different revision activities

You may well have worked out much of the agenda which follows for yourself, and may have already found the revision processes which work really well for you. Check my responses to each of the activities just in case there are one or two additional ideas that you can bring to bear on your revision, to make it efficient, effective, and more enjoyable.

1   *Reading your lecture notes, handouts, books, and articles over and over again.* This does not usually have high learning pay-off. It is also boring and wasteful of time. One of the problems is that it is easy to spend too much time reading things you already know. This is quite enjoyable, and reassuring, but in fact is rather a waste of time and energy. It is much better to use your lecture notes and other resources to concentrate on things that you don't yet know, and to use other means for finding out exactly *what* you don't yet know before turning to your sources to find the information that you need. Of course, you have to read your source materials *sometime*, but it is best not just to read them, but to turn them into something that you can use more actively in your revision. Turn them into concise summaries, mind-maps, and, particularly, lists of *questions* which will help you to interrogate your knowledge and understanding during your revision.

2   *Making summaries of your source materials as you read them.* The learning pay-off of making summaries is quite high. It is a relatively slow process, but a very useful one. Making summaries helps you to make sense of what you are reading. More importantly, the summaries themselves then start to save you time. You can now use your summaries instead of your original source materials as revision aids. You can spend more time with your summaries than with the original materials, checking out as you use your summaries how much of the important detail you can remember from the original materials, and only consulting the originals when there is something important that you need to remind yourself about. Whenever you need to go back to your original sources for something important, it is usually worth adding a prompt or two to your summary, so that you are reminded of the detail of the points that you needed to look up, and of the fact that they had slipped your mind at least once. This helps you to keep tabs on those pieces of information, or ideas, that are most likely to need some attention, to keep them well polished in your mind.

3   *Writing important things out over and over again.* This is quite a good way of learning those things that you may need to get exactly right, for example mathematical expressions or key definitions. It is, however, too slow and boring to use this as a general strategy for revision. Writing things out over and over can seem like useful revision, mainly because it

keeps you busy, and there is something tangible to see as a result. But it can easily degenerate into copying things out, and this is not a high-level task. It is possible to make transcriptions of notes, handouts, or extracts from other sources without actually thinking about what you are writing! Overall, this is rarely one of the key revision habits of students who earn good degrees.

4 *Practising writing out full essay answers.* If your examinations will involve you in writing out essay-type answers, this is highly relevant practice, especially if you are unused to essay-style questions. The more essays you write during your revision, the more likely you are to have done the exam questions at least once before the actual exam. You also can develop your technique and speed at the same time, and become better able to write a given essay in a given time span. It is a technique that is well worth using for *some* of the time you spend revising. The problem is that the learning pay-off can only be regarded as 'medium' rather than 'high'. This is because of the time that it takes to write full essay answers. It makes you feel busy when revising, but is not covering the ground as fast as some of the other options discussed below. Writing full answers involves a little bit of thinking, then a lot of routine writing.

5 *Making essay plans for essay question possibilities.* This technique has high learning pay-off. In the time it would take for you to write one full essay answer you may be able to make essay plans for half a dozen essays at least. This means that you do a great deal more *thinking* in this period of time, and also that you cover much more of your subject matter than you would have done writing a full answer. You can then cover even more of the possible essay questions that might come up in your exam. Your essay plans are useful revision aids in their own right, as you can refer back to them and *plan* how you would turn them into fully-fledged essays. It is indeed worth turning some of them into full answers, to give you some practice at getting the timing right. Meanwhile, you can paste your essay plans around your walls as an exhibition of your thinking, and make adjustments to any of the plans whenever you get a bright idea about something important that you could add to any of the essays. Remember not to make the plans too detailed. Restrict them to important, relevant ideas, and whenever you think of a more important idea to add, put brackets round a less important idea that you may then miss out were you to write a full answer.

6 *Practising writing out answers to old exam questions.* This has quite high learning pay-off. There is no doubt that it is relevant practice, as exams essentially measure your ability to write out answers to exam questions. Old exam questions are particularly useful for giving you an idea of the standard of the questions you may expect, and for helping you to check out your speed. It is well worth developing your ability to write out good

answers to some old questions within the timescale that you would have had available in the exam. The disadvantage is to do with the speed. You can lull yourself into thinking you are revising well because you are slogging away at something with a visible result. You may not be covering as much ground as you could have done using some of the other techniques in this list.

7   *Working out hundreds of short, sharp questions of your own, and practising writing out answers to these.* This has high learning pay-off. The key is that they are short, sharp questions. This means that you won't need to spend very long writing out the answers to them, as they will be short, sharp answers. Any long exam question boils down to a collection of several short ones. If you become well practised at answering lots and lots of short questions, you become better able to combine the answers to make up an answer to a longer exam question. Another advantage of hundreds of short, sharp questions is that you soon begin to be able to sort them out into three categories:

   • Ones where you always seem to be able to remember the answers.
   • Ones where you often have to look up the answers.
   • Ones in between.

   The short, sharp questions that you always get right can be put in a box that you only look at occasionally, to check that you can still get them right. There's no need to spend much time on things that you always get right. The ones to which you often have to look up the answers can be put in another box which you consult much more often. These are the questions you need most practice with. The in-between questions can be worth spending time with now and again, until you can safely file them with the 'always right' set.

8   *Practising* speaking *the answers to past questions, and to short, sharp questions that you have written for yourself.* This has *really* high learning pay-off. What's the difference between this and writing out the answers? Mainly the fact that you can speak a lot faster than you can write. Why speak? Why not just think? The reason is that it is easy for us to con ourselves into believing that we know the answer to a question, but we often only find out whether this is true or not when we try to *express* the answer. Examiners can only measure the answers that you actually express – they can't measure what you *think*, however good your thoughts are. Practising speaking the answers to questions is really good at helping you to work out what you would write in a written exam, and is much faster than practising writing. It is, of course, worth doing some practice at writing out answers, mainly to make sure that you get your timing right in written exams and can find out how much you can express in writing in a given time. It is particularly worth practising speaking your answers to those short, sharp questions and dividing them into three categories, as

discussed in point 7. Another benefit of speaking answers is that it is excellent practice for any possible oral exam or viva that you may face. Speaking answers as a major revision strategy has some implications for where you can revise. You would not be popular if you were to do this in a quiet part of the library, for example! In such a situation you need to consider *thinking* out the answers, and this is discussed in point 9.

9 *Practising* thinking *through how you would answer questions.* This can be a really good revision activity, and can have very high learning pay-off. You can cover an enormous amount of your syllabus in an hour at the speed of thought, which is far faster than the speed of speech, and infinitely faster than the speed of writing. The only problem with thinking is the danger of believing that you know how to answer a question, rather than *proving* that you know how to answer it by expressing the answer. With a bit of practice, however, you can train yourself to think as you would speak, or indeed to think as you would write.

10 *Practising solving problems.* In subjects like science, maths, and engineering this is one of the best possible things you can do in your revision. Exams in such subjects ask you to solve problems, do calculations, prove or derive equations and relationships, and so on, usually against the clock. The best way to ensure competency at solving problems is to have solved a very large number of them! You can practise with old exam questions and with all the questions that you extracted from your lecture notes and tutorial exercises. Actual exam questions are very often based on problems that you have already seen or done, with perhaps some of the data or variables changed around. You can make your own problems to practise on by doing just this: altering the structure or data of existing problems from lectures or tutorials. You can find a wealth of additional problems in most textbooks or learning resource materials. In subjects where solving problems is relevant, the skills, and particularly the *speed*, with which you can apply those skills, to solve the problems, are probably the main things measured by the exams. This means that to get a good degree, you need to be better at solving problems against the clock than most of your fellow students. In some subjects, problem solving is much more important than writing essays and you may need to take this into account when deciding on how you balance the different kinds of relevant practice that you build into your revision.

11 *Getting fellow students to quiz you and quizzing them.* This has excellent learning pay-off for a number of reasons. First, being quizzed by fellow students puts you on the spot. You don't know what question is coming next. This is good practice for thinking on your feet, and for tuning in rapidly to new questions – just the thing you want to be able to do in your forthcoming exams. Second, it's not so easy to con yourself that you know how to answer the questions: your fellow students may put you right

when your answers aren't good enough. Third, it's much more sociable to work with fellow students than to be locked away in a private world of revision. Fourth, working with fellow students helps you to see how your revision is really going, as you can compare your standard with theirs. Fifth, reciprocating and quizzing fellow students gives you information both about mistakes you need to make sure that *you* don't make and about right answers that you would not have thought of by yourself. Working with other students in self-help groups has been demonstrated in research by the Open University to be very beneficial for students' learning. However, excellent as this activity is, it is important to strike an appropriate balance between it and several of the somewhat slower, less efficient activities described above. You *do* need to practise writing, and you also need to practise getting the timing right.

How to prepare a revision timetable

Have you prepared a revision timetable before? 'Yes!' most students reply. Did it work for you, and did you stick to it? 'No.' most students reply. The fact is that many students spend quite a lot of time preparing a revision timetable, and often set it out very neatly and in several colours, showing exactly what they intend to be revising exactly when, all the way up to the exams. Invariably, it doesn't quite work out like that. Usually, something happens which gets them 'behind' in their work. Maybe something takes them just a bit longer to revise than they intended. Or something else in their lives turns up and interrupts their timetable. Then the rot sets in. They can't catch up. They feel they have let themselves down, and that their revision is doomed. They abandon the timetable and maybe spend quite a lot of time making a new one. They may feel that their lives are dominated by the timetable and find all sorts of ways to escape from it.

The problem with most timetables is that they are inflexible, boring to follow, and too ambitious. They are too rigid to cope with the unexpected. It is a good job that the sort of degree you get does not depend on how sophisticated is your revision timetable. It is usually the most detailed timetables that are abandoned soonest.

However, it *is* worth making some kind of timetable. Here are some suggestions for making a timetable that will be a useful tool in your learning strategy, rather than a noose around your neck, which could in fact damage the effectiveness of your revision.

Make your timetable early

This is just another way of saying 'start your systematic revision early'. We've already explored why you should do this, not least the fact that making this decision for yourself is one of the characteristics of students who end up with good degrees.

Plan to have a near-normal life

One of the things that gives 'revision' a bad name is that people associate it with a hard grind, sitting in a lonely room, forcing your brain to work hard, involving the absence of all the normal elements of a balanced life, such as friends, hobbies, pastimes, relaxation, and just enjoying yourself or resting. If your revision regime is hostile and restrictive, you will naturally rebel against it and want the things that make for a normal happy life. If, however, you can manage to plan your revision so that it is not much different from your normal life as a student, there won't be anything to rebel about and you will find that you are better able to make realistic revision plans which work out in practice.

Plan to do some revision on most days, but have no days of solid revision

It is normally possible to do some revision on most days. Even just an hour's worth is worthwhile. It is just *not* possible to plan to do a whole day of revision, however determined you are to get through everything you need to learn. Revision, as we have seen in our exploration of those revision activities with high learning pay-off, is hard work when it is being done well. It is tiring. You also need time to make sense of what you are revising as you go along. It is no use filling your mind with so many things that you just forget them all again. So, revision actually happens best when it is done in relatively short instalments, and when you have time off in between. You need that time off not just to rest, or to make your life more normal, but also to allow your brain to digest and consolidate the things you have been thinking about in your spells of revision. If you have full days available, take at least some brief breaks to avoid overload.

Make your timetable humane and realistic

Plan half days and whole days *off*! You can afford these if you start revising early enough. Plan them so that you can accommodate all the other pressures in your life, not least your need to have a rest now and then. Even if you're working quite hard at your revision, it can make a big difference if you know that tomorrow you have a day off, or at least some time to do other things that you enjoy. This helps you to work all the harder today. Also, when you're *having* the time off you can then enjoy it, because it is part of your plans and it isn't just that you are escaping from all that revision which hasn't been done yet.

Plan out your syllabus, approximately, and with 'repeats'

One of the advantages of making a timetable of some sort is that it helps you to plan out your revision such that each subject gets the time that it needs.

You don't end up having spent weeks revising, and then finding out that one subject hasn't been touched. Build in repeats of everything. How much you remember about something depends far less on how long you have spent learning it, and far more on how *often* you have worked with it. Aim to work with everything several times, and with the most important parts of your subject matter *many* times. A little, and often, is the principle.

Plan variety into your revision content

For example, it is better to plan to look at three different subjects in any day's revision activities than just to plough ahead with one topic. This is not least because it gets rather boring if you stick for too long with one subject. It works out better in practice to learn a little of several things in a day than a lot of one thing. The human brain likes variety. As soon as you find yourself sliding into inefficient revision, it is best to stop what you are doing and try revising something else. As a student heading for a good degree, you aren't going to be tempted (are you?) to stop just because something is *hard*.

Plan to work in spurts, not slogs

It doesn't take long to do some useful revision. Here are just a few examples of useful revision elements that you could do in just five minutes each:

- Make a draft essay plan for a possible title that you have thought of.
- Test yourself out on 20 short, sharp questions, and decide which you already know the answers to, and which you will need to research further in your notes, handouts, and resources.
- Write ten questions about a topic you are going to revise tomorrow.
- Write down a summary of the three most important things you remember about topic 'X'.
- Make a list of three 'hard bits' that you intend to have another look at in the next two days.

Plan in a variety of activities

Remember the range of revision activities that we explored earlier in this chapter? It is worth making a conscious decision to use a good variety of the productive ones. Alternate your working between thinking through answers to questions, speaking them, writing them down where this is really useful, making summaries, devising questions, and working with fellow students. The more variety you have in the things you actually *do* as you revise, the faster the time will go by, and the more likely you are not to get bored or rebel against your revision plans.

Some students revise really well using large visual aids that they make for themselves (posters, charts, and so on). Others like to read notes aloud onto tapes and listen to them when travelling. Work out the activities which really suit you and build them into your revision strategies.

Build in eating and sleeping!

These are perfectly normal human needs. If you don't get enough sleep for weeks on end, your health deteriorates. More importantly, your brain power also gets less efficient. Similarly with food. A reasonably balanced diet is best if you are aiming to have your body and brain in good condition for the period of time where your performance is going to count so much. It is also worth avoiding hammering your system with things that interfere with good performance. Hangovers are not very pleasant anyway, so don't have too many of them during important revision phases of your life. There's all the rest of the time *after* you've got your degree if you really like the processes of getting a hangover. Avoiding excesses does not mean going into retreat from all the pleasures of the world: it's just a matter of being reasonable, and using pleasure for relaxation rather than for escape.

What if you can't sleep? What if you're so worried about all the work that is still to be covered that you lie awake fretting about it? And then you start worrying about not sleeping, and how you will be good for nothing tomorrow after a sleepless night? Insomnia is a well documented human condition. Equally well known is that when human beings really need sleep, they tend to go to sleep! If you're lying awake fretting about work, it is probably best to *do* some work, but nothing arduous, just a little polishing of something you already know rather well. You may even find that this process is so relaxing (or boring!) that you're asleep in no time! Alternatively, relax deliberately, read something that has nothing to do with your revision, or listen to some music, or watch some TV, and so on. Worrying about not sleeping is a really useless and destructive thing to do.

Last minute revision

The whole philosophy of this chapter is to make last minute revision unnecessary. If you've worked consistently and steadily at your revision for weeks or months while leading up to your exams, you should not need to spend any significant efforts right at the last minute. You should be able to rest on your laurels, and save your energy for *showing* that your revision has been successful by giving a good exam performance. Look at it another way. If you spend so much time on last minute revision that you are exhausted at the start of an exam, you may indeed *know* a lot, but just not have the energy left to read the paper well or, importantly, to structure your answers to the questions well.

It can be quite hard to *stop* revising, however. You may have an overactive conscience nagging you along the lines of, 'The exam is tomorrow. Now is my last chance to make that difference which will get me a good degree'. Your conscience may be right, but you've also got to protect your energy levels.

Usually, a compromise helps. Do *some* revision, but keep to the following relatively easy processes:

- Do a little polishing of things you already know well, rather than reading things that you find you don't yet know well. It does little for your morale if you find out at the last moment that there are some things that you don't yet know. You may begin to wonder, 'How much *else* don't I know properly?' It is better not to go into the downward spiral of morale that can then happen. Keep to the familiar territory in your final polishing.
- Do a little gentle practising. Map out again in your mind (or on paper) the answers to questions that you have already addressed in your revision. Show yourself that you can gather up your thoughts efficiently and calmly, and will be able to do so again, shortly, in the actual exam.
- Treat last minute revision like warming up in the gym. Use it to stretch your mind and to raise energy levels, rather than to exhaust yourself before the actual exam.

You may need to remind yourself that you have *already done* a great deal of revision and that your revision has already been deliberately effective, efficient, and focused. If you know that your revision has already earned you your good degree, you may find it easier to call it a day just before your exams start and to conserve your energy for *proving* this to your assessors.

Exams – the days of reckoning

Why should you take another look at your exam technique?

We've already explored a lot about exam technique in this chapter, particularly when looking at what exams really measure, and how to adjust revision processes to prepare for what is required. In many ways, all the rest is common sense. However, when we're stressed, things that are just common sense may elude us, so in the remainder of this chapter I will remind you of many aspects of exam technique that you will already be well practised in, but which should still not be forgotten, particularly in those exams which have most to do with getting yourself that *good* degree. There are some reasons why, however good your exam technique already is, it is worthwhile taking another look at it. These include:

- If you have put a great deal of intelligence into making your revision effective, efficient, and focused, it would be tragic if your exam performance did not do you justice.
- The fact that you're reading this book makes it likely that your exam

technique is already good, to have got you this far in your studies. Now is the time to polish it up if and where necessary, to make sure that it serves you well for the most important exams of your life.

- All through this book, we have been looking at the habits and behaviours that distinguish candidates who get *good* degrees. Exam technique is no exception. There are many ways in which exam technique can be your passport to communicating what you know, understand, and can do, to the people who will be making important assessment decisions about what they *see* as a reflection of what you knew, understood, and *actually did* under exam conditions.

Not surprisingly, exam technique makes a very significant difference to exam performance. Some of the main differences which distinguish those candidates who end up with good degrees are that they have sorted out the fine points of exam technique. Among these are those actions which help successful candidates to arrive at the exam in a non-stressed state, ready to give their best.

We will look at exam technique at different stages of the process of sitting exams, and look separately at:

- The day before an exam.
- The day of an exam.
- The first few minutes of an exam.
- Writing to score.
- Editing and scoring even more marks.
- After an exam.
- After your last exam.
- Preparing for a viva.

The day before an exam

Perhaps it's best to start thinking the day *before* an exam. We've already looked at the issue of whether or not to do yet more revision then. There are, however, some useful things that you can do on the day before an exam which can save you anxiety and stress for the exam day. These include the following.

1 *Get together into one place everything that you will need during the exam.* This will depend on what sort of exam it is. For most exams you will need writing implements such as pens and pencils, maybe with more than one colour (but not red!). You may need a ruler. You may need a calculator, and it may be the time to get a new battery for this. You may need drawing instruments. You may wish to take in an eraser or some correction fluid. You may have a favourite kind of pen, which is comfortable and makes the most of your handwriting. It could be worth having a spare one of these. Putting all these things into one wallet or folder means that on the day of the exam you

have just *one* thing to remember to pick up and take with you, rather than scrabbling around looking for all of the bits and pieces you need.

2 *Check out exactly where the exam is going to be held. Double-check the starting time.* If you have never been to the room or building, it could be worth making an exploratory trip, so that on the day you know exactly where you're going, and don't have to waste any energy on getting stressed about finding your way to the right place.

3 *Decide what you're going to wear and put your clothes out ready before you go to sleep.* It's surprising how stressful it can feel, on any important day in our lives, not to be able to find an item of clothing! Wear layers, so that if the exam room is hot you can remove some, and if it is cold you can add some. Don't wear anything tight or uncomfortable.

The day of an exam

1 *Make sure you're going to be awake.* Get up reasonably early, so that you're going to be reasonably alert by the time you set off for the exam. Set an alarm if you have any worries about oversleeping. If you're really anxious about oversleeping, take other precautions, such as getting someone you can trust to call for you, or ring you, and so on. There's no point staying awake all night worried in case you don't wake up! You'll sleep all the better if you know that you're not going to be allowed to miss waking up in time.

2 *Get to the venue in good time.* Don't put yourself in for the kinds of stress that accompany such events as the car not starting, or the bus or train not running that day. It is better to be within walking distance of the exam venue an hour or more *early* than to be still on your way, getting anxious about whether or not they are going to let you in if you're late.

3 *Beware of the pre-exam huddle!* You will remember the gatherings of candidates which occur outside the exam room or building. Everyone is keyed up. This disease is infectious. Everyone is asking, 'Do you think there will be a question on so-and-so?' 'Could you make any sense of such-and-such?' 'Did you manage to revise Dr Jones' stuff on the effects of elephants on transport policy?' and so on. Every time you hear someone say something that you *don't know* much about, your spirits fall. You don't actually notice when people mention things that you *do* know a lot about, your ears seem to miss these bits out. All in all, the pre-exam huddle is a place of stress and it is best avoided. Go a few minutes walk away from this huddle, maybe to some other building's coffee machine. There may indeed be another pre-exam huddle there, but all the students will be quizzing each other on whether they've revised subjects that aren't of any concern to you, so you won't catch their disease.

The first few minutes of an exam

These minutes are naturally the most adrenalin-raising of the whole event. Particularly with unseen written exams, this is the time when the great unknown becomes known: you see what the questions actually are! It is perfectly natural to be excited by this, and pulse rates and blood pressures rise automatically. This is a healthy response to the stimulus involved.

There is often a temptation, when you see the questions, to write down furiously everything that flashes through your mind in answer to them, just in case you might forget something important. Tempting though this is, it is quite impossible and would be a waste of a lot of mental energy. It could be worth making a compromise and writing down one or two really important ideas, keywords, maybe even mathematical equations, particularly ones that you have had difficulty remembering in the past, just to reassure yourself that you've captured these again and can use them when you need them in your answers.

Whether or not you are feeling stressed in the first few minutes of any exam, there are several things you need to do. These are not at all difficult, and can be a way of giving yourself time to gain your composure. They include:

- Check that you are confronted by the right exam paper! Exam halls often have several different exams going at once, and it is not unknown for candidates to find themselves looking at some other exam paper. It is also not unknown for them to actually try to answer such a paper! Checking this just takes a few seconds.
- Check the timescale available to you: this too takes seconds. However, from time to time candidates who were expecting a three-hour exam find themselves sitting a two-hour one. You can guess what happens if they don't notice this in time!
- Look carefully at the rubric: the part of the paper, usually at the top, often in italics, that tells you what you have to *do*. In particular, check out whether or not any of the questions are compulsory. Check whether the question paper is divided into sections, and whether, for example, you have to attempt *two* questions from Section A, *one* question from Section B, and so on. Check also whether or not all the questions carry equal marks. A good principle of time management in any exam is to devote equal time to equal mark-scoring opportunity. In other words, if a question is worth 20 percent of the marks, spend on it 20 percent of the time available.
- Put your name and/or candidate number on anything that you are required to. This may include loose sheets such as graph paper, drawing paper and so on, as well as on the paper or booklet on which you are going to write. If you don't put your identity on your script, it may be quite hard for the examiners to award the credit you earn to you.
- Plan out your timing for the exam. The things you are doing in these first few minutes mean that you should subtract (say) ten minutes from the

total. It is well worth subtracting a further 20 minutes from the total, which you will save for editing and polishing your answers. Then divide the remaining time according to the number of questions you are asked to attempt, bearing in mind how many marks go with each question.

- If you have a choice of questions it is worth making your selection very carefully indeed. In such cases it is better to spend an extra five minutes at the beginning of the exam making a wise and considered choice than to rush into answering any question only to find out that you would have been better off with another choice. False starts don't necessarily lose marks, but they penalize you in terms of the time you have available for the questions you decide to answer fully.

- When making your selections of which questions you will attempt, it can be worth making a decision about each and every question on the paper. Read each question slowly, deliberately, and more than once, until you are quite sure that you know exactly what the question is asking. It can help to highlight or underline key words, including important process words such as 'discuss', 'explain', 'decide', 'show that', 'compare and contrast', and so on. For each question, decide whether it could be a *really good* question for you and, if so, mark it with your own code on the question paper (such as two ticks). Maybe it is a *possible* question for you, where you know that you can score most of the available marks but are not certain about some parts of the question. Mark such 'possible' questions with another code (maybe a single tick). Don't be afraid to decide that a given question is a *bad* one for you. This could be because you don't like the subject, or you don't know the subject, or you don't feel sure about how you would approach the question because you haven't practised on this sort of question already. Marking such questions with another code (maybe a cross) helps you to avoid wasting time re-reading them later, and reminds you that you have already made a conscious, considered decision that these are not questions for you.

- Normally, there will be at least one *good* question and one or more *possible* questions by this stage. Work out next in what order you are going to attempt the questions. Most candidates start with the 'best' question for them, which is perfectly sensible in that it helps them to gather some confidence, and they continue to answer the less favourable questions in better spirits. You will probably feel like starting with a good question too. Be aware, however, that the danger with a *good* question is that you know far more with which to answer it than could possibly be written down in the time available to you in the exam (if it's a time constrained exam of course). What can you do to distinguish yourself here from other candidates who are answering their 'best' question? One thing is to be deliberately concise, and to make sure that you get as much relevant content down on paper as you can in the time available, covering all your thinking but not getting into unnecessary detail or elaboration. You may well have time later in the exam to go back to your best question and polish it up or expand on it. Doing so, however, tends to earn very few additional marks. If you've already written a good answer, spending twice as long on it will only add the odd mark or two, if anything. Spending that amount of extra time on a different question that you have answered less well may bring you several more extra marks, perhaps making the difference that leads you to your good degree classification.

- Don't worry when, as you reach the end of these processes during the first ten minutes or so of your exam, you look around the exam room and see everyone writing busily. By adopting this logical approach and planning the campaign for scoring marks in your exam, you will have given yourself the possibility of scoring far more marks than they have already won.

It looks like a long list for 'the first few minutes'! However, it does not take long at all in practice; the only part of the above sequence which takes a significant time is the decision making process about which questions you are going to answer.

Writing to score

The following headings are all about getting marks from your examiners. There is nothing here that is not just common sense, but to get your good degree, you need to display rather *more* of this common sense than other candidates! The points below are not in any particular order. Which of them you will need to keep in mind at any given moment depends on many things about the exam structure, and your own performance so far in the exam.

Keep to time (within reason)

Even if you spend a long time on a question you can't get more than the maximum score available for that question and you will be robbing yourself of mark-scoring opportunities on other questions. If you run out of scheduled time for a question it is usually best to leave some space and go on to another question. Before moving off, spend maybe one minute jotting down in pencil a few keywords to remind you of what you would have done if you'd stayed with the question for the next five or ten minutes. Then, when you return to the question later (if you have time to do so) you can quickly pick up the threads of where you left off, and continue without having to spend time thinking yourself back into the question.

Decide whether to spend up to five minutes 'mapping' your answer

With essay-type questions it is usually worth making some kind of essay plan in miniature before starting to answer the question. An egg diagram is as good a way as any of doing this. The advantage is that it helps you to plan out the sequence of your answer, so that you know where you are starting, and how you are leading up to your conclusion. It can be worth leaving the introduction till last, just as in a coursework essay. Leaving half a page to come back to *after* you know what's in your answer is a way of helping you to write an introduction which really does lead into your actual answer. This is one of those features which scores the extra marks that could make the difference between a good degree and a less good one!

Read the question, again and again

This is to make sure that you keep answering the question as written, and not answering what you thought the question asked. The greatest cause of lost marks in exams is candidates wandering off on tangents to the question. All the available marks are for points that are directly relevant to the question. There aren't any more marks for additional knowledge, wisdom, or expertise – however brilliant – that is not required by the question.

Don't panic when solving problems

With calculation-type questions, you don't know that you've cracked it until you've actually cracked it. This feels different from writing essay-type answers, where you've more or less cracked it once you've made your essay plan. When doing calculations, there may be several different stages on your way to the final solution or answer. It can be worth jotting down in pencil before you start the key equations, formulae, or relationships which you expect to be using in your solution to the problem. This makes sure that if you find yourself struggling in the middle of your solution, you don't get the additional worry that accompanies having temporarily forgotten a key formula. If, halfway through solving a problem, you really feel lost, it can be worth moving on to a different question at least for a while. The hazard with calculation-type questions is that if you don't make real headway towards the correct solution you may not get any marks. It could then be better to go for a question where you know you can get at least some of the marks. But give yourself a bit of breathing space first. When you return to a problem after a few minutes of doing something else, you often find that you can see what was eluding you before, and can press on towards a successful solution.

Show all your working when doing anything with numbers

In mathematical parts of questions everything seems to depend on coming up with the right answer for every computation. Normally you'll be using a calculator to do anything fairly numerical. However, it is extremely dangerous in exams just to use your calculator and write down the number that it gives you as your answer. The examiner can't then see what may have gone wrong if you arrive at an incorrect answer. There's no danger at all if you happen to get the right answer for a calculation; the examiner will just assume that you were doing the right sum to get it. If you get the wrong answer and the examiner can see exactly *why* you made a mistake you can end up getting most of the marks for that part of the question. If the examiner can't see where you made your mistake you get exactly *zero* marks for that part of the question. That can be a big difference. In a couple of calculations it can make the difference between a good degree and a much less good one! You need to 'talk your examiner through what you've done with your calculator'. For example, if you are substituting numbers into a formula, write the formula down first, then below it write the numbers in exactly the places where you are substituting the terms in the formula, *then* write the answer given by your calculator. Most mistakes in calculations are made by substituting one of the terms in a formula with the wrong value for the data concerned. When an examiner can see that this is what happened, marks will still be awarded for using the correct formula *and* for any subsequent operations which are correct scientifically, but which are now distorted by the numerical values being incorrect.

Keep addressing the question

This may seem to be the same as the point made above about reading the question again and again, but it is different! 'Addressing' the question is the art of making your answer an excellent response to the process words in the question. These are important 'instruction' words or phrases such as compare, contrast, decide, show that, analyse, evaluate, critically discuss, and so on. It is often useful, especially in essay-type answers, to bring words from the question itself into the first sentences of each paragraph of your answer. This helps the examiner to see that, point by point, your answer is directly related to the question.

What if your mind goes blank?

This is very frightening when it happens, but is entirely avoidable. It almost always happens when candidates have forgotten something and are struggling to remember it. The human brain does not like to be forced to do anything (like its owner), and can rebel against such pressure and temporarily close down memory circuits. To avoid mental blanks, if and when you feel your brain beginning to rebel against your constant requirements to summon up information from your 'hard disk', move on to a different question for a while. If you find yourself struggling for too long to recall something important, move on to something that is still readily available from your memory. It does not pay to try to force your brain to deliver something that may have been on the 'tip of your tongue' but has now slipped back. It is very likely indeed to come back to your conscious mind, but only when you stop trying to force it back.

Keep the needs of the examiner in mind

Remember that (except in computer-marked exams, of course) examiners are human beings. They are probably tired human beings when they mark your scripts. They may well be stressed human beings, with looming deadlines by which they have to get all their scripts marked. It helps a lot if they can find their way round your script easily. This means not just reasonable handwriting, but making your answers easy to *find*. Number your questions carefully, and start each new page with the question number in the margin, such as '(5 cont.)'.

Don't write anything in red!

Red, traditionally, is the examiner's colour. Examiners underline your mistakes in red. They enter your subtotals and totals in red. If *you* write things in red too, the situation can get very confused. Not least, examiners may feel that you have invaded their territory, and this does not put them into the best of moods!

Leave margins uncluttered

Examiners often enter subtotals and comments into the right hand margin of candidates' scripts. If this margin is filled by your own writing it becomes harder for them to find *where* to enter their subtotals, and they may miss entering one or two of these due to lack of a convenient space. This means no less than you may lose out on some of the marks that you have earned. It's worth leaving that margin clear, and if there's not a margin ruled on your exam paper, you may like to rule one yourself. Just a centimetre or so will do.

Use diagrams or illustrations whenever you can justify them

Reading a lot of handwriting is a tiring job for examiners. Even looking at a numerical calculation provides some kind of break from reading sentence after sentence. A much nicer kind of break for examiners is to see something visual, such as a diagram, sketch, or other kind of illustration. They don't have to read something for a moment or two, they can rest and just *look*. There's more to it than that, of course. A good illustration can show examiners at once that you understand something. (The reverse applies: a bad one can show them at once that you don't understand something!) It is often possible to show examiners that you understand something through an illustration which takes less time to draw than it would take to explain the whole thing in words. So, visual elements in answers can be a break for examiners and can save you time as well. Not every examiner likes illustrations, but most do. By the time you take your exams you should have a good idea what the people who will be marking your work feel about illustrations. You will have been able to try them out in coursework assignments, where you will soon find out if words are preferred to diagrams and sketches.

Editing and scoring even more marks

In our discussion of the things that are worth doing in the first few minutes of a time constrained written exam I suggested saving about 20 minutes in reserve for things to do at the end of your exam. These minutes can be used to score a considerable number of marks – many more marks, in fact, than if you simply continued finishing off your answers to any questions not yet complete. You can make the best use of the time near the end of an exam by *editing*.

The first stage is something that you almost certainly won't want to do! *Read what you have written* in the preceding hours. This is absolutely necessary if you are to pick up the additional marks that remain available to you. As you read, you will find the following kinds of adjustments you can make, there and then, to what you have already written.

Occasions where what you actually wrote was not what you meant to write

In other words, you will see sentences where your intended meaning is just not there. If *you* can't see it, it is quite certain that the examiner won't be able to see what you intended your writing to mean. Quickly adjust your text so that your intended meaning comes across loud and clear. You may be able to do this by squeezing in a few extra words here and there. Sometimes, you may need to add a footnote, or a few sentences written at the end of your answer, in which case make it really clear in the body of your answer where the continuation pieces are to be found.

Mistakes

When you find a mistake, whether it is in words or in numbers, now is the time to put it right. Don't, however, spend so long putting *one* mistake right that you rob yourself of time to find several other mistakes. Put the straightforward mistakes right first, quickly, then go back to anything which is going to take a little longer to rectify. It is surprising how often you can find your own mistakes, when you read your answers afresh.

Further thoughts

It will now be some time since you wrote your first answers. Ever since writing them your subconscious mind will have continued to work at the questions. When you re-read your answers towards the end of an exam there will be many further thoughts at the surface of your mind, and now is the time to slip them in, particularly if they are important additions to your original answers. There may be several marks to be earned from these further thoughts. Again, use footnotes and additional paragraphs where necessary.

These corrections and additions can be worth, cumulatively, a very significant number of marks. It is often the case that exam candidates can score an *extra* 20 marks in 20 minutes right at the end of an exam. That is more marks per minute than they are likely to have scored in *any* 20 minutes during the rest of the exam. Such an additional score can certainly be the difference between a good degree and an ordinary one! Make it part of your strategy for getting your good degree to be determined not to miss out on the marks you can get by improving what you have already written in the main part of your exams rather than using any time available just continuing your final answer.

After an exam

Can you remember what most people do immediately after an exam? It's called a post-mortem! That is indeed what it is: the moment time is up, and you hand in your script, that exam is dead as far as you are concerned. There is nothing whatsoever that you can do about it from then onwards. From your point of view, the exam is now history. Whether you did brilliantly or badly, the time has gone where there is any mileage in thinking about that exam. It is over. Despite the logic of all of this, students seem unable to resist post-mortems. Hours after they have handed in their scripts they are to be seen in huddles, trying to work out what the answer to question 5 really was, and comparing notes on what they did and did not remember to put into other answers. Post-mortems are a bad idea because:

- They almost always demoralize you, when you find out all sorts of things that fellow students did that you did not think of. You hardly notice the things that *you* did that your fellow students did not think of. It is the bad news that sticks. This can demoralize students so much that even when they did well in the exam concerned they do much less well in their *next* exam.
- They are a waste of mental energy. If you've got another exam coming up shortly it is tragic to waste any energy on something that is over and done.

Could it be that students *enjoy* exams so much that they want to relive the whole experience, this time in slow motion? To avoid participating in the inevitable post-mortem requires some self-discipline. You may even have to be somewhat antisocial and stay away from the company of fellow students who took the same exam until they have got it out of their systems.

What can you do instead? The best solution seems hard, but if you try it once or twice you will be convinced of its merits. Do a little *gentle* revision, straight away, for your next exam! You won't feel like doing this, but once you start it you will be surprised how relaxing it is. You may *want* to switch off altogether and really relax but with the extra adrenalin in your system from the exam you have just taken you aren't quite ready to relax. You can use up this adrenalin usefully in thinking about your next exams and reminding yourself of some of the main points you will need soon. It's almost as though you are flushing out the old knowledge from your last exam and replacing it with the knowledge that you will need for your next one. You may also feel a sense of righteousness, that *you* are doing something worthwhile and productive while your friends are indulging in the ritual of a post-mortem.

After your last exam

There's no harm in doing a post-mortem after your *last* exam. It still won't change your mark for the exam, but at least there is no longer the risk that it will demoralize you and affect future performance. However, it's much more productive to find something else to do. Some students find that they suffer quite badly with post-exam blues, feeling weepy and depressed when all their mates are out celebrating and drinking. This sense of anticlimactic malaise is quite normal and nothing to be amazed by. Cures include sleep, physical exercise, being alone, being sociable, and just waiting for it to pass. If you're affected in this way, work out what suits you best and give yourself time to get over it. You will.

Preparing for a viva

Elsewhere in this book I've given some suggestions about preparing for vivas or oral exams. After you've finished your written exams, there may be the possibility that you will have a viva. This may be a process used to consider candidates who happen to straddle a borderline between different degree classifications. If you find you have a viva, however, this does not mean that you are necessarily on a borderline; you may be participating as a 'frame of reference' candidate who is already firmly in one of the classification zones. You may indeed already have won your good degree. Or you may be about to have your chance to upgrade to one. After your last exam, it can be worth making sure that all the material that you learned for your exams is still relatively well polished in your mind. This does not mean rigorous revision yet again. It is usually sufficient to check out that you still are in control of the main ideas and knowledge from your subjects, perhaps concentrating a little more on anything that you know you *didn't* do too well on in one of your written exams, just in case the viva is a chance to show that this was not characteristic of your overall performance.

Conclusions

As long as exams play such an important part in getting a good degree your revision strategies and exam technique remain worth investing in. Even if you know your subjects backwards, to get credit for your knowledge and understanding you still have to communicate your mastery of your studies through exams. Even when you don't know a particular subject brilliantly, really good revision and exam technique can make a very significant difference to your results – and this can be the difference that captures for you the good degree you're chasing.

As I'm sure you will now know, getting a good degree is mainly about developing and maintaining good habits, those that help your studies to be effective and efficient and others that make sure that you do yourself justice in all assessment contexts, including coursework and exams. It should not be a matter of luck. That said, however, I also wish you the best of luck in your efforts towards a good degree, and hope that:

- All of your assessors will be in the most favourable of moods when they mark your work.
- Exam questions are chosen which will allow you to show how well you have mastered your subject matter.
- You will show yourself at your optimum potential throughout.
- Your increased effectiveness, efficiency, and confidence will help you to *enjoy* the journey towards your good degree all the more.

Best wishes,
Phil

References and further reading

There is a wide range of books on various aspects of study-skills development. Quite a lot of the available literature tends to address surviving at university and passing exams, rather than thriving at university and excelling in your overall performance, though nowadays there is also a lot of useful guidance on some of the more specialist skills and techniques you may need in your journey towards your degree (and beyond) including developing critical argument skills. When you look at other sources be careful to select the advice which will really help you to excel in your own particular degree context, rather than that which could compromise your ambitions and standards. And whatever else you do, don't let reading all about how to study well be at the expense of getting down to working towards your degree – reading too much about it can become a study-avoidance tactic! Some of the sources which contain valuable advice are listed below (but you may well find others).

Allison, B. and Race, P. (2004) *The Student's Guide to Preparing Dissertations and Theses*. London: Routledge. (Some detailed advice here about writing longer assessed work.)

Barnes, R. (1995) *Successful Study for Degrees*, 2nd edn. London: Routledge. (Illustrated with examples from interviews with students and lecturers.)

Bell, J. (2005) *Doing Your Research Project: A Guide for First-Time Researchers in Education, Health and Social Science*, 4th edn. (A really useful text if your degree depends significantly on a research project in these areas.)

Creme, P. and Lea, M. R. (2003) *Writing at University: a Guide for Students*, 2nd edn. Maidenhead: Open University Press. (Particularly useful for in-depth discussion of writing style, and organizing your writing.)

Chamber, E. and Northedge, A. (1997) *The Arts Good Study Guide*. Milton Keynes: Open University. (Useful advice tailored to arts disciplines.)

Cottrell, S. (2003) *The Study Skills Handbook*. Basingstoke: Palgrave MacMillan. (An important contribution to the study skills literature.)

Cottrell, S. (2005) *Critical Thinking Skills: Developing Effective Analysis and Argument*. Basingstoke: Palgrave MacMillan. (Especially useful in disciplines where demonstrating critical thinking is important in getting you a good degree.)

Cottrell, S. (2006) *The Exam Skills Handbook*. Basingstoke: Palgrave MacMillan. (If exam technique is one of your key concerns, a really useful starting point for improving them.)

Cryer, P. (2006) *The Research Student's Guide to Success*, 3rd edn. Maidenhead: Open University Press. (Particularly useful if you decide to go on to a higher degree, but also directly relevant to higher-level work in your first degree, such as projects and dissertations.)

Dunleavy, P. (1986) *Studying for a Degree in the Humanities and Social Sciences*. Basingstoke: Macmillan. (A sound source of good advice if your degree spans any of these disciplines.)

Fairbairn, G. J. and Winch, C. (1996) *Reading, Writing and Reasoning: A Guide for Students*, 2nd edn. Buckingham: Open University Press. (A practical and pragmatic book, easy to read and full of useful advice.)

Fairbairn, G. J. and Fairbairn, S. (2001) *Reading at University: A Guide for Students*. Buckingham: Open University Press. (Expert advice if you need to develop your skills at extracting the sense from the published literature.)

Luck, M. (1998) Undergraduate research projects: motivation and skills development, in S. Brown, S. Armstrong, and G. Thompson (eds) *Motivating Students*. London: Kogan Page SEDA Series.

Northedge, A. (2005) *The Good Study Guide*. Milton Keynes: The Open University. (A deservedly best-selling study skills volume, providing insights into a wide range of processes and skills you need in higher education.)

Perrett, J. (1996) *Job Hunting after University or College*. London: Kogan Page. (An interactive book, full of exercises and activities, providing a lot of detail about marketing yourself well to potential employers.)

Phillips, E. M. and Pugh, D. S. (2005) *How to Get a PhD: A Handbook for Students and their Supervisors*, 4th edn. Maidenhead: Open University Press. (If you already have your sights on a doctorate, it is never too early to start using this book, so popular that it's now in its 4th edition!)

Pirie, D. B. (1985) *How to Write Critical Essays: A Guide for Students of Literature*. London: Routledge. (Goes into more depth about writing styles appropriate for this discipline area.)

Powell, S. (1999) *Returning to Study: A Guide for Professionals*. Buckingham: Open University Press. (This book is particularly useful if you're returning to study as a mature student, and helps you to tune in to the higher education context.)

Race, P. (2003) *How to Study*. Oxford: Blackwell. (Some further advice on a wide range of topics, but not quite going into the depth of the present book.)

Race, P. (2005) *Making Learning Happen*. London: Sage. (A book where I go into a lot more detail about how learning *really* happens, and about the various teaching-learning contexts used in higher education.)

Race, P. (2006a) *The Lecturer's Toolkit*, 3rd edn. London: Routledge. (A book for your lecturers, hopefully resulting in better teaching and fairer assessment for you.)

Race, P. (2006b) *In at the Deep End: Starting to Teach in Higher Education*. Leeds: Leeds Metropolitan University. (A simple guide I wrote for new lecturers, which could be useful regarding preparing your first big presentations or lectures, especially if you move on into a post where you need to teach in higher education.)

Race, P. and Pickford, R. (2007) *Making Teaching Work*. London: Sage. (Another book for lecturers, suggesting a range of practical ways they can improve your learning experience.)

Redman, P. (2005) *Good Essay Writing: A Social Sciences Guide*. London: Sage. (Especially for social sciences students.)

Saunders, D. (ed.) (1994) *The Complete Student Handbook*. Oxford: Blackwell. (Contains chapters by various authors (including me!) on a wide range of aspects of surviving in higher education, and includes a good section on 'Getting out of college', which goes into useful detail about job hunting.)

Talbot, C. (2003) *Studying at a Distance: A Guide for Students*. Maidenhead: Open

University Press. (Particularly useful if you're studying for a degree as a distance learner.)

Tamblin, L. and Ward, P. (2006) *The Smart Study Guide: Psychological Techniques for Student Success*. Oxford: Blackwell. (A lively look at how our minds work, with an extensive list of references to other literature.)

Tracy, E. (2006) *The Student's Guide to Exam Success*. Maidenhead: Open University Press. (Probably the most readable and comprehensive guide to preparing for exams, and tackling them successfully.)

Wyse, D. (2006) *The Good Writing Guide for Education Students*. London: Sage. (Especially for education students.)

Index